HAWAI'I WEDDINGS

MADE SIMPLE

HAWAI'I *Weddings* MADE SIMPLE

*Everything You Need to Know
to Plan the Perfect Island Wedding*

Keri Shepherd

MUTUAL PUBLISHING

The information listed in this book is current at press time, but may have changed since the time of publication. If the names, phone numbers, addresses, websites or other information have been changed or are no longer in operation, please forward those changes to Keri Shepherd at keri@wedding-planners.net. The resources will be updated for the next printing. If you are not listed as a wedding resource and would like to be or would like your information updated, you may also contact Keri at the aforementioned e-mail address. Neither the publisher, nor the author makes any guarantees as to the availability, quality or business practices of the vendors mentioned in this book. Likewise, mention of any product, service, vendor or organization does not signify endorsement or recommendation by the author or publisher.

How To Get Listed: If you have a wedding-related service that is not listed, please forward your information to keri@wedding-planners.net. We may list you in the next edition of *Hawai'i Weddings Made Simple*. If you are listed but your information has changed or is incorrect, please forward that information as well.

Library of Congress Catalog Card Number: 2003104516

First Printing, July 2003
Second Printing, April 2006
2 3 4 5 6 7 8 9

Design by Mardee Domingo Melton

Photo and Other Credits:
Many photos shot on location in Hawai'i taken by Sri Maiava Rusden, (808) 384-7029, www.maiavarusden.com or e-mail ruzandsri@hawaii.rr.com; and by Chrissy Lambert Photography, (808) 979-0001, www.chrissylambert.com or e-mail info@chrissylambert.com
Hair and Makeup done by Leslie Gallagher (808) 261-1004 or www.lesliegallagher.com.
Some wedding dresses shown provided by Bridal Emporium (808) 596-8281.
Some tuxedos shown provided by Phil's Tux Shop (808) 596-9872.

ISBN 1-56647-598-8

Mutual Publishing, LLC
1215 Center Street, Suite 210
Honolulu, Hawai'i 96816
Ph: (808) 732-1709 Fax: (808) 734-4094
e-mail: mutual@lava.net
www.mutualpublishing.com
Printed in Taiwan

Dedication

You can't do a resource book without a wealth of resources to pull from. And I have been blessed with an abundance of resourceful, talented friends and family who have given of their time and talents to help make this book a reality.

Here are just a few—my thanks to...

- Mom and Grandma June. The "resource girls" behind the resources. When I say I couldn't have done it without you both…I mean it!

- Marcia Zina Mager for encouraging me to pursue this and pointing me in the right direction.

- Leslie Gallagher, Machi Ueno and Cathy Chun. You guys are the best hair and make-up girls in the biz and I so appreciate your help on this.

- Leslie, Karen and the girls at the Bridal Emporium for letting us borrow your beautiful gowns for shoots.

- Phil at Phil's Tux Shop for lending us your tuxes whenever we needed them and always with a wonderful smile and a word of encouragement.

- Lianne for doing all the "fun" research for the ethnic chapter, you're wonderful!

- Fern for being an editor's editor and a great friend.

- Polly, my own personal art director, you are amazing grace personified!

- Lynn and Lissa my fellow wedding planners and "sisters." Thanks for all your encouragement and lots of laughs.

- Sri and Ruz Rusden for all your beautiful photography. You helped make this a reality—and oh-so-fun! Love you DQ!

- Ayn and Jimi Hazen for all the extra time you spent loving my kids, Janaye and Zion, while I finished this up. You guys are the best!

- Mom and Dad—they don't make them any better than you two! May God bless you tenfold for your unconditional love and support.

- And to Tim, who allowed me the time and freedom to pursue this project in my "spare" time. You are a wonderful father, husband and my #1 fan! Everyone should be so blessed!

- And finally....to God be the glory!!

Sri Maiava Rusden

Contents

Chris McDonough Photography

Sri Maiava Rusden

courtesy of Hyatt Regency Waikiki

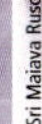
Sri Maiava Rusden

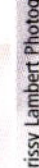
Chrissy Lambert Photography

courtesy of Hyatt Regency Waikiki

Introduction

HAWAI'I. It's the place people dream about. And the place where thousands of couples tie the knot every year. Few places conjure up more fantasies of a beautiful, tropical wedding than Hawai'i. Its lush green valleys, turquoise blue ocean and white sand beaches are the ideal backdrop for a dream wedding. But whether you are kama'aina (Hawai'i resident) or a visitor, planning a wedding in Hawai'i takes time, money and resources.

If you're like most people, you've never planned a wedding, and you don't even know where to begin. There are usually two types of novice wedding planners: (1) those who think it's easy and are naive to the enormity of the task at hand and (2) those who fall ill at the mere thought of having to put together, plan and detail such an event. Settle into a happy medium with a realistic notion that this is one of the, if not *the* biggest events of your life. It takes a lot of work and planning, and with the right tools and guidance, it can be one of the most enjoyable and memorable experiences of your life.

Everyone has his/her own idea of what a perfect Hawaiian wedding is. For some, their perfect wedding is on the beach, walking barefoot down the sandy, make-shift aisle wearing a haku lei (a floral head band) and fitted white mu'umu'u. Others prefer a staunch chapel with stained glass windows, a robed clergy and tuxedos and tails. This book will not try to tell you what's right for you. But we will help you look at all your options and offer you information on everything you'll need to plan *your* perfect Hawai'i wedding.

If you're not familiar with the state of Hawai'i and the uniqueness of each island, refer to pages 5-9 for a brief overview of the islands and what each has to offer.

Hawai'i Weddings Made Simple

PART One

Where to Begin?

First things first. Take some time to think about your wedding. Envision it. Dream about it. Let the whole day play out through your mind. Do this individually and then sit down as a couple and discuss your "dream" wedding together. Write down what you see. This process will help you prioritize later, if and when you have to start cutting things out due to financial constraints. Make a list of the most important elements of your wedding (beautiful flowers as far as the eye can see and a huge Hawaiian-style buffet stocked with the best poi and lomi lomi salmon that money can buy…or maybe it's a wedding in a beautiful chapel followed by a sunset dinner cruise…you get the idea).

Now, after you've envisioned it, prioritized it and discussed it, here comes the sometimes stressful part—setting your budget. Approximately how much money are you going to spend on your wedding? (And when we say wedding we mean everything from the rings to the honeymoon.) Some people have a set budget that they will not exceed and others have a ball park figure that keeps them within a reasonable range. Discuss it with your fiancé, parents, in-laws-to-be and whomever else is helping finance your wedding and decide what you have to work with. Be practical when setting your budget. You want to avoid having to cut corners at the last minute because you've completely gone over your budget, and it can keep you from going into debt just to finance your wedding. For a "typical" wedding, major expenses include: site fee, reception (food, drinks), flowers, photography, invitations, wedding rings and attire. A wedding does not have to be expensive to be memorable!

Hawai'i Laws and Regulations

You'll need to make a visit to the Hawai'i State Department of Health to get your marriage license. A marriage license is valid for thirty days in the state of Hawai'i. There are no residency or citizenship requirements to file. The bride and the groom must bring the $60 cash fee, valid driver's license, passport or valid photo ID. There are no state residence or U.S. citizenship requirements and blood tests are not required. The marriage license is good only in the state of Hawai'i and expires thirty days from the date of issuance, after which it automatically becomes null and void. If you do not get married within the thirty days, you may return the unused license in the pre-addressed envelope provided to you for invalidation.

The legal marrying age in Hawai'i is eighteen. Couples who are sixteen or seventeen years of age who wish to marry require the written consent of both parents, legal guardian, or the family court. The parents or legal guardian do not have to be residents of the state. Consent forms may be obtained from a marriage license agent.

Proof of age is required. A certified copy of a birth certificate must be presented for anyone eighteen years or younger. A valid ID or driver's license may be presented for anyone nineteen years or older.

After the ceremony, the officiant must send the signed marriage license to the Department of Health. This document then becomes the official marriage certificate on file with the Hawai'i State Registrar. You can expect to receive a legal copy of your marriage license approximately twelve to sixteen weeks after your ceremony. For more information, call the Hawai'i State Department of Health on the island you are planning to get married on (see page 4). The office will send out marital packets to out-of-state parties interested in getting married in Hawai'i. For

**Hawai'i State Department
of Health Marriage
License Information
By Island**

Hawai'i (Big Island)
(808) 974-6008
Kaua'i
(808) 241-3498
Maui
(808) 984-8210
Moloka'i
(808) 553-3663
Lāna'i
(808) 565-6411
O'ahu
(808) 586-4545 or
(808) 586-4544
1250 Punchbowl Street
Honolulu, HI 96813

information about obtaining a licensed marriage performer, you can visit The Hawai'i Visitors and Convention Bureau website at www.gohawaii.com, call them at (808) 923-1811 or see the list of officiants on pages 176-178.

Information about marriage licenses may also be obtained via the telephone system, any day or any time, by calling (808) 586-4545. Or you can download a marriage license application form on-line at www.hawaii.gov/doh/records. Now, no matter where you are in the world, you can download the form, complete it and bring it to the Hawai'i Department of Health office.

Introducing the Islands

This chapter provides information for those interested in basics about specific islands. If you live here or are from here you can probably skip this chapter, unless of course you're contemplating marrying on an outer island you're unfamiliar with. Hawai'i is the 50th state and is full of tradition, cultural diversity and history. But we are not going to delve into all of that. There are hundreds of other books that have been researched and written for the sole purpose of providing readers with an in-depth look at everything from who "discovered" the islands to Hawaiian legends, gods and the Hawaiian language. Hawai'i is as multifaceted as any place in the world and we are certainly not going to pretend to be qualified to summarize it for you. However, for purposes of this book, we will give you some general information about each island and offer some insight as to where you may or may not want to tie the knot.

There are eight land masses of varying sizes that make up the state of Hawai'i: the Big Island of Hawai'i, Maui, Kaho'olawe, Lāna'i, Moloka'i, O'ahu, Kaua'i and Ni'ihau. Each island is wonderfully unique but only six of the islands are accessible to us regular folks and only four of them are considered the "main" islands where couples regularly get married. For suggestions on ceremony and reception sites on each island, see the resource section of this book beginning on page 88. Here are the eight main islands in alphabetical order.

1. Hawai'i

Appropriately dubbed "the Big Island" for its 4,038 square miles of land mass, this isle is renowned for erupting volcanoes, jungle gorges, gardens and Hawaiian temples. It has many superlatives: the tallest mountain when measured from the ocean floor is Mauna Kea at 33,476 feet. South Point is the southernmost point in the 50 states. The world's most active volcano is Kīlauea. The nation's rainiest city is Hilo, averaging 140 inches per year. It is the dwelling place of the volcano goddess Pele and the cradle of Hawaiian civilization. It is the only island with its own desert and annual snowfall atop the Mauna Kea and Mauna Loa summits. Each of the Big Island's districts is as large as any one of the other islands, so whether you're in Hilo,

Notes:
____

____

____

____

____

____

____

____

____

____

____

____

____

Kona or volcano country, give yourself some time to tour. The Big Island grows most of the state's food including macadamia nuts, coffee, ginger root, produce, herbs and exotic flowers. Big Isle hot spots to marry are: Lili'uokalani Gardens in Hilo and 'Anaeho'omalu Bay in Waikoloa. (Visit www.gohawaii.com/vacationplanninghawaii/ or www.thisweek.com for more on the Big Island of Hawai'i.)

2. Kaua'i

Enjoy the island's blooming flowers, flowing waterfalls and movie backdrops that have earned the island its nickname, "The Garden Isle." Waimea Canyon, Fern Grotto and Hanalei are some island "must-sees." The island's lush valleys, fluted mountains and scenic coastal strips are the perfect reasons for booking an unforgettable helicopter ride. Flightsee tours are a great way to view the entire island; a lot of it is otherwise inaccessible by vehicle, especially if you're short on time. The island is the home of the menehune, the legendary race of little people said to work only at night. A favorite shooting location, Kaua'i has had more than 60 movies and TV shows filmed on location. Kaua'i offers diverse gardens; Limahuli boasts the title of 1997 Natural Botanical Garden of the Year. Fern Grotto is the most popular place to get married on Kaua'i and Ke'e Beach, where they filmed *The Thornbirds*, is a popular spot for couples honeymooning. (Visit www.gohawaii.com/vacationplanningkauai/ or www.thisweek.com for more on Kaua'i.)

3. Kaho'olawe

is a barren island 11 miles long and 6 miles wide with 29 miles of coastline. It is uninhabited and was once used as a target by U.S. Navy and Air Force, which are now cleaning up unexploded shells. No one is allowed to go ashore without permission. Needless to say, you won't be getting married on Kaho'olawe—nor do you probably want to!

Hawai'i Weddings Made Simple

4. Lāna'i This island is approximately 140 square miles, measuring 18 miles north to south and 13 miles east to west with about 47 miles of coastline. It is home to about 2,500 residents. Almost the entire island was a Dole Company pineapple plantation but is now phasing in tourism. If money is no object, Lāna'i is a secluded treasure island for a perfect Hawai'i wedding. Just ask Bill Gates, who rented the entire island for his wedding.

Lāna'i has two main resorts, the Lodge at Kō'ele and the Mānele Bay Hotel. The Lodge at Kō'ele is a country estate that combines the charm and refined atmosphere of a traditional English country manor, and the awe-inspiring natural beauty of Lāna'i. This exclusive resort, nestled within the dense pine forests and lush valleys of upcountry Lāna'i, is the perfect setting for a dream vacation and dreamy wedding. The Mānele Bay Hotel is only a hop and skip away from the Hulopo'e Beach (named America's most beautiful shore) and is strategically located for great sunbathing and water activities. The Mānele Bay Hotel has been ranked #1 among Hawai'i resorts by *Condé Naste Traveler* as "The Best Places in the World to Stay." It is renowned for its luxurious accommodations, gourmet cuisine, and numerous activities. It attracts even the most discriminating travelers who return as often as they can to soak in what only this world-acclaimed resort can offer. (Visit www.gohawaii.com/vacationplanninglanai/ for more on Lāna'i.)

5. Maui It is nicknamed the "Valley Isle" and was originally two islands. A flat, central isthmus—the "valley"—connects the older West Maui Mountains to the eastern dormant volcano, Haleakalā. Named after the prankster demigod of Polynesian folklore, Maui is the second largest of the Hawaiian Islands. Maui County includes the neighboring

Island Hopping

♥♥

Getting from island to island is affordable and quick. Flights average 30 minutes. There are two main carriers that travel daily to the neighbor islands: Aloha Airlines, www.alohaairlines.com or (808)484-1111 and Hawaiian Airlines, www.hawaiianair.com or (808)838-1555.

Chrissy Lambert Photography

Notes:

islands of Lāna'i, Moloka'i and Kaho'olawe. Maui boasts the oldest American school west of the Rocky Mountains, Lahaina Luna, founded in 1831. It has earned distinction as one of the best places in the world to whale watch from December to April. Humpbacks are Hawai'i's state mammal, and if you're lucky enough to be here in season, don't pass up an opportunity for a whale watch tour. Year round, hit the ground running with scores of other exciting ocean activities. You can take a historic walking tour in Lāhainā, tee up for championship golf in Kā'anapali and Kapalua and dive into an underwater park at the volcanic islet of Molokini–or get married! Popular areas to marry are the beautiful resorts and estates in Wailea and in Kā'anapali.

(Visit www.gohawaii.com/vacationplanningmaui/ or www.thisweek.com for more on Maui)

6. Moloka'i

It is also known as "The Friendly Isle" and it is 260 square miles with a population of more than 6,000. The island's most popular landmark or institution is the Moloka'i Ranch. It's located eight miles from Maui. Points of interest include: Hawai'i's longest beach (the three-mile Pāpōhaku), the sea cliffs of the Pali Coast, Waikolu Valley Lookout, Kamakou Preserve, Hālawa Valley and the Kalaupapa Lookout. It is home to a predominantly Hawaiian populace, due in part to the Hawaiian Homestead acreage at Ho'olehua. Only the island of Ni'ihau has a higher ratio of Hawaiian residents. Some popular places to marry on Moloka'i are: Moloka'i Ranch, Kaluakoi Hotel and Golf Club, Kapuāiwa Coconut Grove/Kiowea Park and many other public beach parks.

(Visit www.gohawaii.com/vacationplanningmolokai or www.hawaiianweddings.net/molokailocations.html for more on Moloka'i.)

7. **Ni'ihau** "The Forbidden Isle" is owned by the Robinson family and is sparsely populated with Hawaiian-speaking residents. Kaua'i's offshore neighbor is best known for its museum-quality Ni'ihau shell lei. The tiny island has few modern conveniences and its visitors are few and far between due to a limited access policy enforced by the island's owners. Unless you're very connected with the Robinson family or a long-time resident, not only will you not get married here—you will probably never even step foot on this island. But don't fret—beauty is in no short order in this state.

8. **O'ahu** The most popular and populated island, probably because it offers the best of both worlds. With nightlife, five-star restaurants, bright city lights and world-class shopping, it affords visitors the amenities of a big city, yet is only a thirty-minute drive from deserted, sun-kissed beaches, desolate roads and miles of sugar cane and pineapple fields. Home to 76 percent of the state's million-plus population, it's no wonder O'ahu is referred to as "The Gathering Place." O'ahu is also home to the state's largest city, Honolulu.

Top sites include the Arizona Memorial, the USS *Missouri*, The Polynesian Cultural Center, Hanauma Bay, Diamond Head and the National Cemetery of the Pacific (Punchbowl). Popular places to marry are hotels, picturesque golf courses, beaches and private estates. (Visit www.gohawaii.com/vacationplanningoahu/ or www.thisweek.com for more on O'ahu.)

For more suggestions on ceremony and/or reception sites on the four main islands see the 'Outdoor Wedding' section on page 15 and the resources beginning on page 88.

If you want to add a nice Hawaiian flair to your champagne, Hawai'i does have its own locally made bubbly. It's made in Maui and is available throughout the state. Maui Brut is a little pink in color and tastes great.

For information on the champagne and other Maui-made wines, call **Tedeschi Vineyards** (877) 878-6058 or visit www.mauiwine.com.

Hawai'i: 50th State. Comprised of eight major islands (Hawai'i, Kaho'olawe, Kaua'i, Lāna'i, Maui, Moloka'i, Ni'ihau, O'ahu)

Currency: U.S. Dollar

Primary Language: English

Phone Area Code: (808) statewide

Daylight Savings Time & Time Difference: Hawai'i has no daylight savings time, however, there is a time difference between Hawai'i and everywhere else. During standard time (November–March), Hawai'i is two hours behind the Pacific time zone. And during daylight savings time (April–October), Hawai'i is three hours behind the Pacific time zone.

Weather: 77° average year-round temperature

Climate: Subtropical

Avg. Humidity: 56–72 percent

Tradewinds are named after the breezes that brought merchant ships to the islands. Short, intermittent showers are called "blessings." Sometimes you hardly feel the drops, and when you look around, you see a rainbow.

Average Temperature on Major Islands:

Kahului, Maui: 67°–84°	Honolulu, O'ahu: 70°–84°
Hilo, Hawai'i: 66°–82°	Līhu'e, Kaua'i: 70°–81°

Weather Service Reports for Major Islands

Maui: (808) 877-5111	Big Island: (808) 961-5582
O'ahu: (808) 973-4381	Kaua'i: (808) 245-6001

State Flower: Hibiscus

State Mammal: Humpback Whale

State Bird: Nēnē (Hawaiian goose)

State Name: Kamehameha the Great, who hailed from the Big Island of Hawai'i, unified all the islands and named his kingdom after his island home. The Territory of Hawai'i became the 50th state in 1959.

State Flag: Eight alternating red, white and blue stripes represent the large islands. The flag resembles Great Britain's Union Jack as many of King Kamehameha's advisors were British.

State Motto: "Ua mau ke ea o ka 'aina i ka pono—The life of the land is perpetuated in righteousness."

State Fish: The black and yellow reef triggerfish or humuhumunukunukuapua'a was made popular in the song "I Want to Go Back to My Little Grass Shack."

State Gem: Black coral

State Tree: The kukui, or candlenut, is used in torches.

State Tax: A state excise tax of 4.166 percent is added to Hawai'i purchases. Foreign visitors must pay duty at customs upon arrival home.

Quarantine Regulations: Federal law prohibits taking or sending certain fresh fruits, vegetables and plants to the U.S. Mainland. Some quarantined items may be shipped if they are inspected by the U.S. Dept. of Agriculture (USDA) before shipment. Call USDA's 24-hour recorded hotline for information: (808) 541-1991; or call (808) 861-8490, 9 A.M.–3 P.M., Monday–Friday.

On the Roads: Speed limits in Hawai'i are generally lower than anywhere else. Wearing seat belts is mandatory for driver, front seat passengers and backseat passengers fourteen-years or younger. Toddlers age four and under must ride in child safety seats.

To report lost or stolen credit cards:

American Express: 1-800-528-4800

VISA: 1-800-336-8472

Diners Club: 1-800-234-6377

Mastercard: 1-800-627-8372

Harrington Photography

Harrington Photography

From the moment we got engaged, we both knew we wanted a grand wedding—one that would symbolize the momentous occasion, one that would help us commemorate our union as husband and wife.

After selecting the date and church, all of our attention turned to the reception. We had attended dozens of weddings the previous two years and Hyatt Regency Waikīkī always stood out for us. Since we had a lot of guests from the mainland and beyond, we knew the heart of Waikīkī would be the perfect location. We liked the logistics of having the ballroom separate from the hotel as it added to the sense of privacy. And it was also large enough to comfortably seat our 400-plus guests.

From our first phone call to the Hyatt catering department, we knew we had selected the perfect venue. Heather Chong, our catering manager, was very professional and accommodated our every need. She made us feel as if our reception was as important to her as it was to us. We knew we were in the right hands.

Jason Nishikawa & Joy Nakagawa

♥♥

HYATT REGENCY WAIKIKI

To this day, we are still getting compliments on our wedding and reception. The romantic ambiance that filled the room was magical. And people haven't stop raving about the food, from the pupu buffet that greeted them upon arrival to the lavish dinner buffet. We can truly say that the entire wedding day experience surpassed our expectations. Everyone from the valet service, bellmen, waiters, bartenders and of course, catering staff, went out of their way to assure us of the perfect wedding day. Everyone dreams of their wedding day and Hyatt Regency Waikīkī helped make that dream come true for us.

(For more information on the Hyatt Regency Waikīkī see page 95.)

Plan Accordingly...

Keep in mind the following state holidays and major events when planning your wedding in Hawai'i. It may affect flight availability, hotel and car accommodations. (*Holidays celebrated that are unique to the state of Hawai'i.)

New Years Day- January 1st. The first month of the Gregorian calendar year.

Martin Luther King Day- Observed on the third Monday in January.

Presidents' Day- Observed on the third Monday in February.

***Prince Kūhiō Day-** March 26th is the day Hawai'i celebrates the birthday of Prince Jonah Kūhiō Kalaniana'ole, Hawai'i's second delegate to Congress. Kūhiō was known as the "Citizen Prince" and was in line to become king before the monarchy was overthrown in 1893.

Good Friday- Observed the Friday before Easter Sunday.

Memorial Day- Observed on the last Monday in May.

***King Kamehameha Day-** Observed on June 11. Kamehameha V designated June 11 as a public holiday to honor the memory of his great-grandfather who was the first ruler of the united Hawaiian Islands.

Independence Day- July 4th.

***Admissions Day-** Observed on the third Friday in August celebrating the anniversary of Hawaiian statehood.

Labor Day- This legal holiday is observed on the first Monday in September. It is considered a day of rest and recreation and is generally the end of the summer vacation.

Veterans' Day- Observed on November 11th.

Election Day- Observed on the first Tuesday in November during election years.

Thanksgiving Day- Observed on the fourth Thursday in November.

Christmas- Observed on December 25th.

Notes:

Island-wide Events

Aloha Festivals (Island-wide)- Aloha Festivals is the nation's only statewide, multi-cultural celebration. Featuring Hawai'i's music, dance and history, it is intended to perpetuate the unique island traditions. The festivals run from August through October. Call (808) 589-1771 for information on each island.

Annual Great Aloha Run (O'ahu)- This 8.15 mile run/walk on Presidents' Day attracts runners from around the country, promotes physical fitness and raises money for numerous local charities. Call (808) 528-7388 for more information.

Honolulu Marathon- Honolulu is host to the world's fourth largest marathon. The annual race happens mid-December and attracts more than 30,000 entrants. For more information on marathon dates and events log on to www.honolulu marathon.org or contact the Honolulu Marathon Office (808) 734-7200, fax (808) 732-7057, or email info@honolulu marathon.org.

Merrie Monarch (on the Big Island of Hawai'i)- A week-long festival of cultural events including Hawai'i's most prestigious hula competition at Edith Kanaka'ole Stadium in Hilo. Call Big Island Visitor Bureau for ticket information at (808) 961-5797.

Pro Bowl All-Star Football Game (O'ahu)- The best football players from the NFC and AFC compete at Aloha Stadium on O'ahu. For information call the National Football League (212) 450-2000 or the Aloha Stadium Box Office at (808) 486-9300.

For more information on island-wide calendar events, festivals, fairs, sporting events, tournaments and more, visit www.thisweek.com or www.gohawaii.about.com.

Outdoor Weddings

More than 50 percent of the people who come to Hawai'i specifically to get married want an outdoor wedding. So it's no surprise that for visitors and residents alike beach, park and other natural landmarks are a very common venue for wedding ceremonies.

There are more than 184 miles of sandy shoreline around the state of Hawai'i and 50.3 miles on O'ahu alone. Although we cannot list all of these areas, we did think it would be helpful to dedicate a little extra time to tell you how you can go about booking and planning for an outdoor/park/beach wedding in Hawai'i.

Popular outdoor sites on O'ahu are private estates and beachside hotels along Waikīkī's world-renowned shoreline. You can also tie the knot aboard a sunset dinner cruise or opt for one of O'ahu's beautiful botanical gardens. O'ahu offers the full spectrum of outdoor wedding options.

Kapalua Bay Beach on Maui's west side was named, "The World's Most Beautiful Beach" by *Condé Naste Travel* magazine for three years in a row. Ka'anapali's westerly exposure results in magnificent back lit sunrises and spectacular Maui wedding sunsets. West Maui has more than twice as many white sand beaches than any other island in Hawaii. The Old Lāhainā Lū'au on Maui was voted as one of the top ten places to marry by the Travel Channel in 2002. Maui Tropical Plantation makes for a lush, garden backdrop to beautiful outdoor wedding. Kīhei, Wailea and Makena (South Maui) are other popular areas to get married on Maui. South Maui is home to some of the best hotels on the island.

Some "in" places for Big Island nuptials are Hawaii Tropical Botanical Gardens, Akaka Falls State Park, Nani Mau Gardens on the east side; Sadie Seymour Gardens at Kona Outdoor Circle and Hulihee Palace on the west side. The Big Island is less crowded than O'ahu and Maui and you can have a beach hideaway or tropical picnic all to yourself.

As we mentioned earlier, Fern Grotto is the place to get married on Kaua'i. You can rent private boats for your wedding party to get there right at the Wailua Marina. Hanalei and Princeville are also popular backdrops. Some beach and cove spots popular with Kaua'i

wedding insiders are Kalapaki Beach, Ninini Lighthouse, Limahuli Botanical Gardens and Hanalei Bay.

For a listing of ceremony and reception sites see pages 88–106.

Hawai'i is known for beautiful year-round climes but for the record, it does have a "rainy" and "dry" season. Typically our rainy season is from November–March, while our dry season is considered to be April–October. Keep these factors in mind if and when you're planning an outdoor wedding. And although these are good guidelines to go by, mother nature has a mind of her own, and doesn't always comply with our preset notion of when it should and shouldn't rain.

Once you've selected the property where you want to get married, you'll need to apply for a permit. There are two main divisions of park and land use: the State and the City & County. We've listed some general guidelines and the contact information for both of these departments.

State Park Use

Most state parks are open year-round. For weddings you need to apply for a special-use permit. Each special-use permit shall be considered on its own merit and must be compatible with the functions and purposes of each individual area. Special-use permit requests must be submitted at least 45 days before the requested date of use. Refer to the contact information for specific fees, permit information and guidelines for usage. For state parks and beach permits contact the district offices and park concessionaires listed below or visit their website at www.hawaii.gov/dlnr/dsp/dsp.html

O'ahu District
P.O. Box 621
(1151 Punchbowl Street, #131), Honolulu, HI 96809
☏ (808) 587-0300
Hours: Monday–Friday, 8:00 A.M. to 3:30 P.M.

Friends of Mālaekahana (Oʻahu)
56-335 Kamehameha Hwy., Kahuku, HI 96731
☎ (808) 293-1736
Hours: Monday–Friday, 10:00 A.M. to 3:00 P.M.

Maui District
54 S. High Street #101, Wailuku, HI 96793
☎ (808) 984-8109
Hours: Monday–Friday, 8:00 A.M. to 3:30 P.M.

Kauaʻi District
3060 Elwa Street, #306, Līhuʻe HI 96766-1875
☎ (808) 274-3444
Hours: Monday–Friday, 8:00 A.M. to 3:30 P.M.

Hawaiʻi District (the "Big Island")
P.O. Box 936, (75 Aupuni St., #204), Hilo, HI 96721-0936
☎ (808) 974-6200
Hours: Monday–Friday, 8:00 A.M. to 3:30 P.M.
(Reservations taken between 8:00 A.M. to 2:00 P.M. only)

Kokeʻe Lodge (Hawaiʻi)
P.O. Box 819, Waimea, HI 96796
Hours: 7 days a week, 9:00 A.M. to 3:45 P.M.

City Parks and Beach Use

Park-use permits and deposits are required for the use of city park facilities for wedding ceremonies—among other things. The first thing you need to do is call the park you're interested in using to check on its availability. You'll need to complete and submit an "Application for Use of Park Facilities" form at least three weeks prior to the date you wish to use the facility. The forms can be obtained at any park or at the Parks Permit Office at 650 South King Street, Honolulu, Hawaiʻi 96813, or by contacting the offices listed below. After your form has been received and processed, you will be notified to pick up your permit at the Parks Permit Office. You can make any required deposits and fees at that time; personal checks are preferred. Checks will be deposited into the City Treasury. If your event did not cause any damage to the event site and you have removed all trash generated by your event, you will be reimbursed

Notes:

Since ancient times, white doves have been regarded as a symbol of love, peace, and purity of heart. As few as two or as many as forty can be released from beautiful white wicker baskets.

Notes:

the amount of your deposit within six to eight weeks. A city treasury check will be issued and mailed to the person and address on the park-use permit.

For permit and park-use information for city and county parks and beaches you can contact:

Oʻahu
Department of Parks and Recreation
1000 Uluohia Street, Suite 309, Kapolei, Hawaiʻi 96707
☎ (808) 692-5585 / 🖷 692-5131

Maui
Department of Parks and Recreation
1580C Kaʻahumanu Avenue, Wailuku, HI 96793
☎ (808) 270-7383
www.countyofmaui.maui.net/departments/Parks/directory.htm
E-mail: parks.dept@co.maui.hi.us
(The County of Maui operates more than 130 park and recreation areas on the three islands of Maui, Lānaʻi, and Molokaʻi.)

Kauaʻi
County of Kauaʻi, Department of Public Works
Division of Parks and Recreation
4444 Rice Street, Moʻikeha Building, Suite 150
Līhuʻe, HI 96766
☎ (808) 241-6660
www.kauaigov.org/parks.htm

Hawaiʻi
County of Hawaiʻi, Department of Parks & Recreation
25 Aupuni Street, Hilo, HI 96720
☎ (808) 961-8311
Hours: Monday–Friday 7:45 A.M. to 4:30 P.M.
www.hawaii-county.com/parks/parks.htm

There seems to be an endless amount of divisions of divisions of divisions and on paper it can look overwhelming. But basically all you need to do is find out the name of the park where you want to get married, contact the number above that most closely matches the area you're interested in, and call it. If you're not calling the right district, the person you're speaking to should be able to direct you to the correct district and answer any of your questions.

The Great Outdoors

♥♥

Outdoor weddings in Hawai'i are beautiful—except when the weather is not. Here are some things to consider when planning your outdoor wedding (on or near the beach).

1) Have a backup plan in case it rains. Passing showers are commonplace in the islands and considered a blessing. But torrential downpours make for a messy ceremony and/or reception—so, if at all possible, have a "Plan B." Options are renting a tent or canopy or booking an indoor backup site. Another option is having your wedding at a beachfront location with indoor capabilities such as a hotel or estate.

2) If you're having your ceremony literally *on* the beach, don't put chairs directly on the sand if at all possible. The sand is uneven and unstable, and many of your guests may not be dressed appropriately for walking and/or sitting on the sand. Look for a grassy knoll to place chairs for guests. If you do want your ceremony on the sand, consider renting some type of flooring for the chairs to be placed on. Another option is having guests stand for the ceremony, which is usually only about twenty minutes.

3) Consider the glare of the sun for you and your guests. Try to position everyone where there is minimal time staring directly into the sun. The beauty of the ocean backdrop gets lost when no one can even open their eyes, through the glaring sun, to see it.

4) If it's a daytime wedding, think about having bottled water available for guests as they arrive. Hawai'i's sun can be hot; and guests—especially older ones—can dehydrate quickly in the afternoon sun.

5) Opt for hand-held fans to distribute to guests as wedding favors or as a nice gesture to help keep the sun out of their eyes and a cool breeze handy.

6) If you're getting married or having your reception at a location that is known for having lots of mosquitoes or other bugs, consider having bug spray or lotion available or using citronella candles.

7) Check with the local weather service with regard to tide and sunset times. And keep those factors in mind when scheduling your ceremony time.

8) Make sure to find out all the rules and restrictions for the beach or park you are "renting." Some guidelines you can expect are restrictions on number of guests; use or availability of electrical outlets; use of amplified sound/music; time allotted. Most public beaches and parks will only allow small ceremonies, so if you're planning a large outdoor wedding you may need to go to Plan C.

We were married on December 21, 2002. This date was chosen for several reasons but was especially significant because of two things. First, it represents the Winter Solstice. Second, it has a numerological translation into the number 1 which represents "new beginnings."

We live on O'ahu and are in love with Hawai'i. We try to travel to a neighbor island at least twice a year. During one of our neighbor island trips, this time to the island of Molokai, we were pleasantly surprised at our find. We stayed at the Sheraton Molokai Ranch & Beach Village. This unique resort has what I like to call a Gemini effect. It is truly two-faced. It has a beautiful rustic lodge

Scott Creel & Jeanne Gibboney

♥♥

SHERATON MOLOKAI RANCH & BEACH VILLAGE

surrounded by a lush tropical garden, wrap-around lanai, sleek infinity pool with ocean views, spa treatments available, a very nice work-out facility and locker rooms, and awesome rooms decorated in Southwestern décor with luxury bathrooms sporting claw foot bathtubs (my personal favorite). In addition to all this luxury, the resort also offers beach front accommodations with its unique canvas tentalows and surrounding redwood decks located at the Beach Village and just a 20-minute shuttle ride from the Lodge.

We especially fell in love with this resort because of the beautiful surrounding ranch lands, flowing with running horses and cattle, not to mention all the activities available including 125 miles of mountain-biking trails. Its foundation is red dirt and is sprinkled with Mesquite trees (Keawe), which is a close reflection of Texas. This sparked a sense of familiarity and comfort for both of us, as we are both from Texas. This beautiful lodge, with its "big" western atmosphere and over scaled décor, stole our hearts and was a natural choice for us when we were deciding where we wanted to get married.

It was a nice surprise to find out that weddings were one of their specialties. We planned our entire wedding using email. We chose the traditional garden wedding at

(continued on next page)

the Lodge using the beautiful greenhouse pavilion and winding paved walkway located just beyond the pool as the site for our ceremony. The wedding coordinator gave us several packages to choose from. We made our choice and then customized it to our expectations. We wanted a small beautiful wedding and that is what we got. Only our very closest friends and our family were in attendance, about 20 people.

We all arrived on a Friday and got settled in our rooms. That evening at approximately 5:30 pm. we all gathered at the front entrance and piled into the shuttle, which took us down to the beach village for the rehearsal dinner (no rehearsal was necessary, just a nice formality.) We had a large tent set up on the beach in a private area. It was beautifully arranged with white tablecloths, all the appropriate dinnerware and accented by tiki torches for soft lighting around the area. We all gathered at approximately 6:00 pm. on the beach with our bare feet in the sand and a glass of wine in hand to witness one of the most gorgeous sunsets we have ever seen. The food was buffet style and was fabulous. The dinner was followed by a nice gathering up at the Lodge bar equipped with a very nice pool table. The guys smoked

> *We wanted a small beautiful wedding and that is what we got.*

cigars, played pool and celebrated with lots of spirits flowing.

Saturday was our wedding day. The time was scheduled for 4:30 p.m. It was a gorgeous day. Everything flowed nicely and the wedding coordinator had all the details worked out so we did not stress about anything. We had about 18 chairs set up in the garden pavilion, which was decorated with tropical flowers. There was also a table with selected pupus, water, tea and coffee at the wedding site for our guests. The woman who married us was a local Hawaiian of 84 years who was born and raised on Moloka'i. She is considered a kahuna and an Ordained Minister. She gracefully blessed us with a Hawaiian prayer at the beginning of the ceremony and then proceeded with some chosen scripture and vows. She again blessed us in Hawaiian tongue and pronounced us husband and wife.

Our reception was located at the Lodge just off one of the main dining areas and out on an extended lanai. We enjoyed a fabulous dinner with wonderful cuisine, good wine, and a Hawaiian guitarist playing soft Hawaiian music. All in all we had a great time and would not change a thing if we had to do it all over again. We can't wait to go back.

Ethnic Weddings and Customs

Hawai'i's ethnic makeup is more diverse than any other state in the nation. And with this diversity comes a creative blending of wedding traditions and customs. We examine how a few couples merge to find just the right mix of both to make their wedding day as unique and interesting as the couples themselves.

And the bride wore silver… Sonia Patel's face, like every newly-wed bride, lights up with excitement as she describes her eclectic wedding ceremony, filled with tradition. "We mixed the traditions from James' Filipino family and my Indian heritage," she said.

One great way to create a one-of-a-kind wedding experience is to incorporate traditions from different cultures into your ceremony, reception or dress. For some, the cultural traditions start before the ceremony is even planned. It is a Filipino custom for the groom's family to ask his intended bride's family permission for her hand in marriage. In Chinese and Korean customs, ancestors are asked for approval and auspicious dates are chosen according to the bride's and groom's birthdates.

Sonia and James found that there were a few traditions in both the Indian and Filipino customs that were similar. Like the importance placed on unity, fidelity and respect of elders, this isn't too shocking. Traditions in India and the Philippines vary by region, and sometimes, between families. Since Sonia's parents are from Gujarat, the Hindu parts of the wedding were modeled after Gujurati tradition. Sonia wore a sari (a traditional costume for Indian women) made for her by the same tailors in India that made her mother's wedding sari. Traditionally, brides wear red, but Sonia opted for a white sari with silver beading. She also wore the wedding jewelry that her mother wore. Sonia chose not to wear the traditional mendhi (henna tattoos).

It is an Indian tradition to include both the groom's and bride's mothers in the ceremony; as it is a Filipino tradition to include many family members: sponsors, siblings, cousins, godparents, etc. In Sonia and James' wedding, they had their mothers pin Sonia's sari to James' suit jacket. The connecting of the bride's and groom's clothes, symbolic of their unity, is taken from both the Indian and Filipino wedding traditions. Another overlapping cultural tradition the couple used was the draping of a jasmine lei around the couple by their mothers, a symbol of their unity.

Sonia and James were married at Luana Hills, in Maunawili. She liked the outdoor setting, especially since she wanted to incorporate a phera into her wedding. Traditionally, a phera is the act of walking around a flame and is usually done around a fire pit. Sonia and James used a candle instead. During the phera, the couple walk around the flame four times—twice led by the groom, and twice led by the bride. This is to symbolize their commitment to the partnership in the marriage. Sonia also fed Indian sweets to James as a show of her willingness to cook and take care of his house. He then fed her as a show of his ability to provide for her.

The traditions didn't stop at the ceremony. As a surprise for their first dance, James changed from his Armani suit to a dhoti, a long loincloth traditionally worn in southern Asia by Hindu men. It's wrapped around the hips and thighs with one end brought between the legs and tucked

Hawai'i Weddings Made Simple

into the waistband. The dhoti resembles baggy, knee-length trousers. Sonia says, "I had no idea he was going to do that. I almost didn't recognize him!"

❦ **Channe and Brandon Lake** celebrated both their Japanese and his Hawaiian culture during their wedding. Like many Japanese brides here in Hawai'i, Channe set to folding gold cranes for her tsuru soon after they got engaged. In Japanese tradition, tsuru are 1,001 origami cranes that are folded and presented at most important occasions—weddings and special birthdays for example. The cranes are a Japanese symbol for longevity. For a wedding, the bride is supposed to fold one thousand cranes as a display of her patience and diligence. The groom folds one crane as an example of his commitment to the marriage. The cranes are traditionally strung together on string and hung from branches, so the cranes look like they're flying. Nowadays, it's customary to leave the cranes folded and have them mounted in a frame in the form of the bride's and groom's family crest, or mon. Brandon didn't have a mon, so he instead designed a scene of Chinaman's Hat, where the couple first made their commitment to each other.

To pay homage to Brandon's Hawaiian roots, the couple chose to serve their guests traditional Hawaiian lū'au food—lau lau, kalua pig , poi, haupia and more. During the reception, uncles from both Channe's and Brandon's families gave the traditional Japanese toasts; one from the guests to the couple and one from the couple to the guests. The toasts, said in Japanese, are wishes for long life and happiness all around. Each toast is followed by a resounding "Banzai!," meaning ten thousand years, said three times.

The tradition of throwing rice has been replaced by throwing birdseed, confetti and rose petals, or even blowing bubbles. Rice was customarily thrown at the bride and groom to encourage fertility.

For Lianne and Kris Thompson, the wedding was a way to not only share their different cultures, but also their interests. Kris loves Hawaiian music, so he hired a local Hawaiian musician. He also comes from a long line of ranchers on the mainland so he paid homage to that past by wearing his favorite cowboy boots. Lianne shared her Japanese culture by making her tsuru—although she didn't fold them all herself. "Kris knows I'm not that patient," she says. They mounted them in a design of the western wedding vows, "Love, Honor and Cherish," written in kanji. It is also a Japanese tradition for the bride to change outfits during the reception, and Lianne had two outfits planned for her reception.

Their appetizer table also featured many traditional Japanese celebratory dishes including chi chi dango and sashimi. When it came time for their first dance, guests came up to them, placing dollar bills on their clothes. The couple then picked the money off each other's clothes with their mouths. This Filipino tradition has been adopted by most of the cultures here in Hawai'i, and it has become such an integral part in local Hawai'i weddings that some brides assign a bridesmaid to collect all the bills from the couple as they pick them up.

All these couples knew when going into the wedding that they had something special they wanted to incorporate into the event. Of course, it isn't necessary to be from a particular ethnic background to adopt a tradition from that culture into your ceremony. To research other wedding traditions, probably the best source is your own family and elders. Many cultural traditions vary from family to family, and if you're planning on incorporating only certain elements into your event, you may want to consult with your family as to which elements are important to the family, and the best way to include them.

Sri Maiava Rusden

Hawai'i Weddings Made Simple

Here are some wedding traditions from various cultures:

❦ **African-American:** Some couples wear African-printed fabrics as part of their traditional American dress. Others choose headdresses or full African dress. At the end of the ceremony, it is customary for the couple to jump over a broom during the recessional. This custom dates back to when the West Africans were brought to America as slaves. They were stripped of their right to marry so they made up secret marriage rituals. In West Africa it was customary for a bride to sweep the home of her in-laws. So slave couples would jump over a broom to the beat of a drum. It is also said to symbolize the sweeping away of evil and their literal jumping into married life.

❦ **Chinese:** The bride's dress may be red, to symbolize the color of love and joy. Some couples choose to honor their ancestors with a tea, where they kneel before older relatives and family, offering cups of tea as a gesture of respect. The reception might also feature the setting off of firecrackers or a lion dance to ward off evil spirits. As with the Japanese tradition mentioned earlier, the Chinese bride may change outfits several times during her reception.

❦ **Fijian:** One of the events leading up to the Fijian wedding is the "Warming." The groom himself provides food for his bride's family and sends it to them. Before the ceremony, the bride is adorned with a necklace, which the groom removes during the ceremony, signaling that she is now married.

❦ **Filipino:** When a couple becomes engaged, they still have to ask the permission of the bride's family. This is called the pamanhikan. If her family approves, it is during this meeting that the details of the wedding will be discussed: guest lists, locations for receptions, etc. It is traditional for

Get With the Program

— ♥♥ —

Many couples will put together a printed program so guests can follow along during the ceremony. This is especially helpful if your guests are unfamiliar with your religion or any ethnic traditions you are incorporating into your ceremony. It also serves as a nice keepsake for your wedding day. The program may include the ceremony order, letters from the bride and groom, the names of the bridal party and their relationship with the bride and groom, music selections, readings, thank-you's, photos, etc. Your ushers can hand them out to guests as they arrive or you can place them on the seats.

Here are some additional resources for a more in-depth look at ethnic weddings and traditions.

Wild Geese and Tea: An Asian-American Wedding Planner (Shu Shu Costa)

Under the Wedding Canopy: Love and Marriage in Judaism (David C. Gross, Esther R. Gross)

Polish Weddings: Customs & Traditions (Sophie Hodorowicz Knab)

Something Old Something New: Ethnic Weddings in America (Gail F. Stern)

The Christian Wedding Planner (Ruth Muzzy and R. Kent Hughes)

Happy Is the Bride the Sun Shines On: Wedding Beliefs, Customs, and Traditions (Leslie Jones)

Interfaith Wedding Ceremonies: Samples and Sources (Joan C. Hawxhurst)

Jumping the Broom: The African-American Wedding Planner (Harriette Cole)

there to be "sponsors" for Filipino weddings. These sponsors can be godparents, family friends, or elders within the couple's families. Sponsors help with the wedding by giving advice and defraying costs such as the bride's dress or parts of the ceremony and reception. The unity candle is an important part of the Filipino wedding ceremony. The bride and groom light a single candle with their own candles, joining them in life. The other popular Filipino tradition is the money dance discussed earlier in this chapter. And in Hawai'i, it is done at weddings of all nationalities.

❧ **Hawaiian:** Many Hawaiian couples will wear maile and/or pikake leis as part of their wedding costume. This custom is adopted by many couples in Hawai'i, regardless of their heritage. Lū'au foods are served to the couple and some people may have a Hawaiian blessing and/or chant as part of their wedding ceremony. The bride may also dance a hula for her new husband during the ceremony. This tradition is also adopted by many brides, regardless of their ethnic background.

❧ **Indian:** As stated before, many Indian traditions vary between states. In addition to those that Sonia used in her wedding, some Indian traditions include the draping of flower garlands from the couple's wedding costumes; the kanyadaan in which the couple's parents wash their feet in milk and water to purify them; and the hastamelap where the bride and groom place their right hands together.

❧ **Japanese:** Brides from the Edo era of Japan wore all-white wedding kimonos, but most Japanese-American brides opt for the traditional American white wedding gown. Some brides-to-be may have their portrait taken in a white kimono as an engagement photo. One Japanese custom adopted by some here in Hawai'i is the san san kudo, which is the sharing of sake from three cups between the wedding couple. The groom leads by taking sips from one cup, the bride follows suit and they progress through the three cups. The sake is then offered to the family. This custom varies between families, and may be done in a private ceremony rather than during a large reception.

Another popular custom taken from Japanese culture is taiko drum performances during the reception. The taiko drum performances are supposed to chase away bad spirits.

Perhaps the most common Japanese tradition carried out in marriages in Hawai'i is the folding of 1,001 Japanese cranes. The crane, or tsuru, represents good fortune, happiness, peace and longevity. In Japan, the crane is said to live for a thousand years when it mates. In Hawai'i, couples add the one extra crane for good luck and have the origami cranes mounted and framed in a unique art piece.

❧ **Jewish:** No single set of rules applies to all Jewish weddings. There are many differences among the Orthodox, Conservative, and Reform branches of the faith. Weddings may take place at any time except on the Sabbath, on Holy Days or festival periods.

There is the signing of the marriage contract (the Ketubah) by the groom. The Ketubah is an illustrated and artistically lettered document in Hebrew detailing what the groom promises to provide for the bride.

The ceremonies are traditionally performed under a huppah (a canopy). As the bride arrives under the huppah, she may walk three or seven times around the groom, symbolizing that the woman is a protective wall for her husband and stepping inside, they have a new status or family circle.

The end of the ceremony is signaled by the groom breaking a napkin-wrapped wineglass underfoot, in remembrance of the destruction of the Holy Temple in

"Something old, something new, something borrowed, something blue, with a sixpence in your shoe."

Why blue you ask? Apparently tradition dates back to ancient Israel when brides wore blue ribbons on the border of their wedding clothes to symbolize love, modesty and fidelity. Blue was also a popular color for Christian brides because it symbolizes the purity of the Virgin Mary. Mary is most often depicted wearing that color in paintings and statues.

Notes:

in Jerusalem, and other tragedies that have befallen the Jewish Faith.

Korean: The traditional Korean bridal gown is the hanbok, once reserved for those of nobility, like the groom's faruotsu (a dark-green robe embroidered with gold symbols). The goose and duck are animals that mate for life and it is because of this fidelity that the Korean groom traditionally gifted the bride's family with a duck or goose. Nowadays, the bride's family receives a wooden fowl as a symbol of the groom's commitment. Another traditional custom is the kunbere, in which the couple share a wine called jung jong. The bride and groom sip the wine from separate cups, traditionally made of gourd; the wine is then mixed together and poured into their cups again. When the couple sips from their cups a second time, they are married.

Samoan: A bride may present her new family with fine mats during the wedding ceremony. "Talking chiefs" dance and give speeches during the wedding feast, set up by both the bride's and groom's families.

Vietnamese: In a traditional Vietnamese wedding, an auspicious wedding date is chosen by an astrologer. The groom brings gifts to the bride's family. Then the bride walks over coals at the groom's house to ward off bad spirits. Both the bride and groom are presented at each other's family altars for the ancestors' approval. Then the officiant ties a red thread around the couple and a wedding altar. Once this is done, the couple is married.

Whatever wedding traditions you choose to incorporate into your wedding ceremony and/or reception, it's a great way to add some culture and character to one of the longest-standing institutions—the institution of marriage.

Blaine Michioka (Rainbow Photography-Kauai)

Blaine Michioka (Rainbow Photography-Kauai)

Dan Obuhanych & Mel Mori

♥♥

KILAUEA LAKESIDE ESTATE

Dan and I were married on a private estate in Kilauea, Kaua'i. What we wanted most was to have a small, simple, and intimate wedding with our closest friends and family in attendance.

I imagine that most brides and grooms get nervous before the big day, but Dan and I were pretty relaxed and at ease because we were surrounded by all the people whom we love. Many of our friends and family arrived several days before our wedding to help in any way they could. The guys took Dan out for a couple golf games and the girls took me out for tea at Princeville and shopping around the island. The week leading up to our wedding was like a mini-vacation for both Dan and me and our guests. So many special memories were made.

We exchanged vows overlooking a beautiful lake with 46 of the most important people in our lives watching and supporting us as we began our new life together. Immediately following the ceremony, our best man and matron of honor gave a champagne toast. All of our guests gathered around and held up their glasses and our photographer was able to capture this moment. It was awesome!

There were two swans that live on the lake which surrounds the estate. Our photographer was able to capture them in several of our wedding photos too. It rained a little before our ceremony and it was a bit windy while we exchanged our vows. My chapel-length veil blew like a sail in the wind. My head was pulled in all directions while I tried to concentrate and say my vows. At one point, my mother and matron of honor had to grab hold of my veil so that it wouldn't whip anyone in the face. I guess that's the chance you take when you have an outdoor wedding. Other than that, everything went as planned.

The location we chose was perfect. It was very private and tucked away near the mountains and it provided the most beautiful scenery for our wedding photos. Dan and I were fortunate to have found such a wonderful location. Our wedding day was just as we had envisioned—even the out-of-control veil and rain couldn't spoil it!

It was one of the best days of our lives.

This is a standard timeline. It's based on the premise that you have nine to twelve months to plan your wedding. There will be those who start planning several years earlier while still others may only have several weeks. Use this timeline more as your list of things to do within the time that you have. Don't get discouraged if you don't have nine to twelve months, some of these things may not even be applicable for your wedding, but it's a good starting point. Now, obviously, if you hire a wedding consultant or planner, she or he can assist with many of these tasks and create a more specific timeline of the list of things you need to get done.

Nine to Twelve Months Before:

❑ Announce your engagement.

❑ Establish a preliminary budget.

❑ Start a guest wish list to help you gauge how many people you will be inviting.

❑ Hire a wedding planner (if you think you need one). If you're not hiring a wedding planner, select and recruit some family and friends to help you with the wedding planning process.

❑ Select a wedding date and time.

❑ Determine the type of wedding you want (size, formality, style, color scheme).

❑ Select and secure your ceremony location.

❑ Select and secure your reception location.

❑ Start shopping for your engagement rings/bands.

❑ Select and secure your officiant.

❑ Begin to select and secure your major vendors (photographer, florist, baker, videographer, caterer, DJ or band, entertainment, etc.).

❑ Go to wedding expos and related events for ideas. (Check for local wedding expo dates, times, and locations.)

❑ Select, contact, and confirm bridal party (bridesmaids, groomsmen, ushers, flower girl, ring bearer).

❑ Select and purchase your wedding gown.

❑ Mail "save the date" cards to out-of-town guests.

❑ Purchase a wedding binder or planner book to help keep all contracts, notes, and important information.

Six to Nine Months Before:

❑ Narrow down the guest list (ask your families to do the same). Start compiling current addresses and contact information.

❑ Shop for the wedding accessories (headpiece, veil, shoes, accessories, etc.).

❑ Start planning for the honeymoon.

❑ Register with a bridal gift registry.

❑ Select and order the bridesmaids' dresses.

❑ Begin planning for your wedding day itinerary and reception program.

❑ Begin compiling a contact sheet with names and phone numbers of all key vendors.

Four to Six Months Before:

❑ Select and order the invitations and stationery. Prepare all maps and directions for the ceremony, reception and rehearsal dinner.

❑ Complete the guest lists with up-to-date addresses and contact info.

❑ Begin addressing invitations/announcements.

❑ Remind mothers to start shopping for their dresses.

❑ Select and order the men's attire.

❑ Finalize honeymoon details and make the necessary reservations. Apply for or update passports and other necessary travel documents.

❑ Assign and confirm wedding responsibilities (coordinator, if you are not hiring one, trouble shooter, reception table, someone to handle passing out the leis and flowers to family and friends, and ushers).

❏ Select wedding music and review with musicians and or disc jockey.

❏ Wedding dress fitting.

Two to Four Months Before:

❏ Shop around for transportation companies. Book one.

❏ Confirm the menu and catering details with the caterer.

❏ Buy or create your own wedding guest book (preferably with removable pages for a quick check-in procedure; some reception sites will provide one if you're spending x amount of dollars).

❏ Set the dates and times with the officiant and ceremony site coordinator for the rehearsal.

❏ Determine your resources for designing and printing the program for the ceremony.

❏ Finalize the florist details, photographer, videographer, musicians, transportation, baker, caterer, hair and makeup persons, etc.

❏ Make reservations for rehearsal dinner, time and place.

❏ Confirm the wedding cake details with the baker, and florist, if necessary.

❏ Go to pre-marital counseling with your officiant, pastor or clergy person.

❏ Select gifts for all your attendants.

Six to Eight Weeks Before:

❏ Decide on wedding vows. (You can write them yourselves, use standard ones from your officiant, or go to the bookstore or library and purchase a book on vows.)

❏ Mail out invitations and announcements.

❏ Purchase, borrow or make wedding accessories such as the ring pillow, flower girl basket, garter, candles, toasting glasses, favors, centerpieces, card box, etc.

❏ Wedding dress fitting.

Four to Six Weeks Before:

❏ Estimate the expected number of guests.

❏ Buy a gift for the groom or the bride (whichever applies to you).

❏ Pick up your wedding rings.

❏ Plan the seating for the reception as well as other details for the ceremony and reception. Start writing placecards, if applicable.

❏ Make sure all bridesmaids' dresses have been fitted.

❏ Create a script or outline for your emcee.

Two Weeks Before:

❏ Make preliminary table assignments, if applicable.

❏ Make arrangements for someone to be in charge of collecting and safe-keeping gifts after guest check-in is complete.

❏ Handle business and legal details such as name changes, address changes, etc.

❏ Make sure all clothing and accessories for you and the bridal party are ready (veil, shoes, jewelry, etc.).

❏ Call any guests who have not responded yet.

❏ Final wedding dress fitting.

One Week Before:

❏ Confirm *everything*! (florists, officiant, photographer, caterer, baker, ushers, videographer, musicians, entertainers, emcee, guest table attendants, ceremony and reception sites).

❏ Give final count to banquet hall or caterer; finalize seating arrangements.

❏ Review any seating details with the ushers and reception table attendants.

❏ Reconfirm your honeymoon reservations. Ensure you have any necessary plane tickets, travel documents and travel insurance.

❏ Finalize all the place cards for the reception.

❏ Review all the final details with your photographer, videographer, etc.

❏ Review timeline with your wedding coordinator and/or those assisting at the ceremony and reception.

❏ Finalize your rehearsal dinner arrangements or other plans.

❏ Meet with coordinator or your point person and equip her with any and all emergency phone numbers for all suppliers and vendors. If not a wedding planner by trade, give her a three-ring binder with copies of all your wedding day contracts, contact names and numbers, a list of those attending rehearsal and/or dinner, copies of wedding day itinerary to give to all vendors, copy of officiant's timeline, flower list, copy of the vows and everything else she might need to help ensure your day runs flawlessly (or at least make you think it is!).

❏ Create a wedding day "emergency kit" (see page 146 for details).

❏ Pack for honeymoon or wedding day if you're staying at a hotel or somewhere other than home prior to or following your wedding.

One to Two Days Before:

❏ Finalize script or outline for your emcee and go over it with him/her.

❏ Get a manicure or massage.

❏ Review and rehearse all the details with your bridal party.

❏ Make sure groomsmen pick up *and* try on tuxes or formal wear.

❏ Confirm last minute details with hair and makeup person.

❏ Make envelopes with vendors names with cash payments for services needed on wedding day (limo, florist, musicians, etc.).

❏ Have rehearsal and rehearsal dinner. Give attendants gifts.

❏ Make final seating arrangements/guest list. Make multiple printouts for coordinator and guest table assistants.

❏ Create and distribute final contact sheet with all key people/vendors' names and phone numbers, preferably cell phone numbers.

The Big Day:

❏ Eat something and make sure you drink lots of water.

❏ Allow yourself plenty of time to get dressed.

❏ Prepare for your hairdresser and makeup appointments.

❏ Give your coordinator or point person the tips or final payments in sealed, labeled envelopes to give to your vendors.

❏ Give your marriage license to the officiant.

❏ Start on time. Relax.

❏ Enjoy every second.

❏ Let your coordinator or point person stress now!!

Marcia Campbell

Marcia Campbell

Brian and I were married at our "dream hotel," the beautiful and elegant Halekulani Hotel in Waikīkī, Hawai'i. We exchanged vows on the grounds of the hotel, where our minister began the ceremony with a beautiful Hawaiian blessing (Brian's family, who traveled all the way from Louisiana to attend our wedding, really enjoyed this part of the ceremony). We chose our site for its picturesque surroundings, impeccable service, and mouth-watering food, since Cajuns know good food. After all, we were told, guests generally don't remember what the flowers looked like or what the program was about, but they remember how good the food was. It was amazing to see the people we cared about most in this world, here in one location to share this special day with us.

My dear sister, bless her heart, had done everything in her power to make sure this day went smoothly. Because everything was so well coordinated I was truly able to enjoy every single moment of this wonderful day. There seemed to be a happy, light-hearted, and magical feeling in the air. I thought that I would be nervous but I felt so exhilarated and excited, that I had an ear-to-ear grin as I walked down the aisle. Our photographer and videographer were worth every single cent as

Brian Johnson & Anne Furubayashi

♥♥

HALEKULANI HOTEL

they captured some of the most precious moments that would've gone unnoticed if it hadn't been for their wonderful work.

The best part of the ceremony was the moving speeches by my four bridesmaids, all of whom expressed the importance of love and friendship; few eyes were left dry (including Brian's Uncle Frank who never cries). Some other memorable moments from our wedding were: 1) Realizing that I forgot to take my wedding gown out of the bag as soon as I got to the hotel so it wouldn't wrinkle. 2) Not knowing the procedure for the cake-cutting portion of the ceremony, locking arms, fumbling around, laughing hysterically and dropping the cake knife on the floor. 3) Our friends singing our "First Dance" song to us. 4) Realizing that my false eyelashes had begun to slowly fall off—too many tears of joy and laughter I think! I didn't realize what was happening until I started to hear comments like, "Oh my gosh, is that a spider on the table?" By the end of the day, I had two remaining false eyelashes attached to my eye with a few still lingering on my cheeks.

As you can tell, although our wedding wasn't flawless, (it never is!) it was a perfect wedding for us and we loved and cherished every single minute of it.

Ceremony
Goody Golf Club
5:00 P.M.

11:00-3:15 P.M.
❏ Women at hotel for hair and makeup

1:15
❏ _______________ to bring everything for set-up, centerpieces, favors, guest table and decorations, programs, rose petals, baskets… (_______________ bringing centerpieces and favors, _______________ and _______________ bringing guest table, _______________ and _______________ will man guest table after ceremony, _______________ and _______________ to help set-up, rose petals sachets in baskets at the entrance) _______________ making, bringing and setting up signs.

1:30
❏ Men arrive at chapel, get dressed and get ready to take photos.

2:00
❏ Florist drops off flowers at chapel. _______________ and _______________ bring flowers and leis for family/out-of-town guests. (Need to have all bridal party flowers there in time for photos.)

2:30
❏ _______________ set up sound system (small amp, mic for soloist and lavaliere for pastor). Sound check.

3:00-3:30
❏ Men take pictures (groomsmen, ring bearer, father of the groom, etc.)

3:20
❏ Limo picks up girls from hotel and takes them to chapel.

3:30
❏ Men back to men's waiting room to hang out, freshen up. Wait for ceremony to start. _______________ to set-up unity candle (candles, lighters, hurricane lamps, etc.).

3:45
❏ Women arrive at chapel. Go to women's waiting room to freshen up for pictures. Make sure best man gets marriage license and rings.

4:00
❏ Guest table attendants arrive and set-up table.
❏ _______________ and _______________ ready to give flowers/leis to family and other assigned guests.

4:00-4:30
❏ Women to take pictures (bridal party, flower girl, mother of the bride, etc.).

4:15
❏ Guest table attendants ready to check in guests.

4:30
❏ Women back to waiting room to freshen up and get ready to walk out.

❏ Ushers ready to seat guests
❏ Prelude music begins
❏ Guests begin arriving, checking in, being seated

5:00
❏ Processional music starts (Cue Song: ________________________)

❏ Grandparents of groom seated
❏ Grandparents of bride seated
❏ Parents of groom seated
❏ Mother of the bride seated (________ to seat her)
❏ Officiant and groomsmen walk to altar

5:04
❏ Bridal Party Music
❏ ________ Bridal Party enters (List names in order of walking)
❏ Flower Girl and Ring Bearer walk

5:06
❏ Everyone rise for bride
❏ Bride and Father of the Bride begin walk (Cue Song: ________________)

Ceremony Outline (Sample only)
Giving away of the bride
Welcome and prayer
Readings (List them)
Wedding homily
Vows to each other
Marriage vows
Giving of rings
Prayer for each other
Communion (Cue Song: ________)

Unity candle (Cue Song if different: ________________________)
Pronouncement
Prayer of dedication
Presentation and blessing
Recessional (Cue Song: ________)
Sign marriage licence

5:25
❏ Pūpū/open bar outside ballroom
❏ Reception table girls go to table for check-in (________ will store gifts in hospitality room and be in charge of locking up)
❏ Guests continue to check-in, seating

5:30-6:10
❏ Pictures with bridal party, family

Reception Program
Beautiful Ballroom
5:45 P.M.

5:45
❏ Ballroom opens

6:10
❏ Ask people to be seated
❏ Bridal party freshen up. Get ready to be introduced

6:15
❏ Emcee announce bridal party entrance
❏ Introduce bridal party (list names in order of introduction) (Cue Song ________)

❑ Introduce Mr. and Mrs.______________
(Cue Song: ______________________)
❑ Everyone seated
❑ Emcee to go over housekeeping (bathroom location, food and drink procedure etc.)

6:25
❑ Blessing for food
❑ Tables dismissed by banquet captain
❑ Head table, bridal party to be served
❑ Cue dinner music (band, entertainer, DJs or cd music)

7:05
❑ Program begins
❑ Family introductions (list of names in order of introduction)
❑ Toast by father of the groom
❑ Toast by father of the bride
❑ Introduction of out-of-town guests, special guests

7:15
❑ Program (i.e., bridal party speeches, special performances, hula)
❑ Other toasts (Bonzai, best man, etc.)

7:40
❑ Cake cutting (Cue Song: ________________________)
❑ Bouquet toss or presentation (Cue Song: ________________________)
❑ Garter toss (Cue Song: ________________________)

7:50
❑ Slideshow

8:05
❑ Centerpiece giveaway
❑ Thank you's
❑ First dance (Cue Song ________________________)
❑ Dance with father/bride, mother/son (Cue Song: ________________)
❑ Money dance (optional)
❑ Mr. & Mrs. ____________ visit with guests
❑ Open up dance floor for everyone

10:00
❑ Limo picks up bride and groom and takes them to honeymoon suite

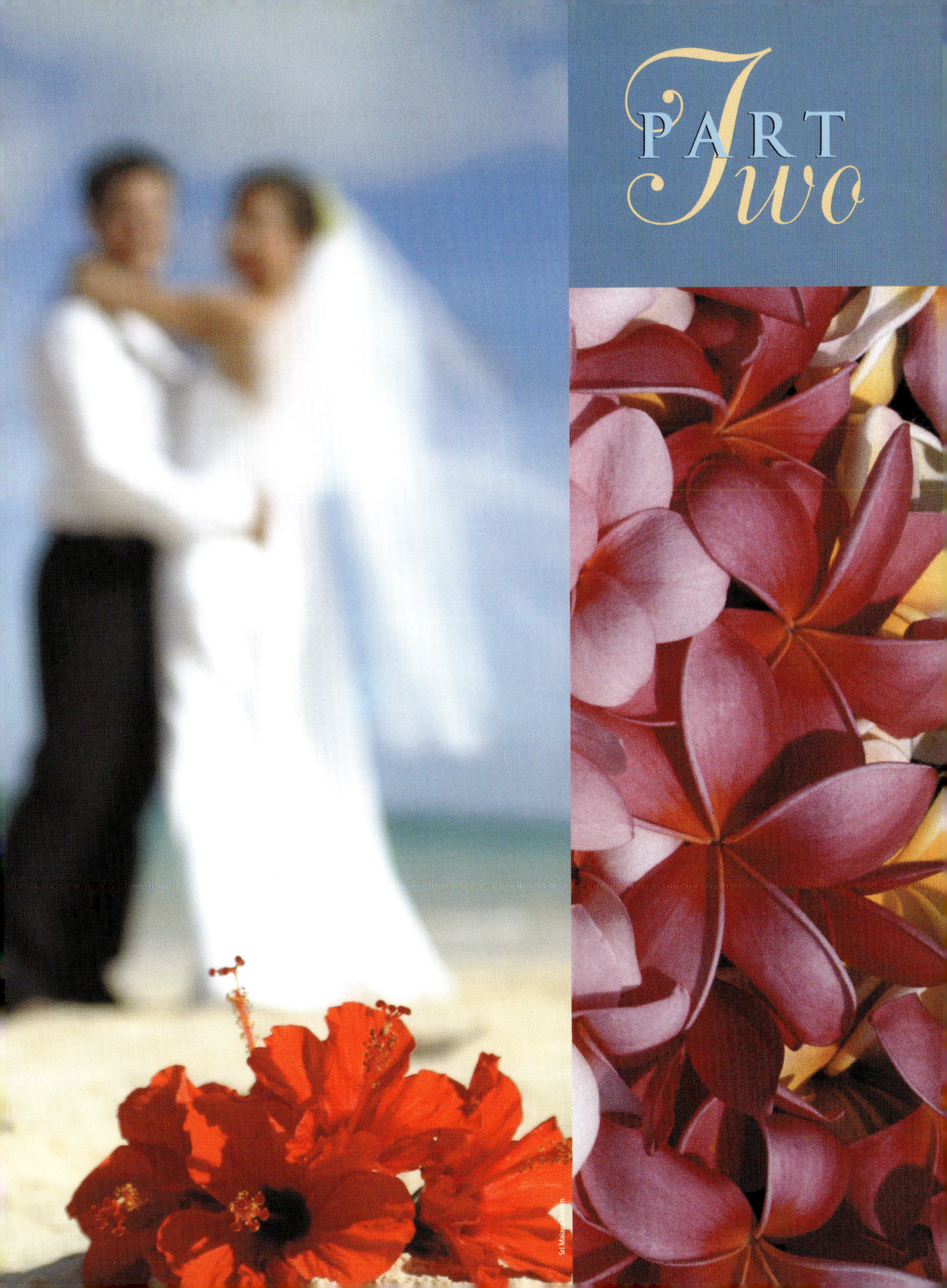

PART
Two

People, Places and Things
for Your Wedding in Hawai'i

This book is strictly a guide to help make *your* dream wedding a reality. That means you need to have some ideas as to what you want. Do you want an outdoor wedding with an indoor reception? Do you want the ceremony and the reception in the same place? Do you want lots of Hawaiian flowers and leis or just simple tropical bouquets? Will your ceremony be traditional or do you want a completely unorthodox wedding? The sky is the limit—it just has to be right for you.

Use this resource book as a guide to your options. It's up to you to make the phone calls, send for information, check out websites, make appointments (if you're on the island), ask for references and start making decisions. In several categories (i.e., beauty, caterers, cakes/bakeries, transportation, photography and videography), we have listed only those who have advertised their businesses as professional, reliable wedding vendors. For additional resources in those categories, we suggest you consult a local phone directory. To order a residential or business phone book for any island call Verizon Hawaii at (800) 888-8448.

We cannot personally endorse these vendors, specifically, and will not be held liable or responsible for their business practices. However, if you do have any complaints or problems, please be sure to forward them to the Hawaii Better Business Bureau (808) 536-6956. You are also welcome to e-mail us your comments at keri@wedding-planners.net.

We have provided you with helpful tips and "questions to ask" (QTA's) in this part of the book. But there are some things you should keep in mind when dealing with ALL vendors. **Always get your agreement in writing, ask them if they have liability insurance, check your potential vendors' references, call the Hawaii Better Business Bureau and, whenever possible, pay with a credit card so that if it's ever necessary to dispute or refund the charges you have at least sixty days to do so.**

We've categorized the areas you need to consider. Remember, this is the most important day of your life—use this book as a guide and enjoy every minute of it—it'll be over and done before you know it. We have divided each resource listing by island. As you will see, the bulk of the resources available are on Oʻahu, or at least based there. However, many of these vendors are willing and able to travel to other islands to be a part of your wedding day. If you're planning to get married on a neighbor island but want to use an Oʻahu based vendor (i.e., photographer, hair and makeup artist), be sure to inquire about any travel or additional charges you may incur.

What are you waiting for? Time's a wasting and you've got a lot of work to do!

Dress Code
Bridal Gowns, Bridesmaids' Dresses, Tuxedos

Nothing creates more excitement and sleepless nights than looking for the perfect wedding gown. There are literally thousands of styles, fabrics, colors, textures, adornments, and cuts to choose from. If you don't have an idea of what you want before you visit a bridal salon or warehouse, you will be completely overwhelmed. The shopping adventure needs to begin with some serious research before you set foot into a bridal salon. Look through recent bridal magazines and go on-line for ideas. If you have a specific gown in mind that you've seen in a magazine or on-line, call merchants in your area to see what they have to offer. Some salons have limited store hours or will see you by appointment only. Find out if they carry the designer you are looking for or if they are able to order it for you. Then gather all your samples and start shopping!

QTA's (Questions to Ask):

❏ Are there any hidden costs (like shipping, steaming or last-minute alterations)?

❏ Do they require a deposit? Is it refundable? How much of the total order price do you pay upon placing your order?

❏ What are their procedures on dresses that arrive damaged or not as you ordered?

❏ Will they hold the dress until the week before your wedding for security purposes?

❏ When do they do the final steaming?

❏ Do they handle alterations in-house? If they have someone outside of the salon do it, who is liable for damages to the gown?

❏ Can you get a written estimate on alteration charges?

❏ If you order your bridesmaids' dresses and bridal gown from the same shop, will they offer a discount?

❏ What are the sample size dresses they carry? (Most salons will only have samples in a specific size, usually between 8-12.)

❏ Does the store have undergarments and shoes in the store for you to use when you're trying on the dresses? (If not, bring what you have.)

Tips:

❋ Shop at "off" times, like mid-day or early evening on a weekday, you'll get more of the sales peoples' time and attention.

❋ If you are ordering a gown from a local salon, allow three to four months for the order to be processed and the dress to arrive. If you're short on time, pay extra for a rush order. It's worth the extra money for the dress to arrive in time for you to make the proper alterations. In some cases, orders shipped to Hawai'i take more than three to four months.

❋ Visit a bridal salon even if you don't plan on buying your gown there. You'll receive some valuable tips on fit and style based on your age and body type. It's worth the time to hear what the "experts" have to say.

❋ Make sure you get all the essential terms of your agreement of purchase in writing. If they don't make a habit of doing that, write up your own agreement and have them sign it.

❋ Don't overspend! Have a budget set for your dress and stick to it. If you find the dress of your dreams and it's completely out of your price range, look into having a seamstress design and make it. More often than not, a seamstress can recreate that same dress at a much more affordable price.

❋ After finding your dress, give yourself at least a day before you order or buy it. That way you make sure you're not acting irrationally or being pressured into buying a dress you're not sure about.

Size Ain't Nothing But a Number

♥♥

Don't stress out if the dress you want doesn't come in your size. You have at least two options. Either take a picture of your dream dress to a seamstress and have them give you an estimate to make it. Or contact any of the following designers who offer their collections in larger sizes: Alfred Angelo, Bianchi, Bonny, Bridal Originals, Eden, Forever Yours, Jessica McClintock, Jim Hjelm, Mary's Mon Cheri, Monique, Mori Lee, Private Label, Sweetheart and Venus.

Clean Up Duty

❊ Keep in mind that your dress should also include accessories (headpiece, veil, shoes, jewelry, etc.). Accessories are a necessity on your wedding day and not something you want to overlook or overspend on.

❊ Let the salon or seller know what your dress budget is so they can show you dresses within your budget.

❊ Plan on at least three fittings—first, when the gown arrives for your initial alterations; the second, for additional alterations; and the third, to ensure everything is perfect. Your last fitting should be about two weeks prior to your wedding.

❊ Wedding gowns tend to run small so plan on ordering your dress one to two sizes larger than your size (don't freak out and think you've gained weight!).

❊ Expect to give an initial deposit of up to 50 percent.

❊ Keep in mind that many "new" styles come with the seasons. A dress you see in the magazines today may not be available in stores until the upcoming season.

❊ Bring your mother or maid of honor with you when you purchase your dress as well as for your fittings. They'll give you an honest opinion (hopefully!). They'll be able to see how the dress is supposed to fit and help with any last-minute, on-site alterations.

Expect To Pay:

❊ Wedding gowns vary from a few hundred dollars to thousands of dollars. Plan to spend approximately 5–6% of your total wedding budget on your gown and accessories. Costs vary from $400–$2,000 and up.

Bridal Party

Ahhhh…the bridesmaid's dress…the source of many a horror story. (Think orange taffeta with big puffy sleeves!) From a bridesmaid's point of view—they'll either love 'em or hate 'em. The bride wants to look good, but so do her bridesmaids. There's nothing worse than a bride who deliberately makes her bridesmaids look silly, fat, or uncomfortable just to make sure she looks good. This is the bride's day and she should pick her bridesmaids' dresses to reflect a theme and feeling that goes with the wedding. But she should also be sensitive to her bridesmaids' feelings and financial constraints.

QTA's:

Use the QTA's for the bride's gown as general guidelines for purchasing your bridesmaids' dresses as well.

Tips:

✳ Be fair to the bridesmaids. Usually the bridesmaids are expected to pay for the dresses. So consider possible financial constraints when picking out their dresses.

✳ Consider having the girls wear the same color but let them pick styles that fit and flatter them. You can select a specific designer and let them choose their own.

✳ The girls may wear alternating colors. For instance, if your wedding colors are pastel, have each bridesmaid in a different pastel color or alternate between two different colors (two girls in cream and two in lavender).

✳ Try and find something they'll be able to wear again—not an easy task, but always a good thing to shoot toward.

✳ Black is a great color to wear for evening and formal weddings. Everyone can use a new black dress and chances are, they'll wear it again—at least once! (White or off-white dresses are great too!)

✳ If you're ordering dresses that are non-refundable or non-exchangeable, make sure you get them on the larger size so they can be altered easily as opposed to ordering a dress that is too small, difficult or impossible to alter.

Island Style Attire

♥♥

This is for my girl-friend Linda (aka Paris Hilton), who made me promise her in my next edition of this book, to add something here for those looking for men's attire for casual but classy weddings. So for those of you in search of men's linen, silk, or dressy aloha shirts here are some places we recommend looking: Banana Republic, Gap, Hilo Hattie, Macy's, Neiman Marcus, Off Sax Avenue at Waikele, Tommy Bahama, and Tori Richards.
If all else fails, and you can't find that cream colored, long sleeve linen shirt you're looking for (Linda!), you can always have it made! See some suggestions for good seamstresses and dressmakers in the Attire chapter beginning on page 42.

The mothers' dresses should reflect the formality of your wedding, but other than that let their own individual tastes shine through. Most mothers want to make sure they're not wearing a color that clashes with your wedding colors or with their mother-counterpart, but beyond that there are no do's and don'ts for mom's attire. Etiquette suggests that the mother of the bride purchase her dress first and then describe or show it to the mother of the groom. This is supposed to alleviate any embarrassing situations like purchasing the same dress or wearing colors that clash.

❋ If the bridesmaids are dying their shoes to match the dresses, make sure all the shoes are dyed at the same place. Often dye lots vary from state to state or store to store and can result in different shades or tones. Give a big enough swatch to color match (the bigger the better, but at least a two-inch square).

❋ If you are ordering the same dress for all of the bridesmaids, let them see the dress, even if it's only a picture, before you order it.

❋ If you have girls in your bridal party who are flying in or traveling from afar, offer to pay for, or help pay for, the dress. They are already incurring significant costs to travel.

❋ Purchase dresses off the rack of your favorite department store. You'll find great deals! Buy them all at the same time to make sure you can get the right sizes and color.

❋ If you don't want a veil, crystal and zirconia tiaras, headbands and hairclips are popular choices for a decorative head piece.

Expect To Pay:

Bridesmaids: Like a bridal gown, bridesmaids' dresses vary in price. You can buy a simple dress off the rack for as little as $50 or $60. Standard bridesmaids' dresses ordered out of magazines or on-line will usually run between $150 and $250. You may have to pay more for shipping costs to Hawai'i.

Groom/Groomsmen

Choosing the tuxedo or the groomsmen attire is considered to be one of the groom's main "jobs." However, unlike the tradition of the groom not seeing his bride's dress until the day of the wedding, most brides and grooms will decide together on what the guys will wear. Like the wedding gown, it's important to have an idea of what you want before shopping. Tuxedos vary in cut, style and formality.

QTA's:

❏ Does the store have the tuxedos in stock to try on or do you have to select from the in-store books or from the mannequins?

❏ Do you get a deal if you rent x amount of tuxes?

❏ What is included in a "full rental" (accessories, shoes, pressing, etc.)? What is the price difference between "full rental" and "a la carte"?

❏ What are their late rental fees?

❏ How far in advance can you pick up the tuxedos and when do they need to be returned?

❏ Can you special order tuxedos from designers not regularly carried in that store? Are there additional fees to do so?

Tips:

✳ Decide on what colors you may want for the vest, cummerbund, bow tie and other accessories.

✳ If you can, take in a swatch of material as a color sample so the tuxedo shop can determine what color most closely matches your wedding colors/theme.

✳ Insure that everyone picks up his own tux and tries it on!

✳ Count studs, cuff links, etc., for proper number. Ask for extras from the tuxedo shop just to be on the safe side.

✳ Each person should return his own tux or designate one person to do this for all the groomsmen.

✳ It is customary, but not mandatory, that the groomsmen pay for their tuxedo rentals.

✳ Place one group order. Don't rely on the groomsmen to order individually. Pay for the rentals at one time if need be. If your groomsmen are paying for their own tuxes, they can reimburse you.

Dads often get left in the proverbial wedding dust. But more often than not, they are "footin'" a good portion of the bill. For that reason and the fact that he is your father and you want him to look and feel special, talk to him about what he wants to wear. Again, other than dad dressing appropriately to match the formality of your wedding, let him wear what he wants to wear and what's comfortable. If he's walking you down the aisle, take extra care in making sure he looks as sharp (well almost!) as you do. Any thing goes...as long as it goes with the rest of the wedding theme. It's not out of the question for dads to sport nice aloha shirts and slacks in Hawai'i.

❊ Rental usually includes a jacket, trousers, shirt, vest or cummerbund, studs, cuff links and a tie.

❊ Guys should wear black nylon socks and black shoes. (White tuxes are the only exception and can be accompanied with white socks and shoes.)

❊ Tuxedos should be ordered two to three months ahead of time.

❊ If your wedding date is during heavy wedding or prom season, visit the tux shop four to six months before your date to ensure you can get the formal wear you want.

❊ Consider the cost of buying a tuxedo. If you'd wear it again, it might be wiser to invest in buying one. They can run from $200–$500.

Expect To Pay:

$75–$160 per tuxedo rental

O'ahu:

AA Waikahala Fashion Center
4210 Waialae Ave., #104
Honolulu, HI 96816
☎ (808) 732-2066
Alterations/custom made.

Anne Namba Designs, Inc.
324 Kamani St.
Honolulu, HI 96813
☎ Toll Free (877) 578-0001
(808) 589-1135
www.annenamba.com
anne@annenamba.com
Custom-made gowns using vintage Japanese uchikake wedding kimonos.

Assi Bang
915 Ke'eaumoku St., #101
Honolulu, HI 96814
☎ (808) 947-2442
www.assibang.com
Wedding gowns, bridesmaids', etc.

B'Ellagance
98-023 Hekaha St., #2D1
Aiea, HI 96701
☎ (808) 484-9333
www.bellagancebridal.webpointusa.com/
bella@bellagance.com
Wedding gowns, bridesmaids' dresses, tuxedo rentals, etc.

Black Tie Affair
3566 Harding Ave., Suite 103
Honolulu, HI 96826
☎ (808) 732-9474
Tuxedo rentals.

Bridal Emporium
250 Ward Avenue, #209
Honolulu, HI 96814
☎ (808) 596-8281 / 🖷 593-0032
www.bridal-emporium.biz
info@bridal-emporium.com
Wedding gowns, bridesmaids' dresses, tuxedo rentals, etc.

Casablanca Bridal & Formals
1024 Māpunapuna, #200
Honolulu, HI 96819
☎ (808) 839-4696
Wedding gowns, bridesmaids' dresses, tuxedo rentals, etc.

Celebrity Tuxedos
91-226 Kauhi Street
Kapolei, HI 96707
☎ (808) 682-2421
Located inside of Sears in:
Ala Moana (Honolulu)
☎ (808) 947-0397
Pearlridge Mall (Aiea)
☎ (808) 487-4341
Windward Mall (Kaneohe)
☎ (808) 247-8390
www.celebritytuxedos.com

Creations by Toy
931 University Ave., #102
Honolulu, HI 96826
☎ (808) 947-0124
www.creationsbytoy.com
toy@creationsbytoy.com
Designer gowns and custom-made gowns.

Designs By Lee, Inc.
1311 Kapi'olani Blvd., #606
Honolulu, HI 96814
☎ (808) 589-2222
Custom-made gowns and alterations.

Do's Fashions
12 S. King St.
Honolulu, HI 96813
☎ (808) 537-6041
Wedding gowns, bridesmaids' dresses, etc.

Emine Bridal & Design
560 N. Nimitz Hwy., #118
Honolulu, HI 96817
☎ (808) 484-4857
By appointment only.

Events in Apparel
☎ (808) 261-6166
kathejames@hawaii.rr.com
Extreme alterations, vintage retrofit, alternative wedding gowns.

H&L Bridal & Formals
94-366 Pupupani St.
Waipahu, HI 98797
☎ (808) 676-2337
info@handlformals.com
The area's largest selection of gowns for brides, bridesmaids, mothers and flower girls.

Hale Niu Tuxedo & Bridals
1014 Kapahulu Ave.
Honolulu, HI 96816
☎ (808) 734-2125
Wedding gowns, bridesmaids' dresses, tuxedo rentals, etc.

Hilo Hattie
700 N Nimitz Hwy
Honolulu, HI 96817
☎ Toll Free: (888) 526-0299
🖷 (888) 526-5696
www.hilohattie.com
See their website for various locations
Aloha wear, apparel and accessories

Island Wind Hawaii, Inc.
1440 Kapiolani Blvd., Suite 108
Honolulu, HI 96814
☎ (808) 951-1135 / 🖷 942-1135
www.island-wide.com
mieko-iwh@hawaii.rr.com

Kiyomi's Bridal & Formals
1050 Ala Moana Blvd.
Honolulu, HI 96814
☎ (808) 596-0079
Wedding gowns, bridesmaids' dresses, etc.

La Mariage Bridal Salon
2555 Kūhiō Ave., #1220
Honolulu, HI 96815
☎ (808) 924-2030 / 🖷 924-2201
Wedding gowns, bridesmaids' dresses, etc.

Lani Roberts
☎ (808) 739-2308
Dressmaker/Alterations

Lina Ariyoshi Wedding Services, Inc.
2155 Kālakaua Ave., #608
Honolulu, HI 96815
☎ (808) 971-0900
Rentals only. Gowns and tuxedos.

Mai-Scherelle Fashion Designer
201 'Ōhua Ave.
Honolulu, HI 96815
☎ (808) 921-0084
By appointment only.

Mamo Howell, Inc.
Ward Warehouse–Ala Moana Blvd.
Honolulu, HI 96814
☎ (808) 591-2002 / 🖷 593-9211
www.mamohowell.com
howell@mamohowell.com
Hawaiian style gowns and bridesmaids' dresses, etc.

Marppy Total Wedding & Studio
808 Sheridan St.
Honolulu, HI 96814
☎ (808) 955-5155
www.marppywedding.com

Masako Formals
716 Cooke St.
Honolulu, HI 96813
☎ (808) 947-2696 / 🖷 946-6419
www.masakoformals.com
masakoformals@masakoformals.com
Wedding gowns, bridesmaids' dresses, tuxedo rentals, etc.

Phil's Tuxedo Shop
250 Ward Avenue, #110
Honolulu, HI 96814
☎ (808) 596-9872 / 🖷 596-9864
Tuxedo and suit rentals.

Princess Bridal
1221 Kapi'olani Blvd., #102
Honolulu, HI 96814
☎ (808) 592-1550 / 🖷 592-1557
www.hawaiiprincessbridal.com
princesb@lava.net
Wedding gowns, bridesmaids' dresses, tuxedo rentals, etc.

Princess Kaiulani Fashions
1222 Kaumuali'i, Honolulu, HI 96817
☎ (808) 847-4806 / 🖷 847-0003
www.pkaiulanifashions.com
sales@pkaiulanifashions.com
Hawaiian style gowns, bridesmaids' dresses, etc.

Ritz, The
650 Iwilei Rd., Suite 102A
Honolulu, HI 96817
☎ (808) 521-6011 / 🖷 595-8591
www.hawaii-ritz.com
info@hawaii-ritz.com
Wedding gowns, bridesmaids' dresses, tuxedo rentals, etc.

Sayumi's Princess Garden Bridal Salon
1 Aloha Tower Dr., #177
Honolulu, HI 96813
☎ (808) 524-2066
Wedding gowns, bridesmaids' dresses, tuxedo rentals, etc.

Sharotte Boutique
1497 S. King St., Rm. 2
Honolulu, HI 96814
☎ (808) 946-1636
Wedding gowns, bridesmaids' dresses, etc.

Tuxedo Junction
1218 Waimanu St.
Honolulu, HI 96814
☎ (808) 597-1196
www.tuxedo-junction.com
info@tuxedo-junction.com
Wedding gowns, bridesmaids' dresses, tuxedo rentals, etc.

Vows Bridal and Formals
1249 S. Beretania St.
Honolulu, HI 96814
☎ (808) 591-6612
www.vowsbridal-formals.com
Wedding gowns, bridesmaids' dresses, tuxedo rentals, etc.

Wedding Emporium
2270 Kālakaua Ave., #401
Honolulu, HI 96815
☎ (808) 923-9853
www.matzki.com/tuxserv.htm
Bridal gowns and bridesmaids' dresses with all the accompanying accessories.

Bridal Emporium
360 Pāpā Pl., Suite Z
Kahului, HI 96732
☎ (808) 893-2230 / 🖷 893-2130
www.bridal-emporium.com
info@bridal-emporium.com
Wedding gowns, bridesmaids' dresses, tuxedo rentals, etc.

Caviar Couture
P.O. Box 330621
Kahului, HI 96733
☎ (808) 875-8654
www.caviarcouture.com
rlabanowski@hotmail.com
Women's custom clothing—bridalwear and eveningwear.

Elly's Formal Wear and Bridals
1295 S. Kīhei Rd., Suite F
Kīhei, HI 96753
☎ Toll Free (888) 522-5477
(808) 879-7280
www.ellysformalwear.com
formals@maui.net
Hawaiian wedding attire and tuxedos.

Gilbert's Formal Wear
104 Market St., Wailuku, HI 96793
☎ (808) 244-4017 / 🖷 879-2576
www.gilbertsformalwear.com
ihultqst@aloha.net
Tuxedos.

L'Amour Wedding
222 Pāpalaua St., Suite 219
Lāhainā, HI 96761
☎ Toll Free (800) 886-5313
🖷 (808) 669-3957
www.lamourwedding.com
lamourwedding@aol.com
Wedding gowns, tuxedos.

Lāhainā Towne Tuxedos

252 Lahainaluna Rd.
Lāhainā, HI 96761
☎ Toll Free (877) 984-4040
🖷 (808) 667-9226
www.mauituxedos.com
info@mauituxedos.com
Tuxedos.

Phil's Tuxedo Shop

360 Pāpā Pl., Suite Z
Kahului, HI 96732
☎ (808) 893-0205 / 🖷 893-0266
Tuxedo rentals.

Big Island:

Attractions

74-5576 Pawai Pl.
Kailua-Kona, HI 96740
☎ (808) 329-1113

Haku Formals Boutique

58 Furneaux Lane
Hilo, HI 96720
☎ (808) 934-9599 / 🖷 934-8599
tkapono@hotmail.com
Tuxedos.

Love N Lace

1221 Kīlauea Ave.
Hilo, HI 96720
☎ (808) 935-3285 / 🖷 935-7812

Kaua'i:

A Formal Affair

P.O. Box 854
Kapa'a, HI 96746
☎ (808) 822-0748

Sophisticated You!

3416 Rice St.
Līhu'e, HI 96766
☎ (808) 245-3800 / 🖷 245-7019
hawaiiweddingplanner.com/html_more/so
phu/sophu.htm
*Located in Anchor Cove Center; largest, most
complete bridal store on Kaua'i.*

Hawai'i Weddings Made Simple

Notes

Jon Mozo

The best thing about getting married in Hawai'i is the beautiful scenery. Our pictures turned out just swell. You know, in all of God's creation. Hawai'i is the ideal place to get married if you want an outdoor wedding.

The ceremony and reception went smoothly. Although, it would have been better if we were able to spend more time talking and mingling with our guests. I know that it was the people who came to our wedding that made the day so special. I wish our wedding day could have lasted forever.

Bobby Olmstead & Janice Gumar

♥♥

PARADISE COVE

I would also make sure that your baker doesn't deliver the cake five hours before the scheduled time of delivery. It doesn't bode well with an outdoor wedding but serves right nicely as a gnat magnet. You should have seen Janice's face when we went to cut our lopsided, melting, gnat-frosted cake. It was hilarious.

Things that we wouldn't change? We would not have changed the site of our wedding ceremony, and the set-up of our tent. Thank God we didn't do it on the sand—which was our original plan—that would have been a disaster. I would also make sure that if you have an outdoor wedding, make sure to check out the location several times with all the parties involved, including your parents and your wedding planner.

I would say the one thing that made our wedding unique was the group picture we took with all our family and guests—some two hundred people plus. It's our favorite photo of the wedding. We also put all the music we used on CDs and gave them out as our wedding favors. We received so many compliments on our wedding favors. It was great because when our family and friends listen to the CD, it reminds them of their great trip to Hawai'i, not to mention it's a very personalized, affordable favor.

Behold This!...

Most hair and makeup artists will come to your site, especially if they're free-lancers. If you book someone from a salon, make arrangements with them as to whether you have to go to their salon or if they'll come on-site. Plan a "practice" session with them so you can decide before your wedding day how you want your hair and makeup done. Bring samples of hair styles, makeup colors and looks you like so your "artist" knows what you like.

Remember the saying "you get what you pay for." There are makeup artists out there who won't charge you much at all, and in most cases, it's because they are new and relatively inexperienced. Ask for references and sample photos of previous jobs they've done.

Some brides like to pamper themselves the day before the wedding and want to enjoy a day at a salon or spa. We've included the names and numbers of some of the most popular ones. There are probably hundreds of nail salons throughout the islands so we are not going to list them all. You can look in the Yellow Pages under nail salon or ask a friend who they recommend.

QTA's (For hair and makeup artists):

❑ Does the artist do both hair and makeup?

❑ How much is it for both services? What if you or a bridesmaid want just hair or just makeup, what is the price difference?

❑ How long will it take to do each person? (Usually the bride will take the longest and the artist will do her last.)

❑ Will they have an assistant? Is her price included in your quote?

❑ Is the cost of the "practice" session less expensive than the cost of the artist's services on your wedding day or is it included in the cost of the service they quoted you?

❑ What forms of payment do they accept? And when is it due?

Pay Day

Tradition dictates that the bride's family incur most of the wedding cost. However, like many wedding traditions, there are no absolute rules. Here are some of the wedding/reception costs broken down by who traditionally pays for things:

Bride/Bride's Family: Gifts for attendants, wedding ring for groom, gift for groom, wedding dress/trousseau, invitations, announcements, mailing, photography, all ceremony costs, flowers for ceremony decoration, limo/transportation.

Groom/Groom's Family: Bride's ring and wedding band, gift for the bride, marriage license, gifts for groomsmen, flowers for bridal party, leis, officiant's fees, honeymoon, bachelor party and rehearsal dinner.

Tips:

❋ Do a practice session with the artist.

❋ Bring pictures of what you want. Don't assume the artist will magically do what you've envisioned. Most make-up and hair people are visual people. Show them what you want and they should have no problem doing it.

❋ Bring your veil or headpiece for the practice session so they can work with it ahead of time.

❋ Take pictures at your practice session. This will give you a good idea of what you will look like in your wedding pictures. You can tell from the pictures if you need more or less makeup.

❋ Call references and ask to see the artist's portfolio. Pictures are worth a thousand words, especially when it comes to hair and makeup!

❋ If you're not used to wearing makeup, tell your make-up artist. Keep in mind that almost any amount of makeup looks like a lot if you're not used to wearing it.

❋ If they have an assistant, make sure whoever worked on you for your practice session is the same person who does your hair and makeup on the wedding day.

❋ Work with the artist to create a timeline for the people who will be having their hair and makeup done the day of the wedding. This ensures that the artists and their assistants will have ample time to work on each person. Let everyone know what time they are to be available to have their hair and makeup done.

❋ If you're looking for a gift for the bridal party, consider paying for their hair and makeup.

❋ Bring some extra hair spray, bobby pins and makeup for after-the-ceremony touch-ups. Hair and makeup artists usually leave before the ceremony even starts, unless you pay them extra to stay.

Expect To Pay: $75 and up for hair and makeup for bride; $65 and up for hair and makeup for bridal party, mothers, etc.; $50 and up for hair or makeup only.

Beauty and Hair

O'ahu:

Alison Hayashi
1120 Koko Head Ave., #102
Honolulu, HI 96816
☎ (808) 988-7807 / 🖨 739-5005
hayashi_makeup@yahoo.com
Call for consultation.

Aloha Bridal Gallery
P.O. Box 701077
Kapolei, HI 96709
☎ (808) 672-0450 / 🖨 232-7547
www.alohabridalgallery.com
alohabride@hawaii.rr.com
By appointment only.

Aveda by Suzie and Janine
1585 Kapi'olani Blvd., #710
Honolulu, HI 96814
☎ (808) 944-8858
By appointment only.

Beauty by Tania
☎ (808) 387-7547
www.beautybytania.com
taniadejesus@hotmail.com
Call for consultation.

Bridal Hair & Makeup by Tammy
☎ (808) 487-8314 / 306-2587 (cel)
tammyhiga@hawaii.rr.com
Call for consultation.

Cassie L. Bader
☎ (808) 282-4240
Call for appointment.
Licensed Makeup Arits/Esthetician

Cathy Chun
1338 Alewa Dr., Honolulu, HI 96817
☎ (808) 595-7321 / 571-2232 (pgr)
Call for consultation.

Cherly H. Adachi
96-226 Waiawa Rd., #41
Pearl City, HI 96782
☎ (808) 455-5046
www.marykay.com/cadachi
cadachi@hawaii.rr.com
Call for consultation.

Cheryl Brown
☎ (808) 255-9603
Call for consultation

Cheryl Cruz
P.O. Box 3018, Aiea, HI 96701
☎ (808) 375-6202
www.mahealaniandcherylcruz.com
CherylCruz808@yahoo.com
Free consultation.

Christine Gardner
Honolulu, Hawaii
☎ (808) 561-5798 / 484-2143
www.christinegardner.com
makeuphair@christinegardner.com
Airbrush & traditional make up & professional hair stylist

Dorys Foltin
3705 Waialae Ave #203
Honolulu, Hawaii 96816
☎ Toll Free: (866) 727-3663
☎ (808)737-3663
www.dorysfoltinphoto.com
dorys@dorysfoltin.com

Flawless
☎ (808) 216-7629 (April-Hair)
☎ (808) 864-3303 (Christie-Make-up)
flawlesshairandmakeup@hotmail.com

Hair and Makeup by Beverly
☎ (808) 366-3203
www.makeupbybev.com
makeupbybv@aol.com
Call for consultation.

Hair Innovations
1400 Kapi‘olani Blvd., Suite A27
Honolulu, HI 96814
☎ (808) 946-6755
Call for consultation.

Jacque Rojas
1411 Kapi‘olani Blvd., B-30
Honolulu, HI 96814
☎ (808) 955-5600 / 782-1001
jacquerojas@hawaii.rr.com
Call for consultation.

Jonathan, 808 Professionals
190 Ke Ala Nohona Rd.
Honolulu, HI 96817
☎ Toll Free (800) 211-1202 ext. 9004

Karen Oshiro
☎ (808) 373-1845
oshirokm@aol.com
Call for consultation.

Kathy
1405 Kālakaua Ave.
Honolulu, HI 96826
☎ (808) 391-5937
Full service salon.

Kim Kubo, Inc.
☎ (808) 479-5299
kim@kimkubo.com
www.kimkubo.com

Kissa Salon
1347 Kapi‘olani Blvd., #102
Honolulu, HI 96814
☎ (808) 947-9955
Call for consultation.

Leslie Gallagher
550 ‘Olohana Street
Kailua, HI 96734
☎ (808) 261-1004
www.lesliegallagher.com
info@lesliegallagher
Call for consultation. Also specializes in spray tan services.

Macy's Premier Salons
Various locations around the island.
☎ (808) 941-2345
www.macys.com
Call for consultation and nearest location.

Mahealani
P.O. Box 3018
Aiea, HI 96701
☎ (808) 779-3785 / 375-6202
www.mahealaniandcherylcruz.com
Mahealani323@aol.com
Call for consultation.

Minnie Ruiz
☎ (808) 387-8064
norfolk@aloha.net

Pattie Kuamoʻo
1585 Kapiʻolani Blvd., #710
Honolulu, HI 96814
☎ (808) 941-7289

Paulette R. Kitchell Fukumoto
167 California Ave.
Wahiawa, HI 96886
☎ (808) 622-6938
Make-up artist.

Rejuvenation Skin Care Salon
98-450 Kamehameha Hwy.
Pearl City, HI 96782
☎ (808) 486-8891
www.rejuvenationhawaii.com

Salon (808)
1585 Kapiolani Blvd., Suite 710
Honolulu, HI 96814
☎ (808) 942-7799

Salon Bobbi N' Guy
1050 Ala Moana Blvd., Bay 5
Honolulu, HI 96814
☎ (808) 591-2899

Salon Honolulu
Marin Tower
918 Smith St., Suite F
Honolulu, HI 96817
☎ 808-566-0714

Sandee Magallanes
☎ (808) 678-1466 / 223-2331 (cel)
www.beautydelivered.com
info@beautydelivered.com
Call for consultation.

Susan Akamine
94-212 Awalua Pl., Waipahu, HI 96797
☎ (808) 688-1033 / 255-2380 (cel)
www.susanakamine.com
susanakamine@hawaii.rr.com
Call for consultation.

Suzanne Eleam
1143A 7th Ave., Honolulu, HI 96816
☎ (808) 739-0866 / 🖷 739-0866
www.senegence.com/youngatheart
sye@hawaii.rr.com
Long lasting cosmetics that won't kiss off, rub off, smear off and are waterproof and guaranteed.

Unique
badkitty@hawaii.rr.com
☎ (808) 389-1355 (Nicole Yamashiro)
☎ (808) 383-2913 (Danah Wong)
Hair and makeup on location

Vicky Choe
1535 Pensacola St., #C5
Honolulu, HI 96822
☎ (808) 396-5487 / 395-2781
www.makeuphawaii.com
vicky@makeuphawaii.com
Call for consultation.

Maui:

Beautiful Brides by Marci
P.O. Box 2232, Kīhei, HI 96753
☎ (808) 879-4634 / 🖷 879-4634
www.mauibeautifulbrides.com
info@mauibeautifulbrides.com
Contact: Marci Guendel

Gwen Elf Inc./Brides & Braids
P.O. Box 625, Kīhei, HI 96753
☎ (808) 281-4758 / 🖷 874-3642
www.bridesandbraids.com
gwen@bridesandbraids.com
Contact: Gwen Elf

Karen Schneider
480 Kenolio Rd., #22-104
Kīhei, HI 96753
☎ (808) 875-1354 / 🖷 891-2353
www.marykay.com/kschneider
Contact: Karen SchneiderLily

Moon Salon

300 Ohukai Rd., #319, Kīhei, HI 96753
☎ Toll Free (866) 875-9080
www.lilymoonsalon.com
lilymoon@mauigateway.com
Contact: Gina Carter

Mariah's Mane

295 Auhana Rd., Kīhei, HI 96753
☎ (808) 875-2181
www.mariahsmane.com
info@mariahsmane.com
Contact: Shelly Hoffman / Sarah Jane Jameson

Maui Bridal Hair

P.O. Box 791452, Pāʻia, HI 96779
☎ (808) 579-6040
www.mauibridalhair.com
Linda@MauiBridalHair.com
Contact: Linda Spears

Maui Make Up and Facials

480 Kenolio Rd., Suite 260-201
Kīhei, HI 96753
☎ (808) 250-2603
mauimakeup@yahoo.com
Contact: Lisa Mascaro

Outlook/Creative Cuts

Anchor Square
222 Papalaua St., Suite 210
Lahaina, HI 96761
☎ (808) 661-6644 / 276-3858
outlookmaui@yahoo.com
Contact: Terri Pascual

Salon Nani

3550 Wailea Alanui St., Wailea, HI 96753
☎ (808) 874-2800
www.salonnani.com
salonnani@hawaii.com
*Located in the Renaissance Wailea
Beach Resort.*

Sue Helmer Wedding Hair & Make-Up

2145 Wai Maka Pl.
Kīhei, HI 96753
☎ (808) 875-1702
www.angelfire.com/biz2/suehelmerweddinghair
tsjandc@aol.com
Contact: Sue Helmer

Big Island:

Ambiance Salon & Boutique

74-5565 Luhia St., #C6
Kailua-Kona, HI 96740
☎ (808) 331-0977

Intrigue Dezign Salon

75-5626 Kuakino Hwy., #8
Kailua-Kona, HI 96740
☎ (808) 329-1457

On Stage Salon

68-1845 Waikoloa Rd., #210
Waikoloa, HI 96738
☎ (808) 883-2200 / 🖷 883-2202
www.onstagesalon.net
sandi@onstagesalon.net

Sherri Fernandez

☎ (808) 325-1878
Sherritwinone@aol.com

Styles Unlimited

2196 Kīlauea Ave., Hilo, HI 96720
☎ (808) 959-9395

Kauaʻi:

A Touch of Elegance Salon

3-3204 Kūhiō Hwy., #107
Līhuʻe, HI 96766
☎ (808) 245-5113
www.atouchofelegancesalon.com
susan@atouchofelegancesalon.com
*Hair, skin, eyes, nails and waxing services
available.*

Regis Hairstylists
Kukui Grove Centre, Līhuʻe, HI 96766
☏ (808) 245-5111

Shear Elegance
5-5161 Kūhiō Hwy.
Hanalei, HI 96714
☏ (808) 826-7742

Pampering

Oʻahu:
Abhasa Waikīkī Spa
2259 Kālakaua Ave., #1A
Honolulu, HI 96815
☏ (808) 922-8200 / 🖷 922-8210
Located in the Royal Hawaiian Hotel.

Ampy's
1441 Kapiʻolani Blvd., #377
Honolulu, HI 96814
☏ (808) 946-3838

Bareskin Hawaii
1481 S. King St., #343
Honolulu, HI 96814
☏ (808) 955-7988
www.bareskinhawaii.com
bareskinhawaii@bareskinhawaii.com
Call for free consultation.

Golden Plumeria Day Spa
Discovery Bay Center
1778 Ala Moana Blvd., #LL10
Honolulu, HI 96814
☏ (808) 947-8777

Heaven on Earth Salon & Day Spa
1050 Alakea St., Honolulu, HI 96813
☏ (808) 599-5501 / 🖷 599-5502
www.heavenonearthhawaii.com
lora@heavenonearthhawaii.com

Helen's Haven Skin Care Specialists
4614 Kilauea Ave., #202
Honolulu, HI 96816
☏ (808) 739-0400
www.helenshaven.com
helen@helenshaven.com

Ihilani Spa
92-1001 Olani St., Kapolei, HI 96707
☏ Toll Free (800) 626-4446
(808) 679-0080
www.ihilani.com / info@ihilani.com
Located in the JW Marriott Ibilani Resort.

Manoa Valley Salon & Spa
2801 E. Mānoa Rd., Honolulu, HI 96822
☏ (808) 988-0101
www.avedahawaii.com
info@avedahawaii.com
An Aveda Hawaii lifestyle salon spa.

Mandara Spa
2005 Kalia Rd., Kalia Tower
Honolulu, HI 96815
☏ (808) 923-7721 / 🖷 923-7724
www.mandaraspa.com/where_hilton
hawaiian-village.html
hawaii@mandaraspa.com
Located in the Hilton Hawaiian Village Hotel.

Marsha Nadalin Salon & Spa
4211 Waialae Ave.
Honolulu, HI 96816
☏ (808) 737-8505 / 🖷 735-4126
www.kahalamallcenter.com/directory/
marsha%20nadalin.html
Full service hair salon and day spa.

Na Hoola Spa
2424 Kālakaua Ave.
Honolulu, HI 96815
☏ (808) 921-6097 / 🖷 924-3409
www.hyattwaikiki.com/Spa/spa.asp
Located in the Hyatt Regency Waikīkī.

Robin & Co. Salon & Day Spa
45-655 Kamehameha Hwy.
Kāne'ohe, HI 96744
☏ (808) 235-8884

Salon & Body
2365 Kālakaua Ave.
Honolulu, HI 96815
☏ (808) 924-2511
Located in the Sheraton Moana Hotel.

Serenity Spa Hawaii
2169 Kalia Rd.
Honolulu, HI 96815
☏ (808) 926-2882
www.serenityspahawaii.com
info@serenityspahawaii.com
Located in the Outrigger on the Beach Hotel.

Maui:

Hyatt Regency Maui Resort & Spa
200 Nohea Kai Dr.
Lāhainā, HI 96761-1985
☏ (808) 661 1234 / 🖨 (808) 667-4497
www.maui.hyatt.com
*The Hyatt Regency Maui Resort and Spa has been
called one of the most spectacular resorts in the world.*

Kā'anapali Beauty Salon
2525 Kā'anapali Parkway
Lāhainā, HI 96761
☏ Toll Free (888) 484-1133
(808) 661-4616
www.kaanapalibeauty.com
dromero187@aol.com
Contact: Deborah Romero

Luana Spa Retreat
5050 Uakea Rd., Hana, HI 96713
☏ Toll Free (888) 898-2772
(808) 248-8553
www.luanaspa.com
luanaspa@luanaspa.com

Mandara Spa
Wailea Marriott, An Outrigger Resort
3700 Wailea Alanui
Wailea, HI 96753
☏ (808) 879-1922 / 🖨 (808) 874-8331
www.outrigger.com/hotels
*Experience a full range of treatments including
floral baths, hydrating facials, and aromatherapy
massage. Full service hair and nail salon also
available.*

Natural Nails By Mimi
☏ (808) 975-6793 / 280-1730
www.naturalnailsbymimi.com
Mobile nail services.

Pamper Yourself
☏ (808) 875-2835
pattilesiuke@yahoo.com
Mobile services, will come to you.

Seaside Salon & Day Spa
2605 Kā'anapali Parkway
Lāhainā, HI 96761
☏ Toll Free (888) 743-0948
(808) 661-4616
www.kaanapalibeauty.com
dromero187@aol.com
Contact: Deborah Romero

Big Island:

Hawaiian Rainforest Salon & Spa
Waikoloa Beach Marriott,
An Outrigger Resort
69-275 Waikoloa Beach Dr.
Waikoloa, HI 96738-5711
☏ (808) 886-6789 / 🖨 (808) 886-7852
www.outrigger.com/hotels
*Experience traditional Hawaiian healing arts,
rejuvenating spa therapies, and a state-of-the-art
fitness center.*

Kalona Salon & Spa
78-6740 Alii Dr.
Kailua-Kona, HI 96739
☎ (808) 322-9373 / 🖷 322-9372
Located in the Keauhou Beach Resort.

Lotus Spa Center
Royal Kona Resort
75-5852 Alii Dr.
Kailua-Kona, HI 96740
☎ (808) 329-3111 / 🖷 (808) 329-9532
www.HawaiianHotels.com/
The Lotus Center provides a wide array of spa options to pamper guests using both Eastern and Western spa techniques.

Kaua'i:
Ala Lani Spa and Tennis Club
3351 Hoolaulea Way
Lihu'e, HI 96766
☎ (808) 245-3323 / 🖷 245-3324
www.alanalispahawaii.com
info@alalanispahawaii.com
Located at the Kauai Lagoons Resort.

Alexander Day Spa & Salon
3610 Rice St., #9A
Lihu'e, HI 96766
☎ (808) 246-4918 / 🖷 246-6218
Located at the Kaua'i Marriott Resort.

ANARA Spa
at the Hyatt Regency Kaua'i
1571 Poipu Rd.
Koloa, HI 96756
☎ (808) 240-6440 / 🖷 (808) 240-6599
www.anaraspa.com
Hyatt Regency Kaua'i Resort and Spa's own ANARA Spa was ranked number 9 among Resort Spas in North America and the Caribbean in the 2003 Condé Nast Traveler *reader's poll.*

Tan in no time
♥♥

Almost every bride wants to have a golden bronze color to them on their wedding day, especially if the aisle their walking down is in Hawai'i. But if you're one of those ladies who has sworn off the sun, don't want to burn or simply don't have the time you need to get a tan before your big day, modern technology has made getting brown a breeze. Leslie Gallagher, one of Hawai'i's most popular hair and makeup artists, has a portable airbrush tanning machine and solution that leaves you with a perfect, overall tan. No orange mess. No sunburn. No peeling. No streaking and it lasts for 5-7 days. For more information on Leslie's service check out her website at wwwlesliegallagher.com or call her at (808) 261-1004.

If you opt not to have a "professional" do your hair and makeup, here are some pointers for doing it yourself. 1) Don't buy new makeup or hair products you haven't tried before. You may have an adverse reaction to them. If you do want to try some new products, do it several months before your wedding. 2) Practice. Practice. Practice. Decide exactly how you want your hair and makeup to look and practice doing it a lot. Gauge how much time it takes and allow yourself more than enough time on the day of your wedding. 3) Don't have a facial done within two weeks of your wedding date. Even if you had them before, the added stress of the wedding can cause your skin to react differently and it can often cause breakouts. If you can afford to have someone else do your hair and makeup for you, it's a luxury we recommend. Your wedding day can be stressful and having the added pressure of doing your own hair and makeup can be more than you want to deal with.

Tell us Your *Hawai'i Love Story*

Hawai'i Love Stories is a 30-minute television show that features couples from Hawai'i as they tell their love story; from the moment they met to their walk down the aisle. Cameras will follow the couple from the time they wake up on their wedding day, until the end of the reception, even after everyone's done the electric slide! The main focus of each episode will be to tell the couple's love story in the context of their wedding day.

If you would like your love story and wedding featured on Hawai'i Love Stories, send in a 5– to 10–minute video (VHS, miniDV, or DVD) telling them why your love story should be chosen. Don't forget to include your names, contact information, wedding/reception date, times, and locations. Send it to:

Hawai'i Love Stories Casting
3807 Maunaloa Ave.
Honolulu, HI 96816

Check out the show on OC 16 to see these couples and more. Then visit the website, hawaiilovestories.com for wedding planning resources and advice. For more information on Hawai'i Love Stories, visit hawaiilovestories.com or call (808) 732-9695.

Steve & Erma Soares

WAIALAE COUNTRY CLUB, O'AHU

Shellie & Moku Paiva

LUANA HILLS, O'AHU

Hawai'i Love Stories airs on Hawai'i's local channel, OC16. Check your listings for times or log on to hawaiilovestories.com for details.

Ask and Ye Shall Receive

Registering for your wedding is a great way to ensure that you get the wedding gifts you want. It will cut down on the exchanges and returns you make after the gifts are opened. Most grooms find this task tedious; but if at all possible, register together. After the planning and excitement of the wedding, it's nice to come home to the things that you chose together that make you feel at home. Your bridal registry allows you to choose your china, silver, and crystal as well as various linens, cookware, bakeware, glasses, cutlery, and household appliances.

QTA's:

❏ How long after the wedding will the store maintain your registry info? (They should maintain it anywhere from twelve to eighteen months.)

❏ Is your registry information accessible on-line?

❏ How do they keep track of purchases?

❏ How often is the registry updated? (It should be done as soon as a purchase is made to avoid duplicated gifts.)

❏ What is their return policy?

❏ Can your gifts be shipped to an address out of town? What is the extra cost?

Tips:

❊ Make sure you register at a place that guests from all over the country can access.

❊ If you are getting married in Hawai'i but live elsewhere, request on your registry sheet that your gifts be mailed to your specified home address. That way you don't have to pack or ship your gifts home.

❋ Be as specific as possible on your registry to ensure you get what you want and need. (List things by brand name and specific color.)

❋ Register about five to eight months before the wedding. That way your list will be in place before any parties or showers.

❋ Make sure the store carries a wide range of products and brands.

❋ Most companies will maintain your registry for at least one year after your wedding date.

❋ Choose your bridal registry location based on customer service, selection, quality, prices and ease of use.

❋ Once you've registered, go back to that store or another location and access your information. Make sure it is accurate and easy to use.

❋ It's hard to keep track of multiple registries; limit your registry to one or two locations.

❋ Keep track of your registry. Check it several weeks before the wedding and update or add if much has already been purchased.

❋ Spread the word through family and friends as to where you are registered. You can include bridal registry inserts in your shower and wedding invitations. Don't print it on your actual wedding invitation—some people take offense at that.

Expect To Pay: Nothing for the bridal registry service. It is free and so should be the time you spend with a registry consultant. Take their advice but register for only what *you* want and need.

O'ahu:

Macy's
Ala Moana, Pearl Ridge Shopping Centers
☎ (808) 941-2345
www.macys.com

Mikasa
94-796 Lumiaina
Waipahu, HI 96797
☎ (808) 676-2422
www.mikasa.com

Neiman Marcus
Ala Moana Shopping Center
Honolulu, HI 96814
☎ (808) 951-3460
www.neimanmarcus.com

Pier 1 Imports
1108 Ahuahi Street
Honolulu, HI 96817
☎ (808) 589-1212
www.pier1imports.com

Sears
Ala Moana, Pearlridge Shopping Centers
☎ (808) 974-0211 / 247-8211
www.sears.com

Williams-Sonoma
Ala Moana Shopping Center
Honolulu, HI 96815
☎ (808) 951-5006
www.williams-sonoma.com

Big Island:

Macy's
Makalapua Center
Kailua-Kona, HI 96740
☎ (808) 329-6300
www.macys.com

Sears
Lii E Puainako Street
Hilo, HI 96720
☎ (808) 981-4029
www.sears.com

Kaua'i:

Sears
3-2300 Kaumuali'i Hwy.
Līhu'e, HI 96766
☎ (808) 246-8301
www.sears.com

Notes

Sri Maiava Rusden

Kris Thompson & Lianne Bidal

♥♥

KO'OLAU GOLF COURSE

For our wedding, I wanted to have a big celebration like the ones I grew up with here in Hawai'i. Kris and I also knew that we wanted to relax, have fun and share good food and a beautiful experience with our loved ones. We also wanted to share not only our culture but also the things that make us unique individuals with our guests. To accomplish this, I delegated a lot of things to people I trusted. I chose my cousins, Rheda and Roann, to be in charge of trouble-shooting at the event and my Matron of Honor was my contact person for the Big Day. I opted to do this so that I wouldn't be bogged down with little details on my wedding day.

Kris is a huge fan of Hawaiian music, so I put him in charge of the entertainment. He hired two local Hawaiian musicians to perform after our ceremony (when the wedding party was taking pictures and the guests were eating pūpū) and during our reception. Kris also hails from a heritage rich with ranchers and cowboys, and he's always loved his cowboy boots. He wore his favorite cowboy boots with his tuxedo to our wedding.

I also put Rheda in charge of the reception table. She's great at organizing and giving people directions. My sister, Kimey, who usually has the reception table job with me at family parties, helped her greet our guests.

Roann was put in charge of all the table decorations. She took the ideas I had and made them happen. This was no easy task, since Kris and I chose the colors lavender and orange, our favorite colors. Don't laugh, my flowers were awesome! Roann made topiaries out of orange Mikasa vases, tulle and lavender flowers for the centerpieces. For the favors, we chose to fill shot glasses with m&ms. The m&ms, our favorite candy, were lavender and orange; since Kris is a mad collector of shot glasses, we felt that would be the perfect choice.

I was blessed with a great florist and site coordinator. I called them "my two Lindas." I really wanted to get married at Ko'olau Golf Course because it was at the foot of the mountains that I had lived with and loved my whole life. The thought of having those majestic mountains to gaze at as I said my wedding vows was thrilling.

So, my first Linda was a site coordinator at Ko'olau Golf Course. I liked her because she explained things to me in layman's terms,

(continued on next page)

answered all of my kooky questions and had great follow-up. I think it can be scary for a lot of couples between the time they first meet with their site planner and the actual event. For many, there can be seven to ten months when nothing happens. Linda was very good about calling me at least once a month (if I didn't call her first) to check on me, meet about menus, etc.

My second Linda was my florist. She was the other person with the difficult job of making lavender and orange look good. It was all so beautiful. Everyone commented on how beautiful our flowers were. Yes, Kris and I had many a naysayer before the wedding, but when they saw it, they walked away believers. I wanted all roses for my bouquet, so I chose a Martha Stewart bouquet of lavender roses. My bridesmaids had a mixture of orange and lavender roses. My florist did what I think a lot of florists are doing nowadays: she made pieces that could work for different parts of the day. For instance, the flowers for our wedding arch were removed and made part of the floral decorations for the cake table and head table.

In addition to Kris' love for Hawaiian music, shot glasses and cowboy boots, his favorite football team, the Denver Broncos, somehow made it into our wedding vows. I believe he actually said something about promising to always put me before the Broncos. How sweet! He also loves fishing. So, we had a marlin ice sculpture at our buffet table, and his step-dad (whom he fishes with) flew in fresh 'ahi for our pūpū table. Relatives and friends made a lot of the pūpū, which included several types of poke, sushi, sashimi, chi chi dango, cascaron and more.

As for my traditions, I tried to fold golden cranes for our tsuru, but I just couldn't fold all one thousand. So, I enlisted my mom, cousins and friends to fold them for me. I think I actually folded thirty. Kris folded his required one. We had them professionally mounted in a design of the wedding vows, "love, honor and cherish" in interlocking circles. I also had two more outfits for my wedding reception, but I was having so much fun mingling with my guests, I never got to change into them.

During our reception, we had the traditional garter and bouquet tosses, cake cutting and first dance (which was turned into a money dance). Because Kris' dad lives on the mainland, he wasn't familiar with this tradition. I wish we had explained it to him, as it caught him off guard. Members of our bridal party gave us toasts, but my favorite toasts were by my two uncles. The Japanese "Banzai!" and the Hawaiian "Imua!" It was wonderful.

Compiling our guest list was a daunting task. We had to pare it down to three hundred. One "problem" I encountered was the fact that it had rained the morning of my wedding, making the ground outside soggy. The ceremony had to be moved inside.

Did I accomplish my goal of having the fun party I wanted? Yes. Well, no uncles broke out their ukuleles and started an impromptu concert, but that's what we paid the musicians for. It was, by far, the most beautiful wedding I'd ever been to, and I think that every bride should be able to say that at the end of her Big Day.

CAKE:
Save Room for Dessert!

Your wedding cake serves as both a beautiful decorative piece and a tasty dessert. Strike a reasonable balance between purpose and price and find a baker who will work magic! Look through wedding magazines and books to get ideas before you visit bakeries. You can always change your mind once you see the baker's portfolio, but it's better to have an idea of what you want before you get there. Bakers who specialize in wedding cakes can do just about anything. Keep in mind, the fancier the ingredients and the design, the more you're going to pay for it. If you are what you eat, then you want this cake to be beautiful! But remember it will be eaten, not framed. It's not worth spending an exorbitant amount of money on a cake that will soon be digested.

QTA's:

❏ Will they "custom-make" your cake based on your individual preferences?

❏ How far in advance will they make your cake? (The closer to your wedding date the fresher the cake will taste.)

❏ Is the baker licensed by the health department?

❏ What kind of ingredients do they use?

❏ How many wedding cakes does the shop do a week? (This will give you an idea of how experienced they are and about how much time they spend on each cake.)

❏ Do they charge extra or require deposits for pillars, cake tops, or columns?

❏ Ask about delivery and set-up charges. Make sure all applicable charges are included in the quote they give you.

❏ Can you drop off your cake topper prior to the wedding so they can put it on? Or, if you are having flowers on your cake, will they work with your florist?

❏ If you're using fresh flowers for the cake, will they be provided and already be in place or is the florist responsible? (Some bakers do not provide the fresh flowers. In that case, arrange the flowers for the cake through the florist.)

❏   Ask about a cake knife. Will the baker bring one you can use? Is there a charge? Does the place you are having your reception provide one free of charge?

Tips:

✳ Ask to see pictures of their work. Most professional cake makers will have a portfolio or photo album of their cakes. Make sure you like their style, creativity and overall look of their cakes.

✳ If there are pillars, columns or cake toppers that need to be returned, find out when they need to be returned and assign someone to be responsible for doing that. If the baker is familiar with the reception site or caterer, he/she may pick up the cake accessories on his/her own after the wedding.

✳ If you plan on having fresh flowers or some outside decorations other than what the baker usually uses, make sure you let the baker know what you are planning to do so he/she can frost and finish the cake appropriately.

✳ Flowers should be used in moderation. You don't want the flowers or decorations on the cake table to draw attention away from the cake.

✳ If you have several tiers, think about having multiple flavors. Multi-flavored cakes are a great way to give your guests a nice selection of cakes to choose from. It also helps if you can't decide on just one cake flavor.

✳ Look at your options in cake frostings and fillings. Bakers can do wonders with various flavors, textures and fillings. Make it fun!

✳ If you're saving your top tier for your one-year anniversary, ask the baker's advice on what will freeze best (i.e., strawberry shortcake won't taste as good as chocolate ganace after a year in the freezer).

Beginning in early Roman times, the cake has been a special part of the wedding celebration. A thin loaf was broken over the bride's head at the close of the ceremony to symbolize fertility. The wheat from which it was made symbolized fertility and the guests eagerly picked up the crumbs as good luck charms. During the Middle Ages, it became traditional for the couple to kiss over a small cluster of cakes. Later, a clever baker decided to amass all these small cakes together, covering them with frosting and the modern tiered cake was born.

❊ Consider a wedding cake with an unusual shape. Wedding bakers can make a cake into almost any shape, from a stack of presents to a pair of wedding rings.

❊ Select and design your wedding cake to go with your wedding theme and/or colors.

❊ To save on costs, look into a smaller wedding cake for the bridal party and family and serve a sheet cake for guests.

❊ If your wedding is outdoors or in an enclosed area that is not air-conditioned, stay away from butter-cream icing, whipped cream and meringue—they melt quickly!

❊ Request a contract with all of the necessary information and discussion points (wedding date, delivery or pick-up time, emergency contact names and numbers, deposit amount, balance, due date, etc.).

Expect to Pay: Anywhere from $1.75–$12 per slice

O'ahu:

Alfredos Bakery
626 N. King St., Honolulu, HI 96817
☎ (808) 847-3161

Bakery Kapiolani
1517 Kapi'olani Blvd.
Honolulu, HI 96814
☎ (808) 949-3111
Multiple locations

Cake Couture
☎ (808) 373-9750 / 🖷 373-9789
www.cakecouture.com
Call for appointment

Cake Creations by Lani
☎ (808) 545-8379
cakecreations.bylani@verizon.net
Custom designed wedding cakes

Cake Gallery, The
☎ (808) 258-9285
cakegalleryhi@lava.net
By appointment only.

Cake Lava
P.O. Box 62181, Honolulu, HI 96839
☎ (808) 277-7594 / 🖷 (808) 942-8928
www.cakelava.com / cakelava@hawaii.rr.com

Dee Lite Bakery/St. Germaine's Bakery
1930 Dillingham Blvd., Honolulu, HI 96819
☎ (808) 847-5396, ext. 24 or 25
www.stghi.com / miyata@stghi.com

Dreams Unlimited
2071-C Beretania St., Honolulu, HI 96826
☎ (808) 941-6164
www.weddingdreamsunlimited.com
Ctandal@aol.com
Floral wedding cakes. Call for an appointment

Kilani Bakery
704 Kilani Ave., Wahiawā, HI 96786
☎ (808) 621-5662

Liliha Bakery
515 N. Kuakini, Honolulu, HI 96817
☎ (808) 531-1651

Mary Catherine's Bakery
2820 S. King St., Honolulu, HI 96826
☎ (808) 946-4333

Napoleon's Bakery
94-1068 Ka Uka Blvd., Waipahu, HI 96797
☎ (808) 677-7710 / 🖷 677-6816

Paalaa Kai Bakery
66-945 Kaukonahua Rd.
Wailaua, HI 96791
(808) 637-9795

Patisserie, The
2115 S. Beretania St., Honolulu, HI 96826
☎ (808) 941-3055 / 🖷 941-3059
www.thepatisserie.com/weddingcakes.html

Tiers of Joy
☎ (808) 922-9693
Call for information.

Veronica's Cakes
☎ (808) 734-2423
www.cakesbylil.com / amylandini@aol.com

Maui:
Cakewalk Pāʻia Bakery
Corner of Hana Hwy. and Baldwin Ave.
Pāʻia, HI 96779
☎ (808) 579-8770
www.cakewalkmaui.com
heidicbo@yahoo.com

Cravings Bakery
335 C Hoʻohana St., Building 7
Kahului, HI 96732
☎ Toll Free (877) 351-6717
🖷 (808) 893-2378
www.cravings.com
CravingsHawaii@aol.com
Contact: Pat or Bill Pimentel

Ghislaine Wedding Cakes
60 B Halelani Pl.
Kīhei, HI 96753
☎ (808) 874-9535 / 🖷 874-9535
Ghiselani@hotmail.com
Contact: Marie Ghislaine Audant

Maui Wedding Cakes
100 Luluka Place
Kīhei, HI 96753
☎ Toll Free (866) 537-8888
🖷 874-1832
www.mauiweddingcakes.com
WeddingCake@hawaii.rr.com
Contact: Casey or Cheryl Logsdon

Big Island:
Leilani Bakery of Hawaii Ltd.
65-1158 Mamalahoa Hwy., # 7
Kamuela, HI 96743
☎ (808) 885-2772

Standard Bakery
P.O. Box 341, Kealakekua, HI 96750
☎ (808) 322-3688

Kauaʻi:
Contemporary Flavors Catering
1610 Haleukana St.
Līhuʻe, HI 96766
☎ (808) 245-2522
www.gtesupersite.com/contemflavor

Kauai Bakery & Cinnamons
Kukui Grove Center
Līhuʻe, HI 96766
☎ (808) 246-4765

Suzi's Date Bar
P.O. Box 1156
Kileaua, HI 96754
☎ (808) 822-9040

Hawaiian Wedding Bands...
And We're Not Talking
Entertainment

Hawaiian heirloom jewelry is almost always on your shopping list if you're visiting Hawai'i. If you've lived here for a while you most likely have several pieces of the beautiful, crafted jewelry. If you haven't already purchased your wedding rings/bands consider adding this very Hawaiian touch to remember your wedding in paradise. Hawaiian heirloom jewelry dates back to 1880 when Queen Victoria presented a piece to Princess Lili'uokalani. It was a solid gold bracelet with the Princess' name engraved and enameled on it. Since then, the people of Hawai'i have adopted this style of jewelry and passed it on from generation to generation. You can get Hawaiian heirloom wedding bands with your names (in either English or Hawaiian) enameled or etched on it or various other styles and pieces.

Dennis and I were married on the small, rural island of Lāna'i where we lived for four years. The island used to be the world's largest pineapple plantation but now is home to two five-star world-class hotels. There are only about 3,000 year-round residents, no stop lights, no fast food franchises; and only 2 percent of the roads are paved. We were married in cooler, upcountry Lāna'i City where almost all the local residents live. It's about 1,700 feet above sea level and boasts of hundreds of stately Cook Island pine trees.

We were married outdoors, under two giant trees in an area affectionately known as Haole Hill. This was where the plantation managers used to live in the old pineapple days. Ours was a small homemade wedding with about 35 close friends. We were perched atop a hill that looked down on the vast blue Pacific in the distance. We had rented a large old-world plantation style Hawaiian home where we would have the food, drinks, and music.

Dennis Aubrey & Marcia Zina Mager

——— ♥♥ ———

LĀNA'I CITY & HOTEL LĀNA'I

There is a third small hotel on Lāna'i, Hotel Lāna'i, a quaint, charming 10-room inn. Since we were friends with the chef at that hotel, we hired him to prepare all the food for the wedding. Another friend living on the island picked all the flowers herself and arranged them magnificently inside the house. Still another friend, who was Hawaiian, hiked to a secluded area on Lāna'i where he collected red wili wili seeds for my haku (head lei). His wife made the beautiful haku which matched my floor-length red and white mu'umu'u which I bought on O'ahu. Another friend who was born and raised on Lāna'i made Dennis and me lovely ti leaf leis.

During the ceremony, Dennis and I had to recite our own wedding vows. Dennis was so nervous that when he began to speak, his voice sounded stilted and very much like a radio announcer. I guess all my nervousness sort of came to a head because I burst out hysterically laughing…and could not stop for about 10 minutes. Every time I thought I was calm, he would begin reciting his vows again…and I would lose it. Soon the minister burst out laughing, then the best man and maid of honor, with the entire wedding congregation eventually following suit. It was definitely the funniest and most memorable moment in our wedding. Finally, Dennis had to put his arm around me and whisper the vows in my ear.

Everyone there said it was absolutely the best party Lāna'i ever had! Our wedding on Lāna'i was truly a dream come true!

Food and Drink for Thought

As far as wedding expenses go, your food bill is usually your largest expense (40–50 percent of most wedding budgets). So spend some time selecting a caterer that meets your needs and desires. Meet with several and talk with them about your budget, the style of your reception, and what types of food you would like served. If you're getting married in a banquet hall or hotel where you aren't able to bring in a caterer, make sure you review their menu options and price lists completely before you book the site. Ask your prospective caterers to do a taste sampling if you are unfamiliar with their food. Be sure you're just as happy with the food and service as you are with the reception site. Don't forget to factor in drinks (non-alcoholic and alcoholic). For many couples, your bar expense can be a big one and you need to include it in your catering/food budget.

QTA's:

❏ How long have they been catering weddings?

❏ Are server tips included in the meal price? If not, have them add that into the estimate so you can break down the per person cost.

❏ Do they have liquor and bartending services?

❏ If you're catering through a hotel or banquet hall, will they allow you to provide your own drinks and bartenders? If so, is there an additional fee?

❏ What do they do with the leftover food? Can they make plates for the bridal party and family? (You may also request that leftovers from buffets and food stations be packed up and given to organizations that feed the homeless. The caterer probably won't deliver it to them, but the organization will most likely be happy to pick it up.)

❏ When is the final count due?

❏ When is the final payment due?

❏ Does the caterer have license and liability insurance?

❏ Do their chefs have a specialty or signature meal?

❑ Can they provide specialty meals such as vegetarian?

❑ Does the caterer work with fresh or frozen foods?

❑ If needed, is your caterer able to provide chairs, tables, linens and dinnerware? At what additional costs?

❑ Will the caterer you booked be on-site at the reception? If not, who will be your catering point of contact? Get the name and contact information. Speak with them prior to your reception to make sure they have been made aware of your requests and the specifics of your reception.

❑ What is the caterer's average per-person cost? (It will vary from breakfast, brunch, lunch or dinner, so be specific so you can ensure an accurate estimate)

❑ Will the caterer be working on other weddings or events on your wedding date? (Avoid this if at all possible.)

Tips:

✳ Ask for two to four references of recent weddings they've catered and then call them!

✳ Ask about the ratio of servers to guests. This can vary depending on the type of reception you have (seated dinner versus buffet). One good rule of thumb is to have one server for every eight to twelve guests.

✳ When determining a final head count for your caterer, be sure to include a meal for your entertainer (DJ or band), and wedding-day coordinator and others who are servicing your reception. Confirm with each of them first to be sure that they are staying for the meal.

✳ If you're trying to keep costs low, stay away from certain foods like shrimp, salmon, lobster and beef tenderloin. You might consider incorporating them into the menu as appetizers—it's less costly.

✳ Food stations are a great way to offer variety and save money. Pasta stations are very economical.

✳ Don't assume that a buffet or food stations is less expensive than a sit-down dinner. Talk with your caterer and discuss the options.

✳ Heavy pūpū (appetizers) are a good way to off-set costs.

✳ Include a "menu board," a list of what is being served. This is especially helpful for out-of-town guests who are not used to seeing "lomi lomi salmon" or other local favorites.

✳ Some caterers also do wedding cakes. Ask to see their portfolio. If you're happy with their work, it cuts down on an extra step. Order the cake through them, and you'll have one less person to coordinate with.

✳ Ask to see pictures of their table displays. Some caterers will include floral arrangements or other decor for their food stations and buffets. Make sure to discuss this so that your other decorations coordinate. If you don't want them to do any decor, tell them that, too.

✳ For couples having early weddings who still want to offer alcoholic beverages, look into serving mimosas (champagne mixed with orange juice) or bloody Marys (tomato juice and vodka) or a light champagne.

✳ Rule of thumb for figuring out amount of alcohol needed: three drinks per person, per hour. You can pour six glasses of champagne per bottle and four people per bottle of wine.

✳ Look into bringing in your own alcohol; it's often cheaper. You can buy beer, wine, soda and juice by bulk at places like Costco and Sam's Club.

Expect To Pay: Per person is almost as specific as we can go here. The sky is the limit—actually your purse strings are—but keep in mind, this is where a big chunk of change for your reception will go. It'll run you anywhere from $8 per person to $75 per person and up!

A Catered Experience
94-1068 Ka Uka Blvd.
Waipahu, HI 96797
☎ (808) 677-7744

Carval Catering
2707A S. King St.
Honolulu, HI 96826
☎ (808) 949-2591 / 🖨 943-6447
www.carvalcatering.com
tlbcarval@msn.com

Cater To Me
33 Aulike St., Kailua, HI 96734
☎ (808) 230-8188
Contact: Christian Schneider

The Catering Connection
P.O. Box 12024
Honolulu, HI 96828
☎ (808) 551-3458

Clam Bake Hawaiian Style Catering
46-174 Kahuhipa St.
Kāne'ohe, HI 96744
☎ (808) 235-8183

Creations in Catering
620 Dillingham Blvd.
Honolulu, HI 96817
☎ (808) 847-7611 / 🖨 841-7500

Current Affairs
1933 Homerule St.
Honolulu HI 96819
☎ (808) 732-9666 xt. 34
www.current-affairs.net

Events by Sheraton
2255 Kālakaua Ave., Honolulu, HI 96813
☎ (808) 931-8111
www.starwood.com/hawaii
For on-site and off-property events.

Kahala Caterers
3458 Waialae Ave., Honolulu, HI 96816
☎ (808) 735-7775 / 🖨 735-7776
www.kahalacaterers.com
info@kahalacaterers.com

Kama'aina Services Inc.
94-252A Pupuole, Waipahu, HI 96797
☎ (808) 677-0067
www.kamaainaservices.com

Ko'olau Golf Club
45-550 Kionaole Rd., Kāne'ohe, HI 96744
☎ (808) 236-0013

Let's Eat Hawaii Catering
449 Kapahulu Ave., 2nd Floor
Honolulu, HI 96815
☎ (808) 739-5637 Ext. 22 / 732-8682
www.samchoy.com / samchoy@lava.net
Cuisine by Chef Sam Choy.

Mānoa Catering Company
Honolulu, HI 96822
☎ (808) 988-1075 / 🖨 833-4355

Marian's Island Wide Catering
79 Mango Pl., Wahiawā, HI 96786
☎ (808) 621-6758 / 🖨 621-3670
www.marianscatering.com
marians@gte.net

Old Waialae Road
2820 S. King St., Honolulu, HI 96826
☎ (808) 951-7779

Maui:

Grace and Style, Inc.
P.O. Box 11041, Lāhainā, HI 96761
☎ Toll Free (888) 524-1310
🖨 (888) 684-7737
www.graceandstyle.com
nikki@graceandstyle.com
Contact: Nikki Grace

Hapas Maui, Inc.
41 E. Lipoa St.
Kīhei, HI 96753
☎ (808) 879-9001 / 🖨 879-5322
mauibarsareus@aol.com
Contact: Stacey Hoeft

Larry Mischle
Caterer Extraordinaire, Inc.
281 Kaikea St., Kīhei, HI 96753
☎ (808) 281-1913 / 🖨 879-1183
mischlel001@hawaii.rr.com
Contact: Larry Mischle

Pacific'O Restaurant
505 Front St.
Lāhainā, HI 96761
☎ (808) 667-4341
www.pacificomaui.com
info@pacificomaui.com

Sheraton Maui
2605 Kā'anapali Parkway
Lāhainā, HI 96761
☎ (808) 661-0031 / 🖨 661-0458
www.sheraton-maui.com
marilyn.knecht@sheraton.com
Contact: Marilyn Knecht

Stella Blues Café
1215 S. Kīhei Rd.
Kīhei, HI 96753
☎ (808) 874-3779 / 🖨 879-3037
stelablu@maui.net
Contact: Kale Boverman

The Catering Company
☎ (808) 244-0500
mauimann@hotmail.com
Contact: Allen Mann
Maui's full service caterer, on-site catering is their specialty.

The Rusty Harpoon
2435 Kā'anapali Parkway
Lāhainā, HI 96761
☎ (808) 661-3123 / 🖨 661-3808
www.rustyharpoon.com
manager@rustyharpoon.com
Contact: Suzzette Metcalfe / Jean Coppers

The Seawatch Restaurant
100 Wailea Golf Club Dr.
Wailea, HI 96753
☎ (808) 875-8080 / 🖨 875-7462
www.seawatchrestaurant.com
jennifer@seawatchrestaurant.com
Contact: Jennifer Sylvester,
Director Sales/Mkt.

Vasi's Catering Company
P.O. Box 814
Ha'ikū, HI 96708
☎ (808) 573-8056 / 🖨 573-8309
www.maui.net/~vasis / vasis@maui.net

Big Island:
Captain's Table Catering
P. O Box 2123
Kailua-Kona, HI 96745
☎ (808) 334-0383
rocokona@aloha.net
www.partypop.com/vendors/683486.htm
Contact: Colin Gould

Hilo Hawaiian Hotel
71 Banyan Dr., Hilo, HI 96720
☎ (808) 935-9361 / 🖨 961-9642
www.castleresorts.com

Keoki's Place
75-5626 Kuakini Hwy., Suite #2
Kailua-Kona, HI 96740
☎ Toll Free (800) 210-7622
(808) 329-7500

King Kamehameha Kona Beach Hotel
75-5660 Palani Rd.
Kailua-Kona, HI 96740
☎ (808) 331-6389 / 🖷 331-6305
www.konabeachhotel.com
kbhcater@hthcorp.com

Kaua'i:
Andy's Kine Catering
3734A Hanapēpē Rd.
Hanapēpē, HI 96716
☎ (808) 335-2810

Contemporary Flavors
1610 Haleukana St.
Līhu'e, HI 96766
☎ (808) 245-2522 / 🖷 245-2744
conflvr@gte.net

Gaylord's at Kilohana
3-2087 Kaumuali'i Hwy.
Līhu'e, HI 96766
☎ (808) 245-9593 / 🖷 246-1087
info@gaylordskauai.com
www.gaylordskauai.com

Heavenly Creations
P.O. Box 167
Anahola, HI 96703
☎ (808) 828-1700
Toll Free (877) 828-1700
www.heavenlycreations.org
thestars@gte.net
Contact: DJ Star

Molokai:
The Plantation House
2000 Plantation Club Dr.
Kapalua, HI 96761
☎ (808) 669-6299 / 🖷 669-1222
www.theplantationhouse.com
tiffany@theplantationhouse.com
Contact: Tiffany Kerstein

Notes

Who's Buying?

T here are several tips to consider when calculating your bar tab. 1) An open bar gives your guests unlimited access to all drinks for the duration of your reception. This is what most couples in Hawai'i opt for; but keep in mind, especially if you have heavy drinkers, this can get very costly. Not to mention any liabilities, both legally and otherwise, should your guests drink too much and get into an accident. 2) The average guest will consume three drinks in the first hour. To be safe, calculate three drinks per person, per hour. Bartenders keep track of the amount of drinks served throughout the evening. 3) You can opt to only have an open bar for x amount of hours. After that, guests are expected to pay for their drinks. Be sure to announce when the open bar is closing. 4) With a cash bar, your guests pay for their own drinks. This is unusual for most Hawai'i wedding receptions. You can split the cash bar and serve water, juice and soda for free and have guests pay for alcoholic beverages (or select alcoholic beverages). 5) If you insist on having an open bar all night, but still want to keep costs down, consider serving select beverages like juice, soda, beer and wine. 6) Have your last call for alcoholic drinks at least thirty minutes before your reception ends to give guests some time to sober up, and if that doesn't do the trick, call a cab for those who need a ride home.

Matt and I met on the fourth of July and it's been fireworks ever since. We set the date for about a year-and-a-half after we got engaged and started the planning. We decided early on that we wanted to invite everyone who had touched our lives, even if we hadn't seen them since grade school. With Matt's large extended family, my relatives from the mainland, and all our friends, this wedding was going to be big!

Matt Sojot &
Jenni Cleve

LUANA HILLS GOLF CLUB

When you're throwing a wedding with 400+ guests, your location options are somewhat limited. We needed to find a place with lots of room, great food, and accommodations for a kickin' party. We also felt, with so many people in attendance, it was important to have the ceremony and the reception at the same site. After a couple of false starts, we found the perfect location. Nestled in beautiful and picturesque Olomana Valley on the windward side of O'ahu ,we discovered the Luana Hills Country Club. It's isolated and has a stunning view of the mountains with the perfect spot to perform the ceremony outside. They had all the elements we needed including tents, chairs, and tables. This was a real stress reliever for us. I enlisted the help of my mom and Keri (the author of this book and one of my bridesmaids) to help me coordinate the wedding; and we were off and running.

On the day of the wedding everything was humming along just fine. Aside from the limo's battery dying as it arrived to pick up the girls from the hotel, we were right on schedule. That was until it started to rain. I know it rains on weddings all the time but this was my wedding; and my ceremony was planned

(continued on next page)

for outside. What to do? Hyperventilate and pray.

There was a contingency plan to move everything inside the clubhouse in case of rain. Keri was already on it. As soon as the first drops fell, she was on the phone with her coordinators to move the whole thing inside. This was not what I had planned. I wanted my wedding outside amidst the glory of the ancient and towering green Ko‘olau mountains, not in the clubhouse next to the bar. Where would we take pictures? There was no aisle to walk down. We hadn't rehearsed this. My vision was getting blurry and I was about to have a "bridezilla" moment when…the skies cleared and the sun came out. The wedding gods were smiling on me! Keri was back on the phone with her coordinators and stopped them in their muddy tracks. This wedding was a go for outside and we were on. The wedding began and I grabbed my dad's arm and started down the aisle to my new life.

In Hawai‘i, rain at a wedding is a blessing. As I scanned the faces of our family and friends who had gathered to celebrate and wish us well, I realized just how blessed I was. I neared the front of the aisle. Matt stood there waiting for me. He looked so handsome in his dark suit. Then I got the first glimpse of our entire wedding party. They looked awesome. Matt is half-Filipino and chose to dress his groomsmen in traditional Filipino wedding shirts, or barong tagalegs. (They are sheer, long sleeved shirts, worn with an undershirt and adorned on the front with intricate embroidery.) I wasn't sure how they would work with my bridesmaids' dresses but they were perfect. My gorgeous bridesmaids were dressed in blush-colored, strapless a-line dresses. The design was flattering for all of them and the blush color made their skin glow bronze. The wedding party was rounded out with my nephew Jackie as the very conscientious, handsome, barefooted ring-bearer and Maggie, my bridesmaid Alicia's four-year-old, as the picture-perfect flower girl. Melissa, a close friend, danced a meaningful hula during the service and George, my minister, performed a warm, personal service.

My wedding was better than I had imagined. The rain was truly a blessing. It held for the pictures and most of the evening. After the service, dinner, and brief program, we partied and danced the night away with the help of a superb band and DJ. We got exactly what we wanted, a big celebration surrounded by the people we love.

My advice to you in planning your wedding is: hire a good wedding planner and don't sweat the small stuff too much. Include the things that make you happy and you can't go wrong. If you enjoy yourself, your guests will too.

Setting Your Sites

The wedding of your dreams requires a dream location. Identifying the wedding ceremony and reception site is a momentous step in the path of wedding planning and preparation. You have two options. You may choose to have your ceremony and reception at the same location or you may choose to have them at two different sites. Some couples choose their wedding date first and then look for a reception/wedding site that will accommodate the date. Others choose the location(s) and then set their wedding date according to the availability of the site. Whichever road you choose, there are several key elements to remember in identifying the perfect wedding location beyond the date. Ask lots of questions and visit every location that has potential and offers possibilities before selecting. The "Questions To Ask" and "Tips" sections of this chapter will become your wedding planning bible and will offer dependable pointers to help guide and direct you.

For couples looking for private estates and other exclusive locations, your best bet is to contact a company that specializes in estate rentals or check with your caterer, often they have great suggestions for estates they have done events at. You can also contact real estate companies who have a separate division for estate rentals. You'll find several location specialists listed in this chapter.

For ceremonies outdoors and/or at public parks and beaches refer to pages 15-18.

QTA's:

- [ ] Are there time constraints on your wedding day? Is there a ceremony before or after yours?
- [ ] What is the protocol of the site for booking multiple weddings on the same day?
- [ ] Is there a place for the bridal party to get ready or wait once they are ready (locker room, spacious bathroom, etc.)?

❏ What kind of sound system do they have? Are there extra costs to use their sound system? Can you bring your own?

❏ Do they have the capabilities to accommodate live musicians for the ceremony and reception?

❏ Is there a flat rental fee to use the property? Is that waived after spending x amount of dollars?

❏ If you're getting married in a church or synagogue, are you obligated to use their officiant or can you bring your own?

❏ What are the restrictions for photography, videography, music, decorations, etc.? (Some sites won't allow you to throw rose petals. Other places will allow it but charge extra for clean-up or may require you to designate someone for clean-up.)

❏ What kind of decorations or "props" are provided or available for your use (archway, pew bows, aisle runners, chairs, unity candle stands, communion bench, pillars, etc.)?

❏ Do they provide an on-site wedding coordinator? What is their role?

❏ If it is an outdoor wedding, does the site have a back-up plan should it rain?

❏ What time will the site be available for set-up?

❏ What can the facility provide (kitchen, tables, chairs, linen, lights, tents, dance floor, sound system, podium, etc.)?

❏ Does the site have liability insurance?

❏ How much of a deposit is required to reserve the site? Is it refundable?

❏ If you're bringing in an outside caterer, what access will they have to a kitchen, refrigerator, stove, etc.?

❏ How many people does the ceremony or reception site accommodate comfortably?

❏ Can you bring in your own "people" (florists, caterers, musicians, coordinator)? If not, what are you required to use of theirs?

Better to Give or to Receive?

♥♥

The receiving line is when the bridal party greets each guest. The school of thought behind this is that it may be the only opportunity your guests will have to personally congratulate you. This works well for small weddings, but can be a very time-consuming process if you have a large wedding. Another option, no matter what the size of your wedding, is to designate some time in your reception program to visit each table. The bottom line is, however you choose to do it, it's important for the couple to be able to personally thank and greet each guest.

The order of the receiving line is usually as follows: maid of honor, best man, bridesmaids and groomsmen, followed by your parents, the bride and the groom.

❏ Can you bring in your own drinks? (You'll usually be charged a corkage fee, but often it still ends up being less expensive to bring your own.) Most large hotels will allow you to bring your own, but they will not allow you to provide your own bartenders. Other off-property sites may allow you to do both…for a fee.

Tips:

✳ Ask about restrictions concerning alcohol, occupancy, tents, photography, noise level, etc.

✳ Ensure that there is sufficient parking, and ask if guests will have to pay to park. If there is a parking fee, consider paying for guest parking or a portion of it. Or offer guests alternative parking suggestions that are free or less expensive.

✳ Ask about cancellation policies and deposit requirements.

✳ For cost-cutting ideas, consider heavy pūpū, lunch, or brunch versus a sit-down dinner or dinner buffet.

✳ Research the option of bringing in your own alcohol. Make sure to check with sites regarding corkage fees, bartender tips, children's costs, etc.

✳ Look into package deals to save on site rental.

✳ As you visit possible wedding and/or reception sites, keep notes of your observations and the information you obtain. This will help you narrow down your options and compare accurately.

✳ Ask whether the quoted price is all-inclusive, or whether there will be additional charges, such as gratuities, overtime fees, and sales tax.

✳ Put everything in writing. Include all the details such as dates, times, prices, and descriptions of services provided.

✳ Discuss payment options. Most sites require a deposit to reserve the facility, with the balance due seven days prior to the date of the event, after the final guest count is given.

❋ Discuss payment options. Most sites require a deposit to reserve the facility, with the balance due seven days prior to the date of the event, after the final guest count is given.

❋ You will be expected to reconcile all additional costs, like bar or additional food costs, at the end of the night.

❋ Pay by credit card or cashier's check. Many places will not accept personal checks. Another benefit of paying with your credit card is that most credit cards will give you sixty days to dispute any charges and offer various kinds of insurance.

❋ Some places charge more for certain days of the week or times of the day. (For example, a Saturday evening wedding may be more costly than a Friday evening or Sunday brunch.)

❋ Check out the bathrooms. Make sure they are clean and suitable to handle the number of guests you will be expecting.

❋ Ask for references from the venues as to whom they frequently work with. But call them and meet with them personally.

❋ If possible check out the venues when there are other weddings or events going on so you can see the set-up and event execution firsthand.

❋ Encourage your outside vendors to visit the site if they're unfamiliar with it. Make the necessary arrangements with the site coordinator, if needed.

❋ Certain times of the year will make your wedding arrangements and accommodations more expensive and harder to book. Avoid holidays and other popular dates and times. (See pages 13-14 for a listing of Hawaiian holidays and major events.)

❋ Send your officiant an invitation and allow him/her to bring his/her spouse or a guest.

❋ Keep in mind that weddings "out of town" may be less expensive but some vendors will charge a travel fee or extra delivery charge. (Ask your vendors ahead of time about this.)

Notes:

❋ Make sure there are outlets for extension cords, sound systems, etc.

❋ Hold your wedding rehearsal at the exact place you'll be having the ceremony. It's helpful to hold it at the same time as this will allow you to adjust certain things regarding sunlight, lighting, weather, etc.

❋ Book your rehearsal date and time as soon as possible.

❋ Invite everyone who has a role in your ceremony to the rehearsal. Your photographer and/or videographer don't have to be there, but your officiant, bridal party, family members, coordinator, ushers, and sound system people should be.

❋ If you're getting married at a public beach or park, make sure you have applied for the proper permits and have them with you on the day of your wedding.

❋ Don't be late! Not only is it rude to make dozens or hundreds of guests wait too long, but some ceremony sites book weddings back to back. In these cases, you only have a certain amount of time to do your thing. And when that time is up, whether you're done or not, they'll ask you to leave.

O'ahu:

Above Heaven's Gate
41-1010 Laumilo St.
Waimānalo, HI 96795
☎ Toll Free (800) 800-2933
(888) 463-6933
www.hawaiiweddings.com
howie@hawaiiweddings.com
Specialize in very small, intimate weddings. Usually there is only a bride and groom, and perhaps a handful of guests.

Ala Moana Hotel
410 Atkinson Dr.
Honolulu, HI 96814
☎ Toll Free (888) 367-4811
🖷 (808) 944-6839
www.alamoanahotel.com
reservations@alamoanahotel.com
Spectacular views, elegant dining and convenient access to shopping and the beach.

Aston Waikiki Joy Hotel
320 Lewers, Honolulu, HI 96815
☎ (808) 923-2300

Aston Hawaii ResortQuest
2155 Kālakaua Ave., #500
Honolulu, HI 96815
☎ (808) 931-1303 / 🖷 922-8785
www.astonhotels.com

Atlantis Cruises' Navatek I
1600 Kapi'olani Blvd., #1630
Honolulu, HI 96814
☎ (808) 973-1311
www.atlantisadventures.com
ores@atlantisadventures.com
Elegant and smooth-cruising ship. An idyllic setting for weddings, receptions, bridal showers and rehearsal dinners.

Atlantis Submarines Waikiki
1600 Kapiolani Blvd., Suite 1630
Honolulu, HI 96814
☎ (808) 973-9811
www.atlantisadventures.com

Bayer Estate
5329 Kalaniana‘ole Hwy.
Honolulu, HI 96821
☎ (808) 377-9359 / 🖶 262-3745
www.bayerestate.com
info@bayerestate.com
Ocean-front garden with seaside ceremony.
Listed on the State Register of Historic Places.

Bishop Museum
1525 Bernice St., Honolulu, HI 96817
☎ (808) 848-4148 / 🖶 841-8968
www.bishopmuseum.org
facility@bishopmuseum.org
Choose from the casual atmosphere of Atherton
Halau, or the spaciousness of the Great Lawn, or their
most regal setting—the majestic Hawaiian Hall.

Blaisdell Center
777 Ward Ave., Honolulu, HI 96814
☎ (808) 594-4023 / 527-5400
www.blaisdellcenter.com

Byodo-in Temple
47-200 Kahekili Hwy.
Kāne‘ohe, HI 96744
☎ (808) 239-4724 / 🖶 239-4714
www.hawaiiweb.com/html/byodo_in_
buddhist_temple.html
rnewby@rightstarhawaii.com
Replica of the actual Byodo-in Temple in
Kyoto, Japan.

Café Laniakea
1040 Richards St., Honolulu, HI 96813
☎ (808) 524-8789
Recently remodeled café and facilities inside
the YWCA.

Calvary By The Sea
5339 Kalaniana‘ole Hwy.
Honolulu, HI 96821
☎ (808) 377-5477
Calvarybythesea@hawaii.rr.com
Ocean front chapel.

Central Union Church
1660 S. Beretania St.
Honolulu, HI 96826
☎ (808) 947-5069 / 🖶 941-9124
www.centralunionchurch.org/
weddings@centralunionchurch.org
Central Union Church has four chapels
or gardens for your formal wedding services.

Dave & Busters
1030 Auahi St., Honolulu, HI 96814
☎ (808) 589-2215
www.daveandbusters.com

Dillingham Ranch
68-540 Farrington Hwy.
Waialua, HI 96791
☎ (808) 637-8088 / 🖶 637-3542
www.dillinghamranch.com/
Beautifully landscaped grounds and the historical
Dillingham estate will make any event memorable
and unique.

Dole Ballrooms
735 Iwilei Rd., Flr. 2, Honolulu, HI 96817
☎ (808) 847-7611
catering@hawaii.cateres.com

Dream Cruises
306 Kamani St.
Honolulu, HI 96813
☎ Toll Free (800) 400-7300
(808) 592-5200
www.dream-cruises.com
nmwatson@dream-cruises.com
Take a brunch, lunch or dinner cruise,
or charter a private yacht.

East-West Center
1601 East-West Rd., Honolulu, HI 96822
☎ (808) 944-7111 / 🖷 944-7376
www.ewc.hawaii.edu/
ewcinfo@EastWestCenter.org
*The East-West Center is located in Honolulu,
Hawai'i, three miles from Waikīkī and adjacent
to the University of Hawai'i. Their 21-acre
campus includes conference facilities, a research
and administration office building and three
residential halls.*

Foster Botanical Garden
50 N. Vineyard Blvd., Honolulu, HI 96817
☎ (808) 522-7066
www.co.honolulu.hi.us/parks/facility/
foster/index.htm
Call for wedding information

Ha'ikū Gardens Weddings
46-336 Ha'ikū Rd., Kāne'ohe, HI 96744
☎ (808) 247-0605 / 🖷 (808) 247-5886
weddings@haikugardens.com
www.haikugardens.com
*Ha'ikū Gardens Weddings specializes in providing
a spectacular tropical garden setting for your
wedding as well as facilities for wedding receptions
and rehearsal dinners.*

Hale Koa Hotel
2055 Kalia Rd., Honolulu, HI 96815
☎ (808) 955-9609 / 🖷 955-9429
www.halekoa.com
information@halekoa.com
Oceanfront, garden setting. Military sponsored only.

Halekulani
2199 Kalia Rd., Honolulu, HI 96815
☎ (808) 923-2311 / 🖷 926-8004
www.halekulani.com
Oceanfront, world renowned resort.

Hawai'i Convention Center
1801 Kālakaua Ave.
Honolulu, HI 96815
☎ (808) 943-3500 / 🖷 943-3547
www.hawaiiconvention.com
rtanaka@hccsmg.com
Located 5 minutes from the heart of Waikīkī.

Hawai'i Prince Hotel Waikīkī
100 Holomoana St.
Honolulu, HI 96815
☎ Toll Free (800) 321-6248
🖷 (808) 946-0811
www.princeresortshawaii.com
reservations@princehawaii.com
*Whether you say your vows next to
a cascading waterfall, swim together in
a sea turtle cove or have a cozy candlelit
dinner overlooking a shimmering beach,
they have the stuff dreams are made of.*

Hawaii Sailing Adventures
407 Coral St., #107
Honolulu, HI 96813
☎ (808) 596-9696 / 🖷 596-8494
www.hawaiisail.com
Joshua@hawaiisail.com
*Hawai'i's only luxury boutique sailing charter
company.*

Hilton Hawaiian Village
2005 Kalia Rd.
Honolulu, HI 96815
☎ (808) 949-4321 ext. 35 / 🖷 947-7898
www.hiltonhawaiianvillage.com
*Located on Waikīkī's widest stretch of beach,
features lush tropical gardens, waterfalls.*

Honolulu Academy of Arts
900 S. Beretania St.
Honolulu, HI 96814
☎ (808) 532-8700 / 🖨 532-8787
Honoluluacademy.org
Enjoy your wedding on the elegant grounds of the Academy in downtown Honolulu. Ample guest parking and a staff experienced with event planning make your job easy! Can accommodate up to three hundred sit-down guests.

Honolulu Country Club
1690 Ala Pu'umalu St.
Honolulu, HI 96818
☎ (808) 441-9401 / 🖨 441-9405
www.honolulucountryclub.com
events@honolulucountryclub.com
Located in Salt Lake, a quiet residential community. Breathtaking view of Moanalua Ridge, just three miles from the Honolulu International Airport.

Honolulu Sailing Co.
47-335 Lulani
Kāne'ohe, HI 96744
☎ Toll Free (800) 829-0114
(808) 239-3900 / 🖨 239-9718
www.honsail.com / info@honsail.org
Charter your own personal yacht.

Honolulu Zoo
151 Kapahulu Ave.
Honolulu, HI 96815
☎ (808) 971-7171 / 971-7174
www.honoluluzoo.org
honzoo@honzoosoc.org
Across from Waikīkī Beach.

Ho'omaluhia Botanical Garden
45-680 Luluku Rd.
Kāne'ohe, HI 96744
☎ (808) 233-7323
www.co.honolulu.hi.us/parks/hbg/hmbg.htm
Call for wedding information.

Hyatt Regency Waikīkī
2424 Kālakaua Ave., Honolulu, HI 96815
☎ (808) 921-6054 / 923-1234
🖨 923-7839
www.hyattwaikiki.com
For intimate weddings (under 50) or larger ones (up to 500), poolside or ballroom setting. For more info on Hyatt Regency Waikiki weddings see the "Real Hawaii Wedding" on page 12.

Hy's Steak House
Waikiki Park Heights Hotel
2440 Kuhio Ave., Honolulu, HI 96815
☎ (808) 922-5555
www.hyshawaii.com/
hyshawaii.verizon.net
Hy's charming Main Room and Broiler Room resemble an old English mansion and possess all the ambiance of a private gentlemen's club.

Ihilani Resort
92-1001 Olani St., Kapolei, HI 96707
☎ Toll Free (800) 626-4446
🖨 (808) 679-0080
www.ihilani.com / info@ihilani.com
On the beach. Various venues—beach, gazebo, etc. Small or large weddings.

Ilikai Seaside Chapel
1777 Ala Moana, Honolulu, HI 96815
☎ (808) 942-2277
www.angelchapelbythesea.com
weddings@chapelbythesea.com

'Iolani Palace
Corner of King and Richards Streets
Honolulu, HI 96813
☎ (808) 538-1471 / 522-0832
www.iolanipalace.org
The only recognized palace in the United States.

Japanese Cultural Center
2454 S. Beretania St.
Honolulu, HI 96826
☎ (808) 945-7633 / 943-0063
info@jcch.com

Kahala Mandarin Oriental, Hawai'i
5000 Kāhala Ave., Honolulu, HI 96816
☎ (808) 739-8888 / 739-8800
www.mandarin-oriental.com
mohnl-reservations@mohg.com
Extraordinary oceanfront setting.

Kalama Beach Club
280 N. Kalaheo Ave., Kailua, HI 96834
☎ (808) 262-5995
www.kalamabeachclub.com
info@kalamabeachclub.com
A touch of old Hawai'i on Kailua Beach.

KawaiaHa'o Church
957 Punchbowl
Honolulu, HI 96813
☎ (808) 522-1333
*"Westminster Abbey of Hawai'i," built of coral
and timber in 1841.*

Ko'olau Golf Club
45-550 Kionaole Rd.
Kāne'ohe, HI 96744
☎ (808) 236-4653 ext. 241
*Located beneath the Pali Lookout. Secluded setting.
Magnificent view of Ko'olau Mountains.*

Kualoa Ranch
49-560 Kamehameha Hwy.
Ka'a'awa, HI 96730
☎ Toll Free (800) 231-7321
(808) 237-8925
www.kualoa.com
kualoaevents@kualoa.com
*Luscious green cliffs overlooking the blue ocean
and Chinaman's Hat island.*

**Lanikuhonua Cultural Institute
The Estate of James Campbell**
1001 Kamokila Boulevard
Kapolei, HI 96707
☎ (808) 674-3360 / 674-3349
*Private beachfront property on O'ahu's 'Ewa
side. Located near Ko 'Olina and Ihilani
Marriot Resort.*

Lili'uokalani Botanical Garden
North Kuakini St.
Honolulu, HI 96817
☎ (808) 522-7060
www.co.honolulu.hi.us/parks/hbg/index.
htm#liliuokalani
Call for wedding information.

Long Life Center
Century Center, 40th Floor
1750 Kālakaua Ave.
Honolulu, HI 96826
☎ (808) 955-8809
www.longlifecenter.com

Luana Hills Country Club
770 Auloa Rd.
Kailua, HI 96734
☎ (808) 262-2139
www.luanahills.com
*Located in the deep valley between Kailua and
Waimānalo and surrounded by the Ko'olau
Mountains.*

Maria Caprio International Locations
P.O. Box 10799, Honolulu, HI 96816
☎ (808) 737-6320
www.hawaiilocations.com/
Maria@HawaiiLocations.com
Locations specialists.

Marlu West
61-529 Kamehameha Hwy.
Haleiwa, HI 96712
☎ (808) 637-6417
www.openhousehawaii.com/marlu
hhimar@aol.com
Estate and Vacation Rentals.

Michel's Seaside Chapel
2895 Kālakaua Ave.
Honolulu, HI 96815
☎ (808) 923-9853 / 🖳 926-6063
jdominis@lava.net

Michel's at the Colony Surf
2895 Kālakaua Ave.
Honolulu, HI 96815
☎ (808) 728-3463 / 🖳 526-3758
www.michelshawaii.com
zizlavsky@mac.com

Mid-Pacific Country Club
266 Kaelepulu Dr.
Kailua, HI 96734
☎ (808) 262-8161 / 🖳 263-4396
www.mpcchi.org
char@mpcchi.org

Mission House Museum
553 S. King St.
Honolulu, HI 96813
☎ (808) 531-0481 / 🖳 545-2280
www.missionhouses.org

Natsunoya Tea House
1935 Makanani Dr.
Honolulu, HI 96817
☎ (808) 595-4489
natsunoya@hawaii.rr.com
Located in Alewa Heights, Natsunoya Tea House is Honolulu's oldest tea house, unsurpassed in cuisine, service, and atmosphere.

New Otani Kaimana Beach Hotel
2863 Kālakaua Ave.
Honolulu, HI 96815
☎ Toll Free (800) 356-8264
🖳 (808) 922-9404
www.kaimana.com
hawaiianweddings@kaimana.com
Located at the far east end of Waikīkī, away from the hustle and bustle of tourism. Beautiful beach setting.

Oceanfront Rentals
619 Kapahulu Ave.
Honolulu, HI 96815
☎ (808) 733-5800
www.hawaiioceanfrontrentals.com/
Contact: Kathy Muller, locations specialist

Olomana Gardens
41-1160 Waikupanaha
Waimānalo, HI 96795
☎ Toll Free (866) 259-0162
🖳 (808) 259-0315
www.olomanagardens.com
olomanagardens@hawaii.rr.com
Has a private, old-style Hawaiian, tropical garden on a pocket-sized horse ranch.

Pacific Beach Hotel
2490 Kālakaua Ave.
Honolulu, HI 95815
☎ (808) 922-1233 / 🖳 922-0129
www.pacificbeachhotel.com
reservation@hthcorp.com
Overlooking Waikīkī Beach.

Pagoda Hotel and Restaurant
1525 Rycroft, Honolulu, HI 96814
☎ (808) 941-6611 / 🖷 955-5067
www.pagodahotel.com
reservation@hthcorp.com
The Pagoda Hotel's facilities include Oriental gardens, ponds and waterfall. All serve as an ideal setting for your wedding.

Paradise Gardens at Paradise Cove
2024 N. King St., #226 (Bus. Office)
Honolulu, HI 96819
☎ Toll Free (800) 775-2683
(808) 842-7911, ext. 226
www.paradisecove.com
info@paradisecove.com

Pearl Country Club
98-535 Kaonohi St.
Aiea, HI 96701
☎ (808) 808-487-1557 / 🖷 488-2041
www.pearlcc.com
Banquet rooms accommodate groups from 25 to 300 persons. Just a 20-minute drive from the bustle and bustle of Honolulu and Waikīkī.

Plaza Club, The
900 Fort Street Mall, 20th & 21st Floors
Honolulu, HI 96813
☎ (808) 521-8905 / 🖷 531-4769
www.plazahawaii.com
contactus@plazahawaii.com
A private facility that is available to non-members for special events. Downtown Honolulu.

Polynesian Cultural Center
55-370 Kamehameha Hwy.
Lāʻie, HI 96762
☎ Toll Free (800) 367-7060
🖷 (888) 722-7339
www.polynesia.com
macatiaa@polynesia.com
About 50 minutes from Waikīkī.

Primarrie Chapel
3259 Lincoln Ave.
Honolulu, HI 96816
☎ (808) 922-8881 / 922-7399
🖷 921-7203
www.takasagodenusa.com
Traditional Japanese and English church weddings are our specialty.

Public Parks and Recreation Facilities
☎ (808) 523-4523 / 587-0285
www.hawaii.gov/dlnr/dsp/dsp.html
See phone book for specific listings.

Radisson Waikīkī Prince Kūhiō Hotel
2500 Kūhiō Ave.
Honolulu, HI 96815
☎ Toll Free (800) 333-3333 (reservations)
(808) 922-0811 / 🖷 921-5507
www.radisson.com/waikikihi
rhi_hoha@radisson.com

Renaissance Ilikai Waikīkī Hotel
1777 Ala Moana Blvd.
Honolulu, HI 96815
☎ (808) 944-6372

Roy's Restaurant Honolulu
6600 Kalanaianaʻole Hwy.
Honolulu, HI 96825
☎ (808) 396-7697
www.roysrestaurant.com
honolulu@roysrestaurant.com

Royal Garden at Waikīkī Hotel
440 ʻOlohana St.
Honolulu, HI 96815
☎ (808) 943-0202 / 🖷 946-8777
www.royalgardens.com
reservations@royalgardens.com
Located on a quiet, tree-lined street off Ala Wai canal.

Royal Hawaiian Hotel
2259 Kālakaua Ave.
Honolulu, HI 96815
☎ (808) 931-7909 / 🖨 931-7425
www.royal-hawaiian.com
rh.concierge@sheraton.com
"The Pink Palace of the Pacific."

Sea Life Park
41-202 Kalaniana'ole Hwy., #7
Waimānalo, HI 96795
☎ (808) 259-2599 / 🖨 259-7373
www.sealifeparkhawaii.com
info@sealifeparkhawaii
Seaside Chapel available.

Senator Fong's Plantation and Gardens
47-285 Pulama Rd.
Kāne'ohe, HI 96744
☎ (808) 239-6775 / 🖨 239-6469
www.fonggarden.com
info@fonggarden.net
*A 725-acre private estate, has five serene valleys and
plateaus filled with exotic fruits and fragrant flowers.*

Sheraton Moana Surfrider
2365 Kālakaua Ave.
Honolulu, HI 96815
☎ (808) 922-3111 / 922-3111 (catering)
🖨 923-0308
www.moana-surfrider.com
*The most historic hotel on Waikīkī Beach.
Several options available for your wedding
ceremony, from the oceanfront Diamond Head
Lawn, to the open-air Roof Garden.*

Sheraton Princess Ka'iulani
120 Ka'iulani Ave.
Honolulu, HI 96815
☎ (808) 922-5811 / 🖨 931-4577
www.princess-kaiulani.com
Across from Waikīkī Beach.

Sheraton Waikīkī
2555 Kālakaua Ave., Honolulu, HI 96815
☎ (808) 922-4422 / 931-8111 (banquet)
🖨 923-8785
www.sheraton-waikiki.com
*Rising on the graceful arch of the world's most
famous beach, the Sheraton Waikīkī Beach Resort
reigns above Honolulu's glittering hub of excitement.*

Shriner's Beach Club
Waimānalo, HI
☎ (808) 259-7223 / 536-9333
*On the beach in Waimānalo. Book over one
year in advance.*

**St. Catalina Seaside Chapel
at Sea Life Park**
41-202 Kalaniana'ole Hwy.
Waimānalo, HI 96795
☎ (808) 259-5666 / 🖨 259-9666
www.gloriabridal.com
info@gloriabridal.com
*Located in the Sea Life Park with the magnificent
view of the ocean and Rabbit Island.*

Star of Honolulu
1540 S. King St., Honolulu, HI 96826
☎ (808) 983-7827 / 🖨 983-7780
www.paradisecruises.com/index_english.html
info@paradisecruises.com
*232-foot, 4-deck cruise ship with 1,500-passenger
capacity.*

Tiki's Grill & Bar
Aston Waikiki Beach Hotel
2570 Kālakaua Ave., Honolulu, HI 96815
☎ (808) 923-8454
www.tikisgrill.com
*Your place for a memorable rehearsal dinner
or wedding reception*

Turtle Bay Resort
57-091 Kamehameha Hwy.
Kahuku, HI 96731
☎ Toll Free (800) 203-3650 (reservations)
(808) 293-8811 / 🖷 293-9147
www.turtlebayresort.com
tbrreservations@benchmarkmanagement.com

Vida Mia
Kewalo Basin Boat Harbor, Slip "Y"
1025 Ala Moana Blvd.
Honolulu, HI 96814
☎ (808) 371-0920 / 🖷 587-7056
www.vida-mia.com
sales@vida-mia.com
Contact: Madeleine Noa
Yacht charters available.

W Honolulu Diamond Head
2885 Kālakaua Ave.
Honolulu, HI 96815
☎ (808) 791-5177 / 🖷 791-5164
www.starwoodhawaii.com/weddings
*Contemporary hotel nestled at the end of
Waikīkī with a breathtaking view of
Diamond Head and Waikīkī Beach.*

Wahiawa Botanical Garden
1396 California Ave.
Wahiawa, HI 96786
☎ (808) 621-7321
www.co.honolulu.hi.us/parks/hbg/wbg.htm
Call for wedding information.

Waikīkī Aquarium
2777 Kālakaua Ave.
Honolulu, HI 96815
☎ (808) 923-9741 / 🖷 923-1771
waquarium.mic.hawaii.edu/index.html
On Waikīkī Beach. Available evening hours only.

Waikīkī Beach Marriott
2552 Kālakaua Ave.
Honolulu, HI 96815
☎ (808) 922-6611 / 🖷 921-5255
www.marriottwaikiki.com
info@marriottwaikiki.com
*Located in the southern most part of the
Hawaiian island of Oʻahu, on the world
famous Waikīkī Beach.*

Waikīkī Shell
2805 Monsarrat Ave.
Honolulu, HI 96815
☎ (808) 527-5400
www.blaisdellcenter.com/venues/
waikikishell.html
*Set at the foot of Diamond Head and Waikīkī.
Beach just across the street, the Waikīkī Shell is
a unique venue for large gatherings.*

Waimea Valley Audubon Center
59-864 Kamehameha Hwy.
Haleʻiwa, HI 96812
☎ (808) 638-9199
*Lush, tropical valley about an hour's drive from
Waikīkī .*

**Waiʻoli Chapel
Gardens and Tea Room**
2950 Mānoa Rd.
Honolulu, HI 96822
☎ (808) 988-5800
www.waiolitearoom.com
*A short drive from Waikīkī and downtown
Honolulu, located deep in Mānoa Valley,
Oʻahu's beautiful "Valley of the Rainbows."*

Willows, The
901 Hausten St.
Honolulu, HI 98626
☎ (808) 952-9200
Hawaiʻi's original Garden Restaurant.

Maui:

A Marriage Made in Heaven
☎ Toll Free (800) 299-8077
www.mauimarriage.com
marriage@aloha.net
*Maui's only private and spacious oceanfront
waterfall wedding estate.*

Atlantis Submarines Maui
658 Front St., Ste. 175, Lahaina, HI 96761
☎ (808) 667-2224
www.atlantisadventures.com
mres@atlantisadventures.com

Blue Hawaiian Helicopters
1050 Kahului Heliport
Kahului, HI 96732
☎ Toll Free (800) 745-BLUE
🖷 (808) 871-8844
www.bluehawaiian.com
Call for other island locations.

Event Masters
☎ Toll Free (800) 771-9931
www.masterweddings.com/
masters@maui.net
Call for unique estate locations.

**Garden of Eden Arboretum
& Botanical Gardens**
10600 Hana Hwy., Haʻikū, HI 96708
☎ (808) 878-3385
www.mauigardenofeden.com
reservations@mauigardenofeden.com
Contact: Judith Brandon / Alan Bradbury

Grand Waikapū/Sandalwood
2500 HonoaPiʻilani Hwy.
Wailuku, HI 96793
☎ (808) 242-6162 / 🖷 244-1188
www.sandalwoodgolf.com
banquets@sandalwoodgolf.com
Contact: Peter Schlee

Grand Wailea Resort, Hotel & Spa
3850 Wailea Alanui, Wailea, HI 96753
☎ Toll Free (800) 888-6100
🖷 (808) 874-2412
www.grandwaileaweddings.com
weddings@gwrmail.com
Contact: William Leakakos, Weddings Mgr.

Hyatt Regency Maui Resort & Spa
200 Nohea Kai Dr., Lāhainā, HI 96761-1985
☎ (808) 661-1234 / 🖷 667-4497
www.maui.hyatt.com
*The Hyatt Regency Maui Resort and Spa has
been called one of the most spectacular resorts
in the world. For more info on Hyatt Regency
Maui weddings see the "Real Hawaiʻi Wedding"
on page 180.*

Island Star Sailing
P.O. Box 381, Lāhainā, HI 96767
☎ Toll Free (888) 667-7238
🖷 (808) 878-3574
www.islandstarsailing.com
ocnraftn@maui.net
Contact: Jeri Robinson

Kaʻanapali Beach Hotel
2525 Kaʻanapali Pkwy., Lāhainā, HI 96761
☎ (808) 661-0011 / 🖷 667-5978
www.kbhmaui.com/vacation/planner.html
*Located oceanfront on world-famous Kaʻanapali
Beach, the Kaʻanapali Beach Hotel offers an
ideal setting for a memorable Hawaiian wedding
and/or reception.*

Kapalua Bay Hotel
1 Bay Dr., Lāhainā, HI 96761
☎ (808) 669-4643 / 🖷 665-4537
www.starwoodhawaii.com/weddings
*Somewhere between magnificent ocean-front
bluffs and intimate tropical gardens, you are
sure to find the perfect Maui wedding setting for
your wedding or honeymoon getaway.*

Kolealea Retreat Center of Maui

1135 Makawao Ave., Suite 226
Makawao, HI 96768
☎ Toll Free (888) 248-7017
www.retreatcentermaui.com
saharah@retreatcentermaui.com
Contact: Saharah Dyson

Maui Prince Hotel Makena Resort

5400 Makena Alanui
Kīhei, HI 96753
☎ Toll Free (800) 321-6248
🖷 (808) 879-8763
www.princeresortshawaii.com
rerwin@mauiprince.com
Contact: Ronda Erwin

Maui Ocean Center

192 Ma'alaea Rd.
Wailuku, HI   96793
☎ (808) 270-7083 / 🖷 270-7070
www.mauioceancenter.com
lorim@mauioceancenter.com

Maui Tropical Plantation

1670 HonoaPi'ilani Hwy.
Wailuku, HI 96793
☎ Toll Free (800) 451-6805
🖷 (808) 242-8983
www.maui.net/~mol/activityland/
plantation.html
pattyokuda@hotmail.com
Contact: Pat Okuda

Mendes Ranch

3530 Kahekili Hwy.
Wailuku, HI 96793
☎ (808) 244-7320
www.mendesranch.com
info@mendesranch.com
Situated on the top of a bluff, the gazebo provides the perfect location for your wedding day.

Old Lāhainā Luau Weddings

1287 Front St.
Lāhainā, HI 96761
☎ Toll Free (800) 248-5828
🖷 (808) 661-5176
www.oldlahainaluau.com
weddings@oldlahainaluau.com
Contact: Jamie De Brunne

Pua Le'a Estate

☎ Toll Free (866) 344-7447
(808) 874-7447
www.pualea.com/prw
Contact: Sylvia and Mickey Eskimo
Historical Hawaiian landmark, beautiful, private, rustic setting.

Renaissance Wailea Beach Resort

3550 Wailea Alanui Dr.
Kīhei, HI 96753
☎ (808) 879-4900 / 🖷 874-5370
www.mauionline.com/lodging/stouffer.html
A luxury resort located on a crescent golden sand beach in the Wailea resort area on the sunny south coast of Maui.

The Ritz-Carlton, Kapalua

One Ritz-Carlton Dr.
Kapalua, HI 96761
☎ Toll Free (800) 262-8440
(808) 669-6200 / 🖷 665-7130
www.ritzcarlton.com/resorts/kapalua
jennifer.camilli@ritzcarlton.com

Royal Hale Hotel

2780-A Keka'a Dr.
Lāhainā, HI 96761
☎ (808) 661-3611 / 🖷 994-3538
Oceanfront, recently refurbished hotel on Kā'anapali Beach.

Royal Lahaina Resort
2780 Keka'a Dr.
Lāhainā, HI 96761
☎ (808) 661-3611 / 🖷 661-6150
Set along the best and most exclusive stretch of Kā'anapali Beach on the island of Maui.

Sea Watch Restaurant
100 Wailea Golf Club Dr.
Wailea, HI 96753
☎ (808) 875-8080 / 🖷 875-7462
www.seawatchrestaurant.com
jennifer@seawatchrestaurant.com
Located in the elegantly-appointed clubhouse of the Wailea Gold and Emerald Golf Courses.

Sheraton Maui
2605 Ka'anapali Pkwy.
Lāhainā, HI 96767
☎ (808) 662-8032 / 🖷 661-9991
www.starwoodhawaii.com/weddings
Sheraton Maui's 23 oceanfront acres flow gracefully from the crest of Pu'u Keka'a, to the shores of Kā'anapali Beach.

Silver Cloud Ranch
1373 Thompson Rd., Kula, HI 96790
☎ Toll Free (800) 532-1111
🖷 (808) 878-2132
www.silvercloudranch.com
slvrcld@maui.net
Contact: Michael Gerry

Sugar Cane Train
975 Limahana Pl., #203
Lāhainā, HI 96761
☎ Toll Free (800) 499-2307
🖷 (808) 661-8389
www.sugarcanetrain.com
info@sugarcanetrain.com
Contact: Barbara Allen / Cici Hehemann

Wailea Marriott, An Outrigger Resort
3700 Wailea Alanui
Wailea, HI 96753
☎ (808) 879-1922 / 🖷 874-8331
www.outrigger.com/hotels

Weddings on Horseback
P.O. Box 1419
Makawao, HI 96768
☎ (808) 573-8652 / 🖷 572-4996
adrianna@aloha.net
Contact: Rev. Adrianna Levinson

Westin Maui
2605 Kaanapali Pkwy.
Lāhainā, HI 96767
☎ (808) 667-2546 / 🖷 662-2752
www.starwoodhawaii.com/weddings
Nestled among 12 oceanfront acres on Ka'anapali Beach, the Westin Maui perfectly blends a luxurious hotel with genuine aloha.

Big Island:

Atlantis Submarines Kona
75-5656 Kuakini Hwy., Suite 303
Kailua-Kona, HI 96740
☎ (808) 973-9811
www.atlantisadventures.com
kres@atlantisadventures.com
A very unique and adventurous wedding experience.

Four Seasons Resort
100 Kaupulehu Dr.
Kailua-Kona, HI 96740
☎ (808) 325-8000 / 🖷 325-8200
www.fourseasons.com
From invitations to wedding cakes, floral creations to memorable farewells, trust Four Seasons to simplify your planning and make your wedding day everything you have ever imagined.

Hapuna Beach Prince Hotel
62-100 Kuana'oa Dr.
Kohala Coast, HI 96738
☎ (808) 880-1111 / 🖷 880-3142
www.princeresortshawaii.com
*Select a sensational outdoor setting, luxurious
banquet room or our spectacular grand ballroom.*

King Kamehameha Kona Beach Hotel
75-5660 Palani Rd.
Kailua-Kona, HI 96740
☎ (808) 329-2911 / 🖷 329-4602
www.konabeachhotel.com
reservation@hthcorp.com

Kona Village Resort
☎ Toll Free (800) 367-5290
(808) 325-5555 / 🖷 325-5124
www.konavillage.com / kvr@aloha.net
*Named one of the top 50 Romantic Getaways
by 2002 Travel and Leisure Magazine.*

Mauna Kea Beach Home
P.O. Box 5366, Kailua-Kona, HI 96745
☎ Toll Free (866) 331-8683
🖷 (808) 331-0945
www.maunakeabeachhome.com
consultah@aol.com
Contact: Bill Campbell

Mauna Kea Beach Hotel
62-100 Mauna Kea Beach Dr.
Kohala Coast, HI 96743
☎ (808) 882-7222 / 🖷 882-5700
www.princeresortshawaii.com
*A stunning backdrop on Hawai'i's picturesque
Kohala Coast.*

Mauna Lani Bay Hotel and Bungalows
68-1400 Mauna Lani Dr.
Kohala Coast, HI 96743-9796
☎ Toll Free (800) 367-2323
(808) 885-6622 / 🖷 885-1484
weddings@maunalani.com

www.maunalani.com/
*Nestled on a white sand beach on the sunny Kohala
Coast of the Big Island of Hawai'i, Mauna Lani
Bay Hotel and Bungalows is like nowhere else.*

Pu'u Wai'awa'a Ranch
Entrance by appointment only
☎ (808) 325-2540
www.puuwaawaa.com
info@puuwaawaa.com
*This historic 100,000 acre Ranch, the 32-acre
Estate is a private, exclusive, and secluded setting
for special celebrations, family reunions, weddings,
corporate meetings, and vacations*

Royal Kona Resort
75-5852 Alii Dr.
Kailua-Kona, HI 96740
☎ (808) 329-3111 / 🖷 329-9532
www.HawaiianHotels.com/
*Overlooking spectacular Kailua Bay, the full-
service Royal Kona Resort is in the heart of the
quaint village of Kailua-Kona.*

**Waikoloa Beach Marriott,
An Outrigger Resort**
69-275 Waikoloa Beach Dr.
Waikoloa, HI 96738-5711
☎ (808) 886-6789 / 🖷 886-7852
www.outrigger.com/hotels
*Indulge yourself at the Waikoloa Beach Resort on
the Big Island's sunny Kohala Coast. A unique
setting for outdoor adventure and utmost relaxation.*

Kaua'i:
Aloha Kauai Villas
P.O. Box 813
Kekaha, HI 96752
☎ (808) 337-2290 / 🖷 337-9990
host@alohakauaivillas.com
www.alohakauaivillas.com
*Private beachfront villas for your ceremony
and/or reception.*

   Hawai'i Weddings Made Simple

Bali Hai Realty
5-5088-D Kuhio Hwy.
PO Box 930, Hanalei, HI 96714
☎ (808) 826-7244 / 🖷 826-6157
Info@balihai.com
www.balihai.com/luxury.htm
Private estates and rentals available.

Chapel by the Sea at Kaua'i Lagoons
Kaua'i Lagooon Resort
3351 Hoolaulea Way, Līhu'e, HI 96766
☎ (808) 632-0505 / 🖷 632-0303
info@gardenislandwedding.com
www.gardenislandwedding.com
*The Chapel rests atop the Kaua'i Lagoons,
graced with a beautiful bridge for the bride to
make her grand entrance.*

Gaylords at Kilohana
3-2087 Kaumuali'i Hwy., Līhu'e, HI 96766
☎ (808) 245-9593 / 🖷 246-1087
www.gaylordskauai.com
info@gaylordskauai.com
*Gaylord's location in the historic home known
as Kilohana affords a romantic setting for
proposals, weddings and receptions.*

**Fern Grotto Cruise with
Waialeale Boat Company**
Wailua Boat Marina, Wailua, HI 96746
☎ (808) 822-4908

**Fern Grotto with Smith's
Tropical Paradise**
174 Wailua Rd., Kapa'a, HI 96746
☎ (808) 821-6887
www.smithskauai.com/weddings.html
smiths@aloha.net
*Smith's Tropical Paradise is nestled alongside
the sacred Wailua River and below the ancient
Malae Heiau temple, an enchanting place once
reserved for Hawaiian royalty.*

Hanalei Bay Resort
5380 Honoiki Rd.
Princeville, HI 96722
☎ (808) 826-6522
www.hanalei-bay-resort.com

Hanalei Colony Resort
P.O. Box 206, Hanalei, HI 96714
☎ Toll Free (800) 628-3004
🖷 (808) 826-9893
www.wedding-in-kaua'i.com
weddings-events@hcr.com
*An intimate secluded resort set on a beautiful
golden beach against the magnificent mountains
of Kaua'i's north shore.*

Hyatt Regency Kaua'i Resort & Spa
1571 Poipu Rd., Koloa, HI 96756
☎ (808) 742-1234 / 🖷 742-1557
www.kauai.hyatt.com
*The ultimate Hawaiian classic oceanfront resort
beckons with 50 acres of exquisite beauty on
Hawai'i's garden isle. For more info on Hyatt
Regency Kauai weddings see the "Real Hawai'i
Wedding" on page 157.*

Kaua'i Coconut Beach Resort
484 Kuhio Hwy.
Kapa'a, HI 96746
☎ Toll Free (800) 222-5642
(808) 822-3455 / 🖷 822-1830
www.kcb.com
*Reminiscent of Hawai'i's plantation era, the
oceanfront Kaua'i Coconut Beach Resort is set
on the secluded sands of Waipouli Beach on the
"Garden Isle."*

Kaua'i Marriott Resort and Beach Club
3610 Rice St.
Līhu'e, HI 96766
☎ Toll Free (800) 220-2925
(808) 245-5050 / 🖷 245-5049
www.marriotthotels.com

Koloa Church

3269 Poipu Rd.
Poipu, HI 96756
☏ (808) 742-9956 / 652-1787
www.hawaiian.net/~zx/Southshore
A beautiful old fashioned church with steeple in one of Kaua'i's most picturesque settings.

Princeville Resort

5520 Ka Haku Rd.
Princeville, HI 96722
☏ (808) 826-2230 / 🖨 826-2258
www.starwoodhawaii.com/weddings
Whether beachside or on the Makana Terrace, spectacular settings abound for your wedding vows at the Princeville Resort.

Sheraton Kaua'i Resort

2440 Hoonani Rd.
Koloa, HI 96756
☏ (808) 742-4037 / 🖨 742-4041
www.starwoodhawaii.com/weddings
Sheraton Kaua'i Resort rests along a pristine section of the island's most romantic shoreline— embracing the crescent-shaped white-sand Po'ipu Beach.

Lāna'i:

Mānele Bay Hotel

P.O. Box 630310
Lāna'i City, HI 96763
☏ Toll Free (800) 321-4666
🖨 (808) 565-3868
www.manelebayhotel.com

The Lodge at Ko'ele

P.O. Box 630310
Lāna'i City, HI 96763
☏ Toll Free (800) 321-4666
🖨 (808) 565-3868
www.lodgeatkoele.com
Condé Nast Traveler *Gold List: World's Best Places to Stay #1, overall ranking in U.S.*

Moloka'i:

Sheraton Moloka'i Lodge & Beach Village

100 Maunaloa Hwy.
Maunaloa, HI 96770
☏ (808) 660-2827 / 🖨 552-2773
www.starwoodhawaii.com/weddings
The Sheraton Moloka'i Lodge & Beach Village is located on 54,000 acres of untouched wilderness.

Notes

Practice Makes Perfect

♥♥

The rehearsal and rehearsal dinner are an integral, and often overlooked, part of the wedding process. This is your opportunity to literally walk through your ceremony itinerary, make any last minute tweaks and changes. Some suggestions to make the most of your rehearsal: **1)** Have your rehearsal at the same place and time as your actual ceremony. This helps everyone get familiar with the location. It also gives you a final chance to take note of little nuances you may not have thought of. (i.e., you're looking directly into the sun at that time of day so you need to change your positioning or there is a large tree that blocks your guests' view). **2)** Have someone else, your wedding planner or point person for your wedding day, to take charge of the rehearsal. You need someone who knows the flow of your ceremony, who will take charge and speak loudly. **3)** Start everyone off where they will end up. Before you even walk through the ceremony, position everyone (even guests who will be seated during the prelude) where they need to be when the ceremony starts. This way when you're actually walking through it, everyone knows where they need to go.

4) Now that everyone knows where they are to end up, walk through the ceremony, once without the music and then three or four more times to the music. If you are walking down to live music that is not at the rehearsal, bring a boom box (with batteries in case the outlets are not on or available) with CDs of the songs you will be walking to. This helps everyone get a feel for the tempo. Be sure that the bridal party is evenly spaced out, the groomsmen's hands are all positioned the same (crossed in front or in back, etc.), and the bridesmaids are all holding their bouquets the same. Little details like this will make a difference in photos. 5) Walk through everything, from the parents and family members being seated to the order that everyone leaves the ceremony and where they walk to afterwards for photos. 6) Confirm your reservations for dinner the day before and double check your head count. The guest list should include your immediate families and the entire wedding party, along with assorted dates or spouses, out-of-town guests and other key persons (officiant, wedding planner, sound guys, ushers, musicians performing at the ceremony, etc.) 7) Take time to enjoy the dinner. Mingle with everyone and take time to show your appreciation for everyone who has helped. It's a good time to do intimate thank you's and give gifts to bridal party. 8) Generally the groom's parents (or the groom) host this event.

Selecting Kaua'i for our wedding location was simple; it is where our hearts reside. I have vacationed on the island yearly since I was a child, and to me there is no place that compares.

After Aaron proposed, we knew that Kaua'i was our wedding destination. And after having checked out several locations, we were sure that the Hyatt Regency was the perfect setting.

The Hyatt offered everything we were looking for in one glorious 50-acre setting. We gave ourselves a year to plan the wedding but we could have done it in six months because everything was so well organized. Our wedding planner, Ella Long, was an angel and made everything go smoothly.

We had a welcome reception on the grounds, followed by a golf tournament at Poipu Bay Golf Course. There was a bridesmaids' luncheon at Tidepools Restaurant, and a rehearsal lu'au dinner on Cabana Beach. The outside gazebo offered us a beautiful, private setting for our ceremony, without sacrificing the breathtaking view of the Pacific Ocean. Our reception took place in the Kaua'i Ballroom and we had a brunch at Dondero's Restaurant. Invitations were sent and we ended up with 120 guests. Ella called and kept us on schedule with our plans, and just the sound of her voice calmed a nervous bride-to-be from 3,000 miles away.

Aaron Cornell & Leigh Rodriguez

♥♥

HYATT REGENCY KAUA'I

On the day of the wedding, we couldn't have been more at ease. Our day was perfection in every way. In every detail it was exactly like the pictures we had sent: from the orchid-covered aisle, to the bouquets with seashells, to our beauty time at the ANARA Spa. The ocean sparkled as if Ella had painted it bright blue just for us. The smallest of details had all been carefully executed. My husband and I were the last ones to leave the wedding reception that evening, not wanting to believe it had ended.

My parents truly gave us the wedding of our dreams. By the time we were on the plane jetting off to our honeymoon our hearts ached to be back at the Hyatt. And as of now, we are counting down the days until we return for our first anniversary, of course!

(For more information on the Hyatt Regency Kaua'i see page 105.)

Sounds Like a Plan

Most brides don't think about hiring a wedding planner or coordinator until after the wedding! Not everyone needs a wedding planner. With the help of this book, it's possible that you could plan and coordinate a flawless wedding, but you'll need more than just this book to pull it off. If you are going to plan your own wedding, you need to be extremely organized, responsible, and you need to have time. Wedding planning takes time and that can be difficult, especially if you work full-time. You'll also need several family members or friends who are willing to help; people who will help you along the way in addition to serving as coordinators on your wedding day. If you don't have all of these elements—and then some!—you should seriously consider hiring a wedding coordinator. If you're worried about incurring the extra cost of a wedding planner, consider that wedding planners are experts in their field and are used to working within a budget. They can often get better deals or rates for you because they have established relationships with vendors.

You pay them to take care of all the little details that you don't even know to think of! The role your consultant plays varies depending on what you hire them to do. Coordinating and working with vendors, directing the rehearsal, assisting the wedding party and creating the wedding day itinerary are just a few of the duties a consultant can take on.

QTA's:

❑ How long have they been coordinating weddings? Is this an actual business or just a hobby?

❑ Do they belong to any organizations or accrediting agencies (Association of Bridal Consultants, Event Planner Association, etc.)?

❑ What do they charge for their services and exactly what is included?

Sunnyside Up

♥♥

If you want to incorporate Hawai'i's beautiful sunrise or sunset into your wedding ceremony, reception and/or wedding photos consult these internet websites for specific dates and times—down to the minute.

Visit:
www.almanac.com/rise/index.php *or*
www.eyeofthe islands.com/pages/sunset.html

❏ What is their role from the minute you hire them to the wedding day? How involved are they from beginning to end?

❏ Ask them about their relationships with vendors. Do they have an extensive list of vendors they use regularly? Are they obligated to use their vendors only or are they willing to use whomever you recommend?

❏ Do you have to pay them a deposit? Is it refundable (or a portion of it) should the wedding be cancelled or postponed?

❏ Will they have an assistant on your wedding day?

❏ How many weddings do they plan a month? A year? Do they do more than one wedding in a day?

Tips:

❋ Make sure you get a written agreement for their services and exactly what they include.

❋ Ask for and call references.

❋ Some wedding coordinators/planners work exclusively with certain vendors (florists, caterers, entertainers, etc.) and receive x amount of dollars from the vendors for each wedding they book for them. Make sure that if this is the case you are completely satisfied with the vendors your coordinator books and have the option of choosing other vendors should you want to.

❋ Some brides are willing and able to plan the wedding but need help on the day of the wedding to make sure everything runs smoothly. Your coordinator may be willing and able to assist you on the day of your wedding only; ask about the fees and charges for this service only.

❋ For a list of consultants in Hawai'i (or your area) call the American Bridal Association (860) 355-0464 or go to www.bridalassn.com

---

O'ahu, Maui, Big Island, Kaua'i, Lāna'i:

Aloha Weddings
1551 S. Beretania St., #208
Honolulu, HI 96826
☎ Toll Free (877) 455-4799
🖶 (808) 983-1401
www.alohaweddings.com
consult@alohaweddings.com

O'ahu, Maui, Big Island, Kaua'i, Moloka'i and Lāna'i:

Hawaiian Island Wedding Planners
☎ Toll Free (818) 991-1076
🖶 (818) 991-1504
www.hawaiianweddings.net

O'ahu:

A Beach Wedding
P.O. Box 10051
Honolulu, HI 96816
☎ (808) 735-2933
www.beachwed.com
info@beachwed.com
Contact: Rev. Kermit Rydell

A Perfect Day
P.O. Box 860994
Wahiawa, HI 96786
☎ (808) 497-3339
www.aperfectday1.com
Kelly@aperfectday1.com

A Perfect Hawai'i Wedding
765 Amana St., Suite 501
Honolulu, HI 96814
☎ Toll Free (800) 988-4759
(808) 951-9534 / 🖶 947-1816
www.perfecthawaii.com
rsvp@perfecthawaii.com

**A Treasured Moment
Weddings of Hawai'i**
3103 Pualei Circle, #210
Honolulu, HI 96815
☎ Toll Free (800) 315-4810
(808) 734-8803 / 🖶 923-1440
www.treasuredmoment.com
ido@treasuredmoment.com

A Wedding in Hawai'i
1350 Ala Moana Blvd.
Honolulu, HI 96814
☎ (808) 591-8487
www.wedaloha.com / wedinhi@aloha.net

A'Ala Aloha Weddings
1777 Ala Moana Blvd., #1618
Honolulu, HI 96815
☎ (808) 942-2277 / 1-800-42ALOHA
www.angelchapelbythesea.com
ilikaich@lava.net
Ordained, non-denominational ministers as well as wedding coordinators.

A-1 Hawai‘i Weddings
44-160 Kou Pl., #2
Kāne‘ohe, HI 96744
☎ (808) 235-6966
www.lovehawaii.com / lele@aloha.com

Above Heaven's Gate
41-1010 Laumilo St.
Waimānalo, HI 96795
☎ Toll Free (800) 800-2933
🖷 (888) 463-6933
www.hawaiiweddings.com
howie@hawaiiweddings.com

Affordable Wedding of Hawai‘i
P.O. 26475
Honolulu, HI 96825
☎ Toll Free (800) 942-4554
(808) 923-4876 / 🖷 396-0959
www.wedhawaii.com
RevRuss@WedHawaii.com

Aloha Beautiful Hawai‘i Weddings
3762 Sierra Dr.
Honolulu, HI 96816
☎ Toll Free (800) 383-5713
(808) 734-5088 / 🖷 739-5322
www.iloveweddings.com
barry@bmphoto.com

Aloha Bridal Gallery
P.O. 701077
Kapolei, HI 96709
☎ (808) 672-0450 / 🖷 (888) 633-3886
www.alohabridalgallery.com
alohabride@hawaii.rr.com
By appointment only.

Aloha Enchanted Weddings
38 Kāne‘ohe Bay Dr.
Kailua, HI 96734
☎ (808) 262-6732

Aloha Wedding Planners
1400 Kapi‘olani Blvd., #A23
Honolulu, HI 96814
☎ Toll Free (800) 288-8309
(808) 943-2711 / 🖷 949-1128
www.alohaweddingplanners.com
aloha.ido@att.net

**Always Yours
by the Wedding Connection**
☎ Toll Free (800) 388-6933
(808) 923-9734
Call for appointment.

Angel Wedding Service
1221 Kapi‘olani Blvd., #345
Honolulu, HI 96814
☎ (808) 596-4855
Call for appointment.

Aubrey's Weddings
484 Ke‘opua St.
Honolulu, HI 96813
☎ (808) 561-6221
aubreysweddings@yahoo.com

Beau Mariage
2345 Ala Wai Blvd., #2211
Honolulu, HI 96815
☎ Toll Free (866) 923-1603
(808) 923-1603 / 🖷 923-1681
www.beaumariage.net
khailey@beaumariage.net

Bridal Dream Wedding Company
3259 Lincoln Ave.
Honolulu, HI 96816
☎ (808) 734-6518 / 🖷 734-6518
www.bridaldreamhawaii.com
BridalDream@cs.com

Creative Planners of Hawai‘i
☎ (808) 262-0480
www.creative-planners.com

E Pili Mai Weddings
☎ (808) 638-6714 / 🖨 638-7900
tinker001@hawaii.rr.com
Contact: Tinker Blomfield

FCB Resources
531 Hahaione St., #9A
Honolulu, HI 96825
☎ (808) 395-9728
fcbresources@earthlink.net

Gayle, Weddings & Lifetime Events
2416 Apoepoe St., Honolulu, HI 96782
☎ (808) 783-3169 / 456-3343
gfujita@hawaii.rr.com

Global Aloha Weddings
2947 Kālakaua Ave.
Honolulu, HI 96815
☎ (808) 922-5176
www.hawaiianweddingplanners.com

Gloria Bridal Services
3050 Monsarrat Ave.
Honolulu, HI 96815
☎ (808) 735-5500
www.gloriabridal.com
Call for appointment.

Happily Ever After
P.O. Box 37997, Honolulu, HI 96837
☎ (808) 551-1649
www.happilyeverafterhawaii.com
info@happilyeverafterhawaii.com

Hawaiian Wedding.net
P.O. Box 89440
Honolulu, HI 96830
☎ Toll Free (877) 393-3614
(808) 486-LOVE / 🖨 991-1504
www.hawaiiweddings.net
wayne-penny@hawaiiweddings.net

Lisa Michele
Special Events Consultant
☎ (808) 286-1475 / 488-1014
www.alahi.net
lisamichele@alahi.net

Pacific Aisles
98-1123 Kaonohi St.
Aiea, HI 96701
☎ Toll Free (877) 720-8235
International (808) 487-2431
weddings@pacificaisles.com
www.pacificaisles.com/weddings

Parasol Events
3030 Pualei Circle
Honolulu, HI 96815
☎ 808-923-3969
weddings@ParasolEvents.com
Contact: Laura Lewis

Perfectly Romantic Hawaii
☎ Toll Free (877) 847-4788
(808) 847-4788
www.perfectlyromantichawaii.com

Social Planners of Hawaii
1088 Bishop St., Suite 503
Honolulu, HI 96813
☎ (808) 225-5414
granthaml001@hawaii.rr.com

TK Wedding Services
☎ (808) 926-2378
Call for appointment.

Unforgettable Wedding Consultants
838 Maniniholo St.
Honolulu, HI 96825
☎ (808) 395-4699
unforgetwc@aol.com

Wedding Planners-Hawaii

1750 Kālakaua Ave., #103-3440
Honolulu, HI 96826
☎ (808) 523-0005 / 🖨 523-1145
www.wphawaii.com
info@wphawaii.com

Wedding Planners, The

Honolulu, HI
☎ (808) 223-4118 / 224-4554
www.wedding-planners.net
keri@wedding-planners.net
Contact: Keri Shepherd / Lissa Wilson

Weddings by Grace & Mona

P.O. Box 2732, Honolulu, HI 96803
☎ (808) 524-5331 / 🖨 524-4148
www.mgweddingshawaii.com/
mona@mgweddingshawaii.com

Weddings In Hawai'i

P.O. Box 1584
Kāne'ohe, HI 96744
☎ (808) 254-5374
Call for appointment.

Weddings in Paradise

3017 McKinley St.
Honolulu, HI 96822
☎ Toll Free (800) 245-6777
(808) 735-7903
arevbev@aol.com

Maui, Big Island, Kaua'i and O'ahu:

Hawaiian Island Weddings, Inc.

P.O. Box 2098, Kīhei, HI 96753
☎ Toll Free (800) 368-5502
(808) 874-9215
www.maui.net/~weddings/index.html
weddings@maui.net
Contact: Tim Clark

Maui:

A Beautiful Beginning

3543 L. HonoaPi'ilani Rd.
Suite H 206
Kā'anapali, HI 96761
☎ (808) 669-7423
www.geocities.com/marryonmaui/
kirkandlaura@juno.com
Contact: Kirk W. Boes, Minister

A Beautiful Island Wedding

P.O. Box 1274
Kīhei, HI 96753
☎ Toll Free (877) 738-4353
🖨 (808) 874-0996
www.mauigateway.com/revhelen/
revhelen@tiki.net
Contact: Rev. Helen Downey

A Dream Wedding Maui Style

143 Dickenson St., Suite 201
Lāhainā, HI 96761
☎ Toll Free (800) 743-2777
🖨 (808) 661-0072
www.adreamwedding.net
dreamwed@maui.net
Contact: Tracy Flanagan

A Happy Maui Wedding
Jeffrey T. Bond, Minister of Peace

5095 Napilihau St., #326
Lāhainā, HI 96761-8800
☎ (808) 667-7007
www.ahappymauiwedding.com
happymaui@hawaii.rr.com
Jeff and his happy team provide very special wedding services that are unique on Maui.

A Maui Lani Wedding
655 Haumana Rd.
Ha‘ikū, HI 96768-5942
☎ Toll Free (888) 747-6284
🖷 (808) 572-4600
www.mauilaniweddings.com
office@mauilaniweddings.com
Contact: Govinda F. Leopold

A Maui Moment
4790 L. HonoaPi‘ilani Rd.
Lāhainā, HI 96761
☎ (808) 205-7770
www.amauimoment.com
sarahann@hawaii.rr.com
Contact: Sarah Davidian

A Paradise Dream Wedding
535 Lipoa Pkwy.
Kīhei, HI 96753
☎ Toll Free (888) 286-5979
🖷 (808) 875-2985
www.mauiwedding.net
aloha@mauiwedding.net
Contact: Gordon Nash

A Perfect Maui Wedding
P.O. Box 293
Kīhei, HI 96753
☎ Toll Free (800) 203-0227
🖷 (808) 879-7144
www.perfectmauiwedding.com
susan@perfectmauiwedding.com
Contact: Susan Moyco

A Promise Made in Paradise
3355 Kehala Dr.
Kīhei, HI 96753
☎ Toll Free (877) 875-6127
www.mauius.com / grodan@maui.net
Contact: Marc Grodan

A Simply Elegant Wedding
1993 S. Kīhei Rd., #404
Kīhei, HI 96753
☎ Toll Free (866) 344-7447
www.asimplyelegantwedding.com
asimplyelegantwedding@verizon.net
Contact: Ellen Chatillon

A White Orchid Wedding
P.O. Box 2696
Wailuku, HI 96793
☎ Toll Free (800) 240-9336
🖷 (808) 242-6853
www.whiteorchidwedding.com
awow@maui.net
Contact: Carolee Higashino

Adams & Eve…beginnings in paradise
P.O. Box 11733
Lāhainā, HI 96761
☎ Toll Free (800) 484-2658
🖷 (808) 669-8430
www.maui.net/~adamseve
adamseve@maui.net
Contact: Margy Adams

**All Ways Maui’d Weddings
& Ceremonies**
P.O. Box 817
Pu‘unene, HI 96784
☎ Toll Free (877) 906-2843
🖷 (808) 242-8019
www.maui-angels.com
aloha@maui-angels.com
Contact: Rev. Kolleen O’Flaherty Wheeler

Aloha Nohea Weddings
40 Nohea Place
Haiku, HI 96708
☎ Toll Free (888) 328-9239
www.maui.net/~friends
friends@maui.com

Ancient Hawaiian Weddings
Suite 581, P.O. Box 959
Kīhei, HI 96753
☏ Toll Free (888) 680-1544
🖨 (808) 875-7781
www.hawaiileihochzeit.com
hochzeit1@aol.com
Contact: Arabelle Bottorff

Anointed Weddings on Maui
P.O. Box 11743
Lāhainā, HI 96761
☏ Toll Free (800) 962-7622
🖨 (808) 665-0251
www.maui.net/~anointed/
anointed@maui.net
Contact: Minister Dyne Neil Shaffron

Ceremonies & Weddings by Two Mermaids
2840 Umalu Pl.
Kīhei, HI 96753
☏ Toll Free (800) 598-9550
🖨 (808) 875-1833
www.twomermaids.com / kawaiola@maui.net
Contact: Rev. Juddee A. Kawaiola

Distinctive Weddings
201 Alohilani St.
Pukalani, HI 96768
☏ (808) 572-0515
mauiwed@aloha.net
Contact: Rev. Joseph R. Narrowe

Dolphin Dream Weddings, LLC
P.O.Box 10546
Lāhainā, HI 96761
☏ Toll Free (800) 793-2933
🖨 (808) 661-8535
dolphindreamweddings.com
dolphin@maui.net
Contact: Rev. Charles Hul

Enchanted Weddings of Maui, Inc.
15 Kulaninakoi St. #9G
Kīhei, HI 96753
☏ Toll Free (800) 648-8697
🖨 (808) 875-8838
www.mauiweddingvows.com
enchantedweddings@hawaii.rr.com
Contact: Lisa Bollhorst

Event Masters
600 F Waiehu Beach Rd.
Wailuku, HI 96793
☏ Toll Free (800) 771-9931
(808) 986-0391 / 🖨 986-0224
www.masterweddings.com
masters@maui.net

Forever Mauied
P.O. Box 2212
Kīhei, HI 96753
☏ Toll Free (877) 686-3686
🖨 (808) 877-5637
www.forevermauied.com
memories@forevermauied.com
Contact: Darlene and David Munn

Hawaiian Romance
159 Luakaha Circle
Kīhei, HI 96753
☏ Toll Free (800) 377-9745
🖨 (808) 875-0845
www.hawaiianromance.com
info@hawaiianromance.com
Contact: Stephanie Hessemer

Heart Path Weddings
P.O. Box 943
Puʻunene, HI 96784
☏ Toll Free (888) 551-5006
🖨 (808) 879-8201
www.heartpathweddings.com
evehogan@aol.com
Contact: Rev. Eve Hogan

Ho'ao Hawaii

1579 Lokia St.
Lāhainā, HI 96761
☎ Toll Free (800) 789-6865
🖷 (808) 667-2121
www.alohahouse.com
hoao@alohahouse.com
Contact: Daniela Clement

Hyatt Regency Maui Resort & Spa

200 Nohea Kai Dr.
Lāhainā, HI 96761
☎ (808) 667-4430 / 🖷 667-4712
www.maui.hyatt.com
ljelliso@oggrmpo.hyatt.com
Contact: Laura Jellison

"I Do" Weddings

129 Ōili Rd.
Ha'ikū, HI 96708
☎ Toll Free (800) 628-4436
🖷 (808) 875-0923
www.idoweddingsmaui.com
info@idoweddingsmaui.com
Contact: Rev. Lewanna Godinez

Island Wedding Memories

688 Imihale St.
Kīhei, HI 96753
☎ Toll Free (800) 811-9577
🖷 (808) 891-2480
www.islandweddingmemories.com
lrobb@islandweddingmemories.com
Contact: Leah and Judah Robb

Kea Lani Hotel

4100 Wailea Alanui Dr.
Wailea, HI 96753
☎ Toll Free (800) 256-4280
(808) 893-0388 / 🖷 893-0943
www.alohadestinations.com/

Magical Maui Weddings

P.O. Box 1450
Kīhei, HI 96753
☎ Toll Free (800) 472-5869
www.magicalmauiweddings.com
mmw@magicalmauiweddings.com
Contact: Rev. Jean Keating

Marry Me Maui

P.O. Box 1156
Kīhei, HI 96753
☎ Toll Free (800) 745-0344
🖷 (808) 879-1882
www.marrymemaui.com
info@marrymemaui.com
Contact: Jan Lyle

Maui Destiny Weddings

P.O. Box 1163
Kīhei, HI 96753
☎ Toll Free (800) 330-1307
(808) 891-2000
www.mauidestinyweddings.com
diana@mauidestinyweddings.com

Maui Dreamtime Weddings

444 Hana Hwy., #209
Kahului, HI 96732
☎ Toll Free (888) 424-5550
🖷 (808) 873-9020
www.hawaiiwedding.com
info@hawaiiwedding.com
Contact: Frank Miholer

Maui Me, Inc.

120 Pearl Road
Haiku, HI 96708
☎ Toll Free (800) 856-3270
(808) 575-2002 / 🖷 575-9744
www.mauime.net
weddingcoordinator@mauime.net
Contact: John Souter / Susan Souter

Maui Prince Hotel, Makena Resort
5400 Makena Alanui
Kīhei, HI 96753
☎ Toll Free (800) 321-6248
📠 (808) 879-8763
www.princeresortshawaii.com
rerwin@mauiprince.com
Contact: Ronda Erwin

Maui Seaside Wedding
160 Keonekai Rd., #20-201
Kīhei, HI 96753
☎ (808) 891-2958
kkmaui@maui.net
Contact: Kyoto Kato

Maui Storybook Weddings
480 Kenolio Rd., #5-101
Kihei, HI 96753
☎ Toll Free (888) 304-3686
www.mauistorybookweddings.com
douglas@mauiphotography.net

Maui Wedding Co., The
415 Dairy Rd., Suite E-218
Kahului, HI 96732
☎ Toll Free (800) 574-7475
📠 (808) 874-2892
www.themauiweddingco.com
info@themauiweddingco.com
Contact: Sian Christensen

Maui Weddings by Kimberly
480-A Kenolio Rd.
Kīhei, HI 96753
☎ Toll Free (800) 593-6789
📠 (808) 879-1916
www.weddingsonmaui.net
kimberly@kcphoto.net
Contact: Kimberly Curtis

Maui Weddings From the Heart
P.O. Box 329, Kīhei, HI 96753
☎ (866) 874-8755 / 📠 (808) 875-7879
www.mauiwed.com
shasta@mauiwed.com
Contact: Shasta Lowery

Paradise Maui's–Weddings in Paradise
P.O. Box 10903, Lāhainā, HI 96761
☎ (808) 891-8526
www.paradisemaui.com/vod
weddings@paradisemaui.com
Contact: Klaus Bandisch

Paradise Weddings
1215 Pi'iholo Rd.
Makawao, HI 96768
☎ (808) 879-8300 / 📠 572-2003
oceanfrontmaui.com
shareen@oceanfrontmaui.com
Contact: Shareen A. Seykota

Romance On Maui
358 Pāpā Pl., #H1-A
Kahului, HI 96732
☎ Toll Free (866) 484-6284
📠 (808) 877-3116
www.romanceonmaui.com
info@romanceonmaui.com
Contact: Anela Gutierrez

Romantic Maui Weddings
P.O. Box 13232, Lāhainā, HI 96761
☎ Toll Free (800) 808-4144
📠 (808) 665-1412
www.justmauied.com
romance@maui.net

Royal Hawaiian Weddings
☎ Toll Free (800) 659-1866
📠 (808) 875-0623
royalhawaiianweddings.com
info@royalhawaiianweddings.com

Royal Maui Weddings
2780 Keka'a Dr.
Lāhainā, HI 96761
☏ (808) 357-1330
www.royalmauiweddings.com
Debbie@royalmauiweddings.com
Contact: Debbie Mauga

Simply Married
P.O. Box 512, Makawao, HI 96768
☏ Toll Free (800) 291-0110
(808) 986-8444 / 🖷 (808) 368-6933
www.simplymarried.com
Contact: Aulani Marks

Wailea Weddings
2930 Kauhale St.
Kīhei, HI 96753
☏ Toll Free (877) 806-7788
🖷 (808) 891-0413
www.waileaweddings.com
kristin@waileaweddings.com
Contact: Kristin Gerring

Weddings Hawaiian Style
188 Kamakoi Loop
Kīhei, HI 96753
☏ Toll Free (888) 583-9529
🖷 (808) 879-8059
www.kamele.com
weddings@kamele.com
Contact: Judy Angel

Westin Maui, The
2365 Kā'anapali Pkwy.
Lāhainā, HI 96761
☏ (808) 661-2546 / 🖷 662-2752
www.westinmaui.com
debbie.graham@westin.com
Contact: Debbie Graham,
Director of Romance®

Big Island:
A Fairy Tale Wedding
P.O. Box 4953, Kailua-Kona, HI 96745
☏ Toll Free (888) 433-0880
(808) 331-1229
www.getmarriedinhawaii.com

A Vow Exchange
P.O. Box 1255, Kīlauea, HI 96754
☏ Toll Free (800) 460-3434
🖷 (808) 828-0336
www.vowexchange.com
vowex@gte.net
Contact: Linda Pasadava

Beach Weddings Hawai'i
82-5824D Nāpō'opo'o Rd.
Captain Cook, HI 96704
☏ (808) 328-9239
www.beachweddingshawaii.com
beachweddingshi@aol.com
Simple beach weddings, renewal of vows.

Kaua'i:
Bali Hai Weddings
P.O. Box 1723
Kapa'a, HI 96746
☏ Toll Free (800) 776-4813
🖷 (808) 822-7379
www.kauai-wedding.com
balihai@hawaiian.net

Barefoot Kaua'i Weddings
P.O. Box 223185
Princeville, HI 96722
☏ Toll Free (800) 826-9237
(808) 826-9737
www.barefootkauaiweddings.com
b.kw@verizon.net
Contact: Claire Vierkoetter

Barefoot Weddings Hawai‘i
2850 Makau St.
Līhu‘e, HI 96766
☎ (808) 246-6257
www.barefootweddingshawaii.com
Wedsite@aloha.net
Contact: Teri Katahara

**Coconut Coast Weddings
and Photography**
1191 Kuhio Hwy. #20
Kapaa, HI 96746
☎ Toll Free (800) 585-5595
📠 (808) 822-2201
www.kauaiwedding.com
coconut@kauaiwedding.com

Garden Island Wedding, The
3510 Rice St. #210
Līhu‘e, HI 96766
☎ (808) 632-0505 / 📠 632-0303
www.gardenislandwedding.com
sayuri@gardenislandwedding.com

Heart to Heart
4826 A Pelehu Road
Kapa‘a, HI 96746
☎ (808) 823-6869
www.hawaiian.net/~heart2heart
heart2heart@hawaiian.net
Intimate ceremonies in nature on Kaua‘i.

Kaua‘i Christian Wedding
☎ Toll Free (866) 822-5554
www.kauaichristianwedding.com
KCW@KauaiChristianWedding.com

Kaua‘i Custom Weddings
☎ (808) 826-1712
www.kauaicustomweddings.com
kauaiwed@msn.com

Portraits of Hawai‘i
2381 Kipuka St.
Koloa, HI 96756
☎ Toll Free (800) 745-7414
📠 (808) 742-7392
www.portraitsofhawaii.com
poh@aloha.net

Wedding in Paradise
☎ Toll Free (800) 733-7431
📠 (808) 246-2676
www.paradiseservices.com
questions@paradiseservices.com

Weddings Hawaii Kauai
5901 Uilani Pl.
Kapaa, HI 96746
☎ Toll Free (800) 394-3646
(808) 821-9393
www.hawaii-wedding.com
iben@hawaii-wedding.com

Weddings on the Beach
P.O. Box 1377, Koloa, HI 96756
☎ (808) 742-7099
www.weddingsonthebeach.com
judy@weddingsonthebeach.com
Contact: Judy Neale

Moloka‘i:
The Perfect Wedding
500 Kapalua Dr., 18-T-7
Kapalua, HI 96761
☎ (808) 250-1624 / 📠 669-8922
www.theperfectweddingmaui.com
cherise@theperfectweddingmaui.com
Contact: Cherise Vonae Shulman

Weddings on Moloka‘i
P.O. Box 56, Ho‘olehua, HI 96729
☎ (808) 567-6773
www.weddingsonmolokai.com
barb@aloha.net

Five months after a beautiful visit to Hawai'i, Mark and I were engaged and excited to return for our wedding. We couldn't think of a better place to get married, and wanted to treat our guests to a vacation they deserved. We thought, "Who wouldn't want to go to Hawai'i and join in on the celebration?"

After looking at different venues at which to have our once-in-a-lifetime experience, we decided that the Star of Honolulu met all of our needs. We dreamt of an intimate setting with great food, entertainment, and service, while treating our guests to something unique and special. Our concerns were that we would be celebrating with strangers, unable to rehearse before the ceremony, unable to personalize our wedding with our own favors and flowers,

Mark Kirsch & Karen Richter

♥♥

STAR OF HONOLULU

and the logistics of transporting our guests to the boat. However, the Star of Honolulu's wedding coordinator, Kayo, resolved all of our fears prior to the event. Regular communication, their flexibility, and attention to details helped to make our wedding day memorable. We were given our own room; were able to choose our linen colors and entrees; we rehearsed prior to our guests' arrival; we had extra flowers and our own favors; and exclusive limousine service for our guests was included! That was all in addition to a ceremony performed onboard by their Captain, a seven-course gourmet dinner, cocktails, live entertainment, wonderful photography and video of the occasion, and non-stop pampering... We were so impressed!

Selecting the Star of Honolulu was a simple but elegant way to have an all-inclusive wedding with the breathtaking natural beauty of the island and ocean as a backdrop. Our favorite memory was seeing whales and a Hawaiian sunset for the first time as husband and wife.

In retrospect, our advice to other couples would be to make your wedding a week-long experience in Hawai'i and then go on your honeymoon alone for another week. If I had to change anything, it would be to invite more family and friends to share in our special day. Other than that, everything was perfect.

For Our Next Act

Entertainment can encompass several different roles in your wedding. For purposes of this chapter, we will offer advice and resources on emcees, disc jockeys, bands and other types of musicians. Two sets of "entertainers" may be required, one for the ceremony and another for the reception. As an option or suggestion, you may choose a harpist and flautist for the ceremony and then opt for a live band for the reception. The music you select for your wedding sets the tone for the entire event. We always recommend selecting music that is reflective of your personalities and interests as a couple. You may select classical music for the ceremony and then kick it up a notch to jazz or hip-hop for your reception. Selecting your emcee is just as important. Many people use family or friends for emcees and usually this works well. However, there are others who prefer to leave the emcee-ing to the professionals. As with each part of your wedding, select an emcee whose style, sense of humor and personality fit with the tone of your wedding.

QTA's:

❑ Do your prospective bands or musicians have audition nights when you can hear them in person? If they don't, can they provide you with several audio- or videotapes?

❑ Do they require a deposit to reserve their services?

❑ Are they able to bring their own sound system, if necessary?

❑ Have they performed at your wedding or ceremony site before? Are they familiar with the layout, set-up, rules and restrictions?

❑ How much time do they need to set up (if they're bringing their own sound system, instruments, etc.)? Are you paying them for the time they set up?

❑ If you are hiring a DJ, do they provide a light show? What sort of packages do they have?

❑ Do they have back-up equipment or instruments?

❑ What's the emergency back-up plan if your entertainers are unable to attend/perform due to an emergency (illness, accident, death in the family...)?

❑ Do they belong to any professional organizations?

There's a general percentage that you can work with that will help you plan ahead on how many people will attend your wedding versus the amount of people you invited. If you're having more than 200 guests you can estimate between 25–28 percent of those invited will be unable to attend. If you are inviting less than 200 guests, the percentage decreases to about 15–20 percent. Other factors to consider are out-of-town guests and the time and date of your wedding. Keep in mind, however, that all families are different and if you have a firm grasp on who will and will not come, rely on that and not on these percentages.

Tips:

❋ Ask your caterer, wedding coordinator or other vendors for recommendations of good entertainers.

❋ Ask friends and family for recommendations.

❋ Ask your entertainers for references from recent weddings they've done.

❋ Often radio disc jockeys or local entertainers moonlight as emcees. Look into their services. Expect to pay more for the well-known ones.

❋ Go over the reception timeline and create a script with key points you want the emcee to include in the program.

❋ Discuss the type of wedding you are having along with the types of people who will be attending. Let the emcee know ahead of time if there are any subjects or topics of conversation that are off-limits or sensitive.

❋ Book your entertainers as soon as you can. The good ones go early and fast!

❋ Have the musicians provide a written contract detailing the services they will provide. If they don't have a contract, create your own.

❋ If you have specific songs or music you want played, be sure to go over that with the musicians prior to the event to ensure they are prepared to perform them.

❋ Provide your entertainers a wedding day itinerary and map with directions to the ceremony/reception.

❋ Some churches and synagogues will not allow you to play secular music during the ceremony. Check with the clergy beforehand and go over music selections as necessary.

❋ If you don't have song preferences for specific events (recessional, cake cutting, garter toss, etc.), ask the entertainers to suggest some songs so that you can decide on them before hand.

✳ DJs tend to be less expensive than live bands.

✳ Some DJs will hook up with videographers or other wedding vendors and offer multiple services through one company. (For example, if you book a DJ, he may offer you a package deal that includes a videographer.)

✳ Ask to see sound/band equipment or at least ask what type of equipment they use.

✳ If you're hiring a band, ask them how long each set is and how many breaks they will be taking during their stint. Make sure you're in agreement with their schedule and work out any differences prior to the wedding.

✳ For a list of professional musicians in Hawai'i (or your area), contact the local chapter of the American Federation of Musicians at (808) 596-2121/(808) 593-2526, (e-mail) local677@afm.org or (website) livemusicbiz.com.

Expect To Pay:

DJs– $350 and up depending on whether or not you want a light show and how long you're booking them for.

Emcee– Anywhere from $150–$650, based on experience, popularity and amount of time spent.

Bands– Usually paid by the hour, anywhere from $200 to $2,500 an hour. This also varies by popularity, amount of time spent, and size of band.

Harpist and/or Flautist– $125 an hour and up.

O'ahu, Maui, Big Island:
Tihati Productions
☏ (808) 735-0292
www.tihati.net/door/
Entertainment company, various islands.

Notes:

A Disco Beat
940A 10th Ave.
Honolulu, HI 96816
☎ (808) 734-8308
DJ

A Disco in Motion
98-1040 Moanalua Rd., #105
Aiea, HI 96701
☎ (808) 833-3330
DJ

A Music Unlimited
P.O. Box 971342
Waipahu, HI 96797
☎ (808) 678-8333
munltd808@aol.com
DJ

Aloha Audio Mobile Sound
P.O. Box 1147
Kailua, HI 96734
☎ (808) 262-1111
DJ

Barrett Awai
☎ (808) 373-4682
Musicians. Hawaiian duo. Also able to book other groups.

Keith and Carmen Haugen
☎ (808) 951-4332
www.hawaiiansong.com
hakumele@aol.com
meahula@aol.com
Hawaiian duo

Chant
☎ (808) 728-0974
paula_shg@hotmail.com
Contact: Paula Carreiro
Band, contemporary R&B.

Clear Sky Music
☎ (808) 637-4635
Clearskymusic@aol.com
www.clearskymusic.com
Varied Musical Styles. Band, Duo or Single. Suitable for any occasion - from black tie to casual events

Disco Fantasy
☎ (808) 677-9955
changg005@hawaii.rr.com
Specializing in weddings. Sound systems, lights and DJ.

DJ Greg Gabaylo
☎ (808) 456-5207
DJ

DJ Music
1001 Dillingham Blvd., Honolulu, HI 96817
☎ (808) 341-7940 / 🖷 847-3504
DJ

Dynamic Sounds
PO Box 893451
Mililani, HI 96789
☎ (808) 627-0602
dynmcsounz@aol.com
Contact: David Louis

Elua Kane
☎ (808) 261-1405
Contact: Tau Greig
Musicians. Duo/Strolling duo.

Flute a la Harpe
P.O. Box 11254
Honolulu, HI 69828
☎ (808) 735-6813
fluteharp@hawaii.rr.com
Musicians. 1993 HOKU Winner.

Gigi Kidder
☎ (808) 224-5010
Musicians. Duo/Trio.

Gregg Hammer Productions
☏ (808) 478-5873
ghamprod@hawaii.rr.com
Emcee services.

Halau Hula Makana A Ke Aloha
66-162 Haleiwa Road
Haleiwa HI 96712
☏ (808) 637-2345

Harpist Pumehana Davis
P.O. Box 240663, Honolulu, HI 96824
☏ Toll Free (877) 737-6422
(808) 737-6422
www.harphawaii.com
harphawaii@hawaii.rr.com
Musicians.

Hawaiian Ryan
☏ (808) 497-3112
www.hawaiilovestories.com
Contact: Ryan Matsumoto
Emcee services.

HawaiiEntertainers.com
P.O. Box 240553, Honolulu, HI 96824
☏ (808) 738-8088
Musicians.

Heartstrings
126-5 Noke St., Kailua, HI 96734
☏ (808) 254-3003
heartstringsduo@juno.com
Musicians.

High Quality Sounds Production
☏ Toll Free (877) 545-1606
(808) 828-5273
Contact: Roger Acebo
Professional sound and lighting specialists serving Hawaii for over 10 years.

Island Disco
P.O. Box 26042, Honolulu, HI 96825
☏ Toll Free (888) 933-6248

(808) 396-9144
www.islanddisco.com
info@islanddisco.com
DJ, entertainment and emcee services.

JMB Productions
☏ (808) 284-0353
www.jmbproductions.com
Master of Ceremonies, DJ music and entertainment.

Jennifer Cleve
☏ (808) 753-5356
Solo vocalist.

Kapena-Dance Band
P.O. Box 6461, Kāneʻohe, HI 96744
☏ (808) 239-4100 / 🖷 239-6612
www.kapena.com / kapena@kapena.com
Contact: Ken Tompson, group manager
Musicians, contemporary Hawaiian.

Keith and Carmen Haugen
☏ (808) 951-4332
www.hawaiiansong.com
hakumele@aol.com / meahula@aol.com
Hawaiian duo

Kilinahe
☏ (808) 384-5450
www.kilinahe.com / kanaia@kilinahe.com
Musicians, Hawaiian.

Kimie Yamamoto
☏ (808) 741-8658
Solo vocalist

Kuuipo Kumukahi
☏ (808) 389-5454
www.ekuuipo.com
Musicians, Hawaiian.

LB Disco
P.O. Box 61453, Honolulu, HI 96839
☏ (808) 988-3111
DJ

Lanai Tabura
☎ (808) 550-9278 / (808) 620-4942 (cel)
Lanai@clearchannel.com
Emcee services.

Lee Eisenstein / Lionel Standish
305 Hahani St., #186, Kailua, HI 96734
☎ (808) 261-8969
members.cruzio.com/~lionel/
eisenstel001@hawaii.rr.com
lionel@cruzio.com
Musicians, Hoku Award Winning Classical Guitarist.

Manoa Strings
☎ (808) 941-6480
String Quartet, String Trio, Violin Duo, Solo Violin

Maohi Nui
☎ (808) 382-1018 / 488-4855
lilom22@yahoo.com
Contact: Mervyn Lilo
Polynesian entertainment including dancers and musicians.

Maxine-Karen Johnson
240 Makee Rd., #4A
Honolulu, HI 96815
☎ (808) 921-9110
Solo Viola or Viola & Piano.

Melissa Makuakane
☎ (808) 227-3702
Hula dancer. Also available to book hula halau and other Polynesian dancers.

Mike Machado
☎ (808) 554-1316
Emcee services

Music With Class
☎ (808) 536-4114
Professional string ensemble.

Music Xpress Productions
P.O. Box 2801, Ewa Beach, HI 96706
☎ (808) 689-7579
www.mxpentertainment.com
manager@mxpentertainment.com
DJ

Musicians' Association of Hawaii/ Local 677
www.livemusicbiz.com/live.htm
Great site for various live musicians.

Mystical Sounds Productions
P.O. Box 27702, Honolulu, HI 96827
☎ (808) 947-3115
www.mysticalsoundsproduction.com
mspsound@excite.com
DJ

Na Kama
☎ (808) 479-4171
Contact: Eric Lee
Musicians, Hawaiian band.

N.Dmixx Productions
91-1512 Ekemauʻu St., ʻEwa Beach, HI 96706
☎ (808) 681-6499
DJ

Ninja Entertainment Productions
☎ (808) 372-9176
members.prodj.com/ninjamusic
(no "www" in web address)
ninjamusic@prodjmail.com
DJ

Pipi's Sound & Lighting
☎ (808) 330-7474
DJ

Piʻilani Crabbe
☎ (808) 486-0522
puakani21@aol.com
Emcee services.

Randy Focht & Associates
94-758 Lumiauau X-1
Waipahu, HI 96797
☎ Toll Free (877) 557-4686
(808) 951-0448
www.randyfocht.com
info@randyfocht.com
Romantic wedding music.

Rebecca Hilary Smith
P O Box 11325
Honolulu, HI 96828
☎ (808) 735-5130
Harp@lava.net
Musicians.

Roslyn
☎ (808) 227-9568
Solo vocalist.

Rhythm Creations
Honolulu, HI
☎ (808) 368-8190
www.rhythmcreations.com
rhythm@lava.net

Sandyz Moblie Karaoke
☎ (808) 306-7464
DJ

Sweet Sounds Entertainment
☎ Toll Free (800) 816-3538
(808) 627-3538
sweetsounds@hawaii.rr.com
DJ

Maui:

A New Beginning…Weddings
P.O. Box 2063
Kīhei, HI 96753
☎ (808) 875-1721 / 276-4260
Hawaiian music, guitar, chanting, conch shell.

CVP Entertainment, Inc.
2746 Kauhale St.
Kīhei, HI 96753
☎ (808) 875-4450 / 🖨 875-4452
cvpentertainment@juno.com
*Authentic Hawaiian entertainment for your
wedding ceremony and reception: Hawaiian
dancers, hula dancers, conch shell blowing,
Hawaiian drummers, Hawaiian chanter, etc.*

Flute Music Maui
P.O. Box 324
Makawao, HI 96768
☎ (808) 572-3483
www.openeye.addr.com/flute/
barry@openeyetours.com
Flute, flute/harp, trio.

Heavenly Harps of Hawai'i
☎ (808) 870-6050 / 🖨 879-1996
www.heavenlyharps.com
harpinfo@heavenlyharps.com
Contact: Celia Canty
Musicians. Will travel to other islands.

James Brent-Bagpiper
150 Kulalani Dr.
Kula, HI 96790
☎ (808) 878-1022
gordone001@hawaii.rr.com
Musicians.

Louise Lambert Entertainment
☎ (808) 875-1891
Musicians.

Musical Options Inc.
50 Poha Pl.
Pukalani, HI 96768
☎ (808) 572-1271 /
www.musicaloptions.com
options@maui.net
Entertainment company.

Maui DJ
P.O. Box 120
Kula, HI 96790
☎ (808) 876-0231 / 🖷 876-0482
www.mauidj.com
DJ

Pia Aluli
4790 Lower HonoaPi'ilani Rd.
Lāhainā, HI 96761
☎ (808) 669-5034 / 🖷 669-2580
home.hawaii.rr.com/piaaluli/
paluli@hawaii.rr.com
Hawaiian minister, guitar and vocals.

Preston Beachwood Music LLC
P.O. Box 120, Kula
HI 96790
☎ (808) 876-0231 / 🖷 876-0482
www.1atheart.com/
Romantic husband and wife duo.

Big Island:
Ed Geer's Force Enterprises
Mobile DJ Co.
PO Box 2177
Kealakekua, HI 96750
☎ (808) 323-9696
DJ

Good Vibrations
www.goodvibrationz.com
dj@goodvibrationz.com
☎ (808) 889-1332
DJ

Kaua'i:
Cindy Combs
P.O. Box, Hanapēpē, HI 96716
☎ (808) 335-3171 / 🖷 335-3834
www.premamusic.com/cindycombs
ccombs@brudda.com
Musicians / slack key.

Da Soundman
5645 Kuamoo Rd., Kapa'a, HI 96746
☎ (808) 823-6258
kealii@aloha.net
Band equipment and musicians.

Celestial Music Artists
P.O. Box 1302, Kilauea, HI 96754
☎ Toll Free (817) 823-5378
(808) 826-0346
www.celestialmusicartists.com
carman@midpac.com
Jazz artists

Hal Kinnaman
P.O. Box 118, Hanapēpē, HI 96716
☎ (808) 335-0322
www.halkinnaman.com
hal@halkinnaman.com
Musicians.

Kaua'i Musical Arts
P.O. Box 1888, Koloa, HI 96756
☎ (808) 742-1090
www.kauaimusicalarts.com
gordon@kauaimusicalarts.com
Musicians.

Kustom Sounds Kaua'i
P.O. Box 2344, Līhu'e, HI 96766
☎ (808) 245-7860 / 🖷 245-7810
www.kskauai.com
mike@kskauai.com
DJ/emcee.

Luau Hawai'i
4268 Rice, Līhu'e, HI 96766
☎ (808) 639-6624 / 🖷 245-2014
Hawaiian music and hula.

Passport Music & Talent
☎ (808) 742-8885 / 🖷 742-2435
www.kauaimusic.com
rich@kauaimusic.com
Live musicians, bands, DJs.

Notes

The final day of our mini-honeymoon at the Hyatt Regency Waikīkī had arrived. We walked happily from shop to shop, searching for an item to commemorate the experience. Among the scenic postcards, Hawai'i T-shirts, and chocolate-covered macadamia nuts, we discovered a box of guava-flavored lollipops, complete with a cute, albeit kitschy, set of wedding figurines which we immediately declared perfect. To someone else, our purchase may have seemed odd, but the souvenir epitomized our total wedding package: sweet, surprising, extraordinary, and a whole lot of fun!

In the movies, wedding planning always looks so easy. Typically, the man proposes to his sweetheart, they get married and go on to live happily ever after. They conveniently leave out the millions of tasks that need to be done between "Will you marry me?" and "I do!"

Shane Imai & Kathryn Fujioka

♥♥

HYATT REGENCY WAIKIKI

We thought we had a lot of time since we had a year and a half until our wedding day. However, after attending our second wedding expo, our heads were spinning. We had some general ideas about our "wedding vision" but needed some guidance.

Early on in our search for a wedding site, we scheduled a consultation with Darren, the Hyatt's Catering Sales/Convention Services Manager. Instead of forcing decisions upon us, he emphasized that our happiness came first, and quickly put our fears to rest. Darren proposed an ideal ceremony site and layout for the reception which would provide for us the perfect settings for our simple but sophisticated wedding.

We chose to have the wedding ceremony on the 3rd floor ocean terrace with a sweeping view of Waikīkī Beach. It is accented with an intimate white gazebo. accompanied with an elegant white carpet runner and space to seat up to 140 guests.

(continued on next page)

We did have some differences of opinions on priorities, but we all agreed that our guests would want to be comfortable and eat delicious food. In choosing the Hyatt, we were assured that those requests would be met.

The weekend of the wedding signaled the arrival of last-minute craziness. But once we had checked into the hotel and heard the sound of the rushing waterfall, our frazzled nerves were calmed and we started to relax and enjoy ourselves. The accommodations and service shown to us by the Hyatt staff were exceptional and allowed us to experience some much-needed relaxation and quality time with our loved ones before the weekend's climax.

Before the ceremony, Darren had gathered the wedding party for a last-minute briefing. That's when the nervousness set in. What were those instructions we had covered during the rehearsal? Wait for Darren's cue before walking down the aisle. Watch for the bend in the carpet runner. Pause and face the guests once the Reverend concludes. There really wasn't that much to remember but of course, we wanted to do it right—after all this was IT!

The wedding party assembled at the start of the aisle, which at that moment seemed to stretch on endlessly. Had it grown since the rehearsal? The instantly recognizable sounds of "Here Comes the Bride" began to play from the speakers. The funny thing was, my maid-of-honor Lauren was still walking up the aisle. Lauren looked a bit confused, and I'm sure some of the guests were too. Perhaps we stretched it out a bit too long.

The miscue turned out to be nothing but amusing and before we knew it ,the ceremony

was over and we were husband and wife. Hand in hand, we turned to face those who had come to help us celebrate the occasion. We remembered all those important directions and paused. We took a moment to smell the salty beach air mingling with pikake, to admire the beaming faces of our parents, to hear each other's intensified heartbeats, and realized what tremendous beauty—both tangible and indescribable—surrounded us.

The magic continued as we stepped into the stunning ballroom and were welcomed by the attentive staff who gave us every reason to relax. Our ceremony was followed by extraordinary cuisine at our reception. We celebrated our nuptials with our family and friends in the Regency Ballroom, where French windows and crystal chandeliers were the perfect backdrop to a picture-perfect day for us.

We would not have been able to immerse ourselves into the special moments of our wedding had it not been for the care shown by the Hyatt ohana (family). Fairy tales are possible after all!

(For more information on the Hyatt Regency Waikīkī see page 95.)

The average wedding costs nearly $19,000 nationwide and can cost thousands more in high-priced cities. For some it's equivalent to a new car or the down payment on a house, items you'd insure without thinking twice about it. Today some couples are opting to insure their weddings. For a few hundred dollars (usually between $200–$400), couples can purchase coverage that reimburses them if a wedding is canceled or postponed. It also will replace lost, stolen or damaged items, such as wedding bands and gifts. You can also include personal liability riders so they're protected in the event of property damage or an accident by one of their guests. It won't cover you if it rains on your wedding day but will cover you if hurricane, tornado or some other unforeseeable weather condition prevents the wedding from taking place. It will also cover you for any other non-voluntary cancellations.

Most coverage often is limited to just a few days before, and up through, the wedding day. You also may be required to pay a deductible before making a claim. And although nothing can replace your wedding day woes, it will help insure that the day is not a complete financial loss. There's no such thing as a sure thing—but there is such a thing as an "insured thing."

Top websites for information on wedding insurance are:

www.wed-safe.com

www.insurancecompany.com

www.firemansfund.com/products/personal/event/navevents.html

Something Borrowed...

This chapter covers equipment and miscellaneous items you may need to rent for your ceremony or reception site. Most weddings held at hotels and banquet rooms will not require you to rent items from outside vendors. But if your ceremony and/or reception is outdoors, at a beach, park or estate, you may need to rent equipment. Commonly rented items include: a tent or canopy, chairs, aisle runners, linen, glassware, gazebos, tables, archways, communion tables, kneeling benches, unity candle sets, lights, podiums, sound systems, stages—even a dance floor. Most rental places will have brochures with a complete listing of everything they rent along with a price list.

QTA's:

❏ Do they deliver? Is the delivery fee included in the price per item listed in their brochures or is there an additional charge added on? Do they set up the equipment? Is the set-up fee additional or inclusive?

❏ How many weddings do they do a month?

❏ Have they done weddings at your site before? Do they have any suggestions for set up?

❏ When do they return to pick up the items?

❏ Do they have insurance? Who is liable if any items are damaged?

❏ Do they require a deposit; if so how much? Is it refundable?

❏ What is your recourse if they are late in setting up? Or if they provide you with faulty equipment?

Tips:

❋ If you are renting lights, sound systems, etc., *make sure* the people who set them up check that everything is working properly before they leave.

Notes:

❋ Most rental places will have photos of weddings or special events they've done. Look through their portfolios. It's a good way to see what the rental company has and how they set up for different events.

❋ Ask to see everything you are going to rent. Make sure it is presentable and not dirty, old or damaged.

❋ Review your itinerary with the manager of the store or the person who will be overseeing your account. Make sure they are aware of your timeline and when rented items need to be delivered, set up, and ready to go.

❋ Make sure you give them your cell number and the numbers of your wedding coordinator and ceremony/reception coordinator.

❋ Find out how many outlets and other electrical power systems you may need.

❋ Coordinate delivery and pick-up with them and the ceremony/reception site coordinator.

❋ If you can afford to pay a little extra a chair—do it! Most places will rent you these not-so-pretty blue or brown plastic chairs for cheap, but for anywhere from 15¢ to $1 more per chair you can get white chairs that look much nicer. It's worth the minimal expense.

❋ Make sure you find out how many people each table seats and plan accordingly.

Expect To Pay: Because there are literally hundreds of items you can rent, we can't give you an estimate of what you'll pay overall. But just as a starting point here are some of the more popular items you might rent and what you'll pay for them:

❑ Tent or canopy: $200–$4,500

❑ Tables: $8–$30 per table

❑ Stages: $80–$1,000

❑ Chairs: $1–$5 per chair

Hawai'i Weddings Made Simple

O'ahu:

A Plus Party Tent Rentals
99-139 Nāpuanani Rd.
Aiea, HI 96701
☎ (808) 488-1889

A to Z Rental Center
45-618 Kamehameha Hwy.
Kāne'ohe, HI 96744
☎ (808) 235-6651

A'a Party Supplies
94-078 Leokane
Waipahu, HI 96797
☎ Toll Free (877) 815-3614
(808) 677-1964 / 🖨 678-1958
*Tents, tables, chairs, china, buffet serving
instruments, etc.*

Accel Party Rentals and Design
99-1405 Koaha Pl.
Aiea, HI 96819
☎ Toll Free (866) 389-7633
(808) 484-2258 / 🖨 484-4458
accelrentals@hawaii.rr.com

Aloha Party Rentals & Supply
340 Uluniu St.
Kailua, HI 96734
☎ (808) 261-0885 / 🖨 261-0451
www.alohapartyrentals.com

Luau Party Rentals
2020C Kahai St.
Honolulu, HI 96819
☎ (808) 845-5828
*Tents, tables, chairs, linens, paper goods, stages
and much more.*

Omar the Tent Man
94-158 Leoole St.
Waipahu, HI 96797
☎ (808) 677-8785
🖨 (808) 677-1973
www.omarthetentman.verizonsupersite.com
omarthet@hawaii.rr.com

Party Pizzazz
1247 Kailua Rd.
Kailua, HI 96734
☎ (808) 262-5553

Maui:

**Larry Mischle Caterer
Extraordinaire, Inc.**
281 Kaikea St.
Kīhei, HI 96753
☎ (808) 281-1913 / 🖨 879-1183
mischlel001@hawaii.rr.com
Contact: Larry Mischle

Big Island:

Big Island Tents
P.O Box 1725
Kamuela, HI 96743
☎ (808) 885 3534
www.bigislandtents.com
bigislandtents@hotmail.com
Contact: Robert Simms
*Chairs, tables, staging, dance floor, lights/torches,
side curtains, and paniolo equipment.*

Pacific Rent-All
1080 Kileaua Ave.
Hilo, HI 96720
☎ (808) 935-2974

Puna Rental, Inc.
16-175 Melekahiwa St.
Keaau, HI 96749
☎ (808) 966-5491
www.punarentals.com
Tables and chairs, chafing dishes, champagne fountains, cooler with wheels, shaved ice machine, popcorn machine, canopy tents (various sizes starting at 20' x 20' to 40' x 80'). Rates includes setup and breakdown.

Kaua'i:

Conrad Tent Rentals
☎ (808) 822-7080
Table and chair rentals.

Custom Party Rentals
P.O. 1198, Kalaheo, HI 96741
☎ (808) 635-2698 / 🖨 332-0811
Contact: Kirk Huffman

Da Soundman
5645 Kuamoo Rd., Kapa'a, HI 96746
☎ (808) 823-6258
Sound systems and stage lighting, band equipment and musicians.

Kaua'i Tent & Party Rental
P.O. Box 963, Kīlauea, HI 96754
☎ (808) 828-1597 / 🖨 828-0233
www.kauaitent.com
Offering tables, chairs, dance floors, staging, and lighting.

Notes

The Newlywed Game

♥♥

For many, the wedding becomes such a costly production that the honeymoon is almost an afterthought. If you live in Hawai'i and can't afford a "real" honeymoon because your wedding has you strapped for cash, consider a neighbor island trip or think about heading out to Ihilani, Turtle Bay or even Waikīkī. The honeymoon is more about the quality time you spend as husband and wife than any destination you're going to. If you're from out of town and have traveled to Hawai'i to get married, this probably *is* your honeymoon. Either way, here are some tips and things to consider when preparing for your honeymoon. This information is also helpful if you're assisting with out-of-town guest accommodations.

1) Set a budget specifically for your honeymoon. Consider everything from airfare, ground transportation, meals, spending money, entertainment and shopping. Write it down and stick to it!

2) Ask your travel agent about the best time of day and week to travel for the best value.

3) Whether you're going to a neighbor island or Paris, talk with a good travel agent, ask lots of questions. Get on the internet or browse through a few bookstores and research your destination, places of interests, language barriers, culture, money exchange rates, travel insurance, etc.

4) Book your flight at a decent time. If at all possible, don't leave the same day as your ceremony and don't leave at the crack of dawn the following morning, especially if you have an evening reception. You will need time to relax after the wedding and sleep in the next day.

5) Inform the resort, hotel or bed and breakfast that this is your honeymoon. They may surprise you with special accommodations—a room upgrade, complimentary wine or something special to help you celebrate.

6) Make sure all your travel documents are up to date. Security is extra tight nowadays and you need to make sure you have a current driver's license or photo ID. If you're traveling overseas, make sure your passport is current.

7) You will want to purchase your airline ticket using your maiden name because your photo ID needs to match the name on the ticket.

Preston Philpott & Robin Bennett

♥♥

WAI'OLI TEA CHAPEL & WAI'OLI TEA HOUSE IN MĀNOA

I really wanted to get married in a "church" and the chapel was perfect in size. I was able to choose who I wanted to "do" the wedding—our pastor of course. It was so very reasonable for both the use of the chapel and to have the reception at the tearoom.

My best friend from Seattle and my sister-in-law-to-be were my bridesmaids and Preston's best friend and his dad were his groomsmen. The girls wore burgundy dresses we bought off the rack at a department store in Ala Moana. I carried a beautiful, solid, reddish-burgundy rose bouquet from Ito Florist and the girls just carried single white roses. It was a simple, but elegant, evening ceremony.

It really was such a beautiful day. Just the fact that I was marrying the man I knew I was meant to…we had waited so long for this day and been through so much to get there…made us feel blessed to have our wedding in such a beautiful place. The staff at the chapel and tearoom was so helpful and added to the beauty of the day without all the extra added stress that can happen when you're not dealing with professionals. All in all, the day was one I will always treasure.

We were planning a small intimate wedding and wanted to incorporate the beauty of the outdoors without actually being outdoors. We got married in December, and I didn't want to run the risk of getting rained on. When I saw the chapel and tearoom, I knew this was the place. It's set on the grounds of a botanical garden and the whole setting of the quaint chapel and tearoom and all the beautiful flowers and plants made for some beautiful pictures and memories.

Budding Romance

Couples focus on different elements in their weddings. Some will spend an exorbitant amount of money on flowers while others want to spend it on their photographer. Still others like to focus on creating a certain theme or ambiance. The type and amount of flowers you use depends on your personal preference and your budget. There are some other factors you'll want to consider to help you decide how much or how little you should invest. Do a site inspection with your florist for your ceremony and reception site. Keep in mind that you spend the most time at your reception site (unless they're one and the same) so you should not invest an extravagant amount of money on the flowers for the ceremony. Unless, of course, you bring those flowers and arrangements and decorate the reception area as well. If the backdrop for your ceremony is a lush area with naturally beautiful flora and foliage, you might just want to line the aisle with rose petals, plumeria or orchids and decorate a few chairs. If your wedding is indoors and very staunch, flowers can dress it up and add some personality and panache.

The types of decorations, favors and centerpieces you choose can vary from simple to elaborate or sometimes none at all. Like many elements in a wedding, there is no right or wrong way to decorate. Most often, the more creative you are, the more you get excited about this part of your wedding planning. If you're strapped for ideas, wedding expos, magazines and on-line wedding sites are great for suggestions. When all else fails, keep it simple! You can either create your own favors and centerpieces, hire someone to do it for you or buy them pre-made.

QTA's (Your florist or decorator):

❑ Does the florist have photos of previous weddings they've done? Do they have wedding bouquets and/or arrangements for weddings in the store that you could look at?

❑ Will the floral consultant you are speaking with be working on your wedding? If it's someone else, ask about their wedding experience as well.

Every bride needs to have an "emergency" kit handy for all the last minute things that can go wrong. Have this handy and you can tackle almost anything. Have your maid of honor help you get it together. Be sure to include: nail polish remover, clear nail polish, nail file, dental floss, stain remover, toothbrush, tape, super glue, thread and needle, sanitary napkins, gum, mints, spare hose, batteries, measuring tape, safety pins, hair pins, small bottle of hair spray, brush, tissue, lighter, utility knife, small scissors, bandaids, straight pins and anything else that you think may come in handy.

❏ Is the florist able to create bouquets and other pieces that will fit the style and budget of your wedding?

❏ Is the florist knowledgeable? Do they offer helpful suggestions? Do they offer less expensive alternatives?

❏ Do they deliver? Is there an extra delivery charge, and if so, how much?

❏ How many weddings has the florist done in the past month? Will they be doing any others on the same day as your wedding?

❏ Will they help set up the floral arrangements and other pieces? Is there an additional fee for on-site setup?

❏ Have they arranged flowers for weddings at your reception and/or ceremony site before? What is their working relationship with the site directors/consultants?

❏ Does the florist require a deposit? Is it refundable? When is the total payment due? When is the final order due?

Tips:

❋ Bring pictures from magazines and books of floral bouquets and other decorating ideas that you like.

❋ Get a written estimate of the total cost along with deposit and total payment dates and amounts.

❋ Ask to tour the flower shop facilities. This is a good chance to see how they operate and you may get to see them working on some actual wedding bouquets and arrangements.

❋ If you're looking for ways to cut your floral expenses, concentrate your wedding dollars where they will get the most attention (altar, arch, head table, etc.).

❋ Lining the aisle with loose flowers is an inexpensive way to add color and charm to the ceremony site, especially for outdoor weddings. Plumeria, orchids and rose petals are all affordable options.

✳ Ask your florist to incorporate ribbon, tulle or other types of festive fabrics to add style and to help offset the costs of floral decorations.

✳ Use candles as part of your decoration theme. Keep in mind the wind factor or other weather conditions.

✳ Use the arrangements and other pieces from the ceremony site for decor at the reception site. If you don't have a full-service florist do your wedding, assign this duty to someone else.

✳ Consultations with a florist should be free.

✳ Consider negotiating better prices for off-peak wedding days and times.

✳ Keep in mind busy flower seasons like proms and heavy wedding seasons. Make sure that your flowers of choice are in season.

✳ Silk flowers are an option, especially in arrangements. Ask the florist if they work with silk flowers and what the cost benefits might be.

✳ If you're on a budget, think simple. The more elaborate the flowers and designs, the more you're going to pay.

✳ Bring a swatch or photo of your bridesmaids' dresses so the florist can match colors and styles.

✳ Make sure your flowers are delivered or arrive before any pictures are taken. Often the bridal party and groomsmen will take pictures prior to the wedding and you'll want to have the flowers on hand for this.

✳ Check to see that the florist included straight pins for the men's boutonnieres.

✳ Make sure your bouquets aren't too heavy. You don't want to carry a massive arrangement down the aisle with you! It will be heavy, awkward and it just might take the focus off of you—and we don't want that!

Often flowers or a single rose are given to each of the mothers during a traditional American ceremony. Couples in Hawai'i often opt to give a lei or tropical bouquets or nosegays. This can be extended to include grandmothers and even godmothers, if you desire. The tradition of the bride carrying flowers has its roots in ancient times when it was believed that strong smelling herbs and spices would ward off and drive away evil spirits, bad luck and ill health.

❊ Make a list of the flowers and arrangements that are to be delivered and give it to your wedding coordinator or a family friend. Have them check the delivery before the florist leaves.

❊ Assign someone familiar with your family and bridal party to be responsible for giving everyone their flowers. Give them a list of family names along with what each person should get.

❊ Standard wedding flowers and decorations include: bouquets (bride's, bridal party, throw bouquet), boutonnieres (groom, groomsmen, fathers, grandfathers), corsages or leis (mothers, grandmothers, aunties), haku (flower girls, bridesmaids optional), leis (out of town guests, close family and friends, people who have helped with the wedding, thank-you's for parents and family), ceremony arrangements (altar, pews, doors, columns, rose petals or bubbles for recessional), reception arrangements (centerpieces, head table, cake or cake table, archway, reception table, podium).

Expect To Pay: $40–$100 and up for bridal bouquets; $30–$80 and up for bridemaids' bouquets; $15 and up for leis/corsages for mothers; $20 and up for groom's lei, $5–$25 for various leis for ushers, family members, entertainers, special guests, etc; $100–$300 and up for ceremony decorations; $100–$300 and up for centerpieces, favors, other reception decor.

O'ahu:

Aloha Ceramics
98-021 Kamehameha Hwy.
Aiea, HI 96701
☎ (808) 488-9722
Ceramic centerpieces and favors

Always Flowers
1639 Liliha St., Honolulu, HI 96817
☎ (808) 536-5522

Bella Rosa
1421 Kālakaua Ave., Honolulu, HI 96826
☎ (808) 951-0787 / 🖨 944-0887
Exotic roses from Ecuador

Ben Franklin Crafts
2810 Pa'a St., Honolulu, HI 96819
☎ (808) 833-3800
Call for O'ahu locations.

Beretania Florist
1293 S. Beretanina St.
Honolulu, HI 96814
☎ Toll Free (800) 234-0538
(808) 591-2288 / 🖨 593-2341

Butterfly Kisses
94-861 Farrington Hwy.
Waipahu, HI 96797
☎ (808) 671-2617 / 227-2617
Centerpieces, favors, butterfly release, etc.

Designs by Hemingway
Honolulu, HI
☎ (808) 539-2409 / 🖨 732-0366
www.designsbyhemingway.com
designs@designsbyhemingway.com
Specializing in florals for your wedding on the island of O'ahu and travel to all outer Hawaiian islands at your request.

Dreams Unlimited
2071-C Beretania St., Honolulu, HI 96826
☎ (808) 941-6164
www.weddingdreamsunlimited.com
Ctandal@aol.com
Flowers.

Fleur'tations
1340 Young St., #3, Honolulu, HI 96814
☎ (808) 597-7673
fleurtationshnl@aol.com

Flora-Dec
373 N. Nimitz Hwy., Honolulu, HI 96819
☎ (808) 537-6194

Floral Artistry
444 Niu St., PH 101
Honolulu, HI 96815
☎ (808) 947-0144 / 🖷 955-4449
floral@hawaii.rr.com

Floral Specialist, The
1541 S. Beretania St.
Honolulu, HI 96826
☎ (808) 983-1400
🖷 (808) 983-1401

Florist Grand
☎ (808) 589-1382
By appointment only.

Flowers By Carole
99-185 Moanalua Rd., #105
Aiea, HI 96701
☎ (808) 487-1007 / 🖷 487-3907
www.flowersbycarole.com

Fujikami Florist
1200 Pensacola St.
Honolulu, HI 96814
☎ Toll Free (888) 848-1631
(808) 537-9948 / 🖷 532-2922
www.fujikamiflorist.com
fujikama@hawaii.rr.com

HatoRie
2752 Woodlawn Dr. #6-100
Honolulu, HI 96822
☎ (808) 734-2221
www.hatorie.com
hatorie@lava.net
*Candles, unique vases, and other items
for decorating and/or favors.*

Home Sweet Home Gourmet
P.O. Box 420
Waianae, HI 96792
☎ (808) 224-0080
home-sweet-home-gourmet.com
Wendy@home-sweet-home-gourmet.com

Honolulu Florist
851 Pohukaina St., Bldg. C
Honolulu, HI 96813
☎ Toll Free (800) 533-3288
(808) 591-9893
www.honolulu-florist.com
honflo@aol.com

Island Gifts and Flowers
507 N. Kuakini St.
Honolulu, HI 96817
☎ (808) 529-8683

JNS Floral Design
920C Kilani Ave.
Wahiawā, HI 96786
☎ (808) 258-9080
www.jnsfloraldesign.net
info@jnsfloraldesign.net
Contact: Suzette Fernandez

Patty's Floral Designs, Inc.
3133 Waialae Ave.
Honolulu, HI 96816
☎ (808) 732-5728

Picket Fence, The
111 Hekili St., #106
Kailua, HI 96734
☎ Toll Free (877)742-5770
(808) 262-7727 / 🖶 262-6096
www.alohatropicalflowers.com
picketfence@hawaii.rr.com

Rainbow Balloons & Flowers
Lāʻie Shopping Center, Lāʻie, HI 96762
☎ (808) 293-9542

Roses are Red
☎ (808) 486-2140

Sears Flower Shop
Ala Moana Shopping Center
Ground Level, Honolulu, HI 96814
☎ (808) 947-0233

Shapes of the Heart
☎ (808) 383-3830
www.shapesoftheheart.com
info@shapesoftheheart.com
Favors and gifts for all occasions.

Spinning W.E.B. Florist, The
1625 Liliha St.
Honolulu, HI 96817
☎ (808) 533-6760 / 533-6019
www.spinningwebflorist.com
info@spinningwebflorist.com

Stanley Ito Florist
1613 Nuuanu Ave.
Honolulu, HI 96817
☎ Toll Free (800) 449-0726
(808) 533-2348

SU-V Expressions
725 Kapiʻolani Blvd., C-118
Honolulu, HI 96813
☎ (808) 593-8989 / 🖶 593-2729
suvexpressions@earthlink.net
Floral designs, favors and invitations.

Sweet Leilani Florist
620 Dillingham Blvd., Honolulu, HI 96817
☎ Toll Free (888) 771-0008
(808) 832-0500 / 🖶 832-0507
www.sweetleilaniflorist.com
sweetleilani@hawaii.rr.com

Terrie Easley Designs
☎ (808) 595-3536
easleydesigns.com

Watanabe Floral Inc
1607 Hart St., Honolulu, HI 96819
☎ (808) 832-9360
www.watanabefloral.com
desingcenter@watanabefloral.com

Wedding Flowers…Plus!
1909 Ala Wai Blvd., #1601
Honolulu, HI 96815
☎ (808) 951-7673 / 🖶 951-5458
wesleywatanabe@yahoo.com

Yvonne Floral Design
45-934 Kamehameha Hwy. #C-125
Honolulu, HI 96744
☎ (808) 239-5220/ 🖶 (808) 239-6950
www.yvonnefloral.com
info@yvonnefloral.com
Contact: Yvonne Chapman

Maui:

Anny Heid Flowers, LLC
P.O. Box 1890, Makawao, HI 96768
☎ (808) 572-7033 / 🖶 572-3508
www.annheidflowers.com
anny@annyheidflowers.com
Contact: Anny Heid

Ben Franklin Crafts
275 Kaahumanu Ave., Kahului, HI 96732
☎ (808) 877-3337

Blossoms of Maui
1606 Halama St., Kīhei, HI 96753
☎ (808) 879-8074 / 🖷 879-1791
blossoms4u2@aol.com
Contact: Denise E. Wallace

Flowers by Kathy Marchetti
15728 Haleakalā Hwy., Kula, HI 96790
☎ (808) 878-8639 / 🖷 878-8655
www.kathymarchettiflowers.com
Contact: Kathy Marchetti

Flowers by Melissa
P.O. Box 323, Kula, HI 96790
☎ (808) 878-3903
www.mauiflowers.com

Stanfield's West Maui Floral
5095 Napilihau St., Lāhainā, HI 96761
☎ Toll Free (800) 336-4861
🖷 (808) 669-4823
stanfieldsfloral@maui.net
Contact: Sheldene Cockett

Town & Country Flowers, Maui Inc.
Four Seasons Resort, Wailea
☎ (808) 875-8822
etco@maui.net

Big Island:
Ben Franklin Crafts
333 Kilauea Ave., Hilo, HI 96720
☎ (808) 935-0005
Call for various Big Island locations.

Elegant Flowers & Gifts
☎ (808) 883-0225 / 🖷 883-2037

Floral Mart
738 Kino'ole St., Hilo, HI 96720
☎ (808) 935-6344

Kui & I Florist
707 Kino'ole St., Hilo, HI 96720

☎ Toll Free (866) 961-5545
(808) 961-9143 / 🖷 935-9003

Novelty Balloons by Fabian
776 Kilauea Ave., Hilo, HI 96720
☎ (808) 961-3255

Kaua'i:
Ben Franklin Crafts
4100 Rice St., Līhu'e, HI 96766
☎ (808) 245-4091

Flowers & Forever
2979 Kalena, Līhu'e, HI 96766
☎ (808) 245-4717

Florescence
P.O. Box 166
3741-B Hanapēpē Rd.
Hanapēpē, HI 96716
☎ Toll Free (877) 339-3310
🖷 (808) 335-3300
florescence@bigplanet.com

Manai Flowers & Gallery
4940 Hauaala Rd., #A
Kapa'a, HI 96746
☎ (808) 639-8364

Mr. Flowers
P.O. Box 223300, Princeville, HI 96722
☎ Toll Free (888) 828-6641
www.kauai-flowers.com
kodea@hawaiian.net

Tammey's Flowers & Gifts
Anahola, HI 96703
☎ (808) 822-1844

Arna Johnson

Getting married in Hawai'i was a must for me, and my husband, who was born in Virginia, was all for it. The majority of my family and friends still live there, and I didn't want to get married without them present. However, living in Phoenix, Arizona, didn't make planning a wedding easy. Thankfully, I had friends and family to help. Since I'd been living on the mainland for over ten years, I couldn't remember all the beautiful places and locations where one can get married. Thankfully, my girlfriend who lives in Hawai'i was planning her wedding during the same time I was. She attended the bridal shows, visited different locations, asked friends and family for recommendations and passed her information along to me.

Sean Pullen & Candida Lum

♥♥

SHERATON MOANA HOTEL

When I think about it now, I would've enjoyed having done those things myself. I would've chosen a different location for my ceremony and reception. But to make things easier on me, I chose to have both the ceremony and reception at the same place—The Sheraton Moana Surfrider Hotel, the oldest hotel in Hawai'i. Plus, I still remembered where and what the hotel looked like. Choosing a hotel to have both the reception and ceremony enabled me to eliminate the need for transportation of the wedding party from ceremony to reception. It provided a place for out-of-town guests to stay without worrying about how they would get to the wedding. Most hotels have fabulous scenery and the Sheraton Moana is no exception. And I didn't have to hire a catering service.

For everything other than the food, I hired people based on my research on the internet and recommendations from family and friends. But it's definitely not the same as seeing and doing things for yourself.

In the end, the wedding ceremony and reception went smoothly. For that my husband and I are grateful. Unfortunately, the night went by too fast. But that is one of the reasons I hired a videographer; and we will be forever thankful for the videotape. One of my most memorable moments was when the ceremony was about to start. A light rain began to fall. It was one of those unique Hawai'i rain showers–short, light and cool. It was a Hawaiian blessing.

During Victorian times, flowers took on an additional significance as couples would send messages to each other using different flowers—each flower having its own meaning. These associations were eventually adopted for the bride's bouquet and are still used today by many brides.

The most popular flowers with their traditional meanings (in alphabetical order) are:

Apple Blossom – Better things to come

Camelia – Gratitude

Carnation – Fascination and love

Chrysanthemum, Red – I love you

Chrysanthemum, White – Truth

Cyclamen – Modesty and shyness

Daffodil – Regard

Daisy – Innocence

Fern – Fascination and sincerity

Flowering Almond – Hope

Forget-me-not – True love and remembrance

Heliotrope – Devotion and faithfulness

Honeysuckle – Generosity

Hyacinth – Loveliness

Hydrangea – Boastfulness

Iris – Warmth of affection

Ivy – Eternal fidelity

Japonica – Loveliness

Jasmine – Amiability

Lemon Blossom – Fidelity in love

Lilac (white) – Youthful innocence

Lily – Majesty

Lily-of-the-valley – Return of happiness

Magnolia – Perseverance

Maidenhair – Discretion

Mimosa – Sensitivity

Orange Blossom – Purity and virginity

Peach Blossom – Captivity

Roses

Red – Love

Yellow – Friendship

Coral – Desire

Peach – Modesty

Dark pink – Thankfulness

Pale pink – Grace

Orange – Fascination

White – Innocence

Rosemary – Remembrance

Snowdrop – Hope

Sweet Pea – Delicate pleasures

Tulip – Love

Veronica – Fidelity

Violet – Faithfulness

Popular Hawaiian Wedding Flowers & Leis

Not only is Hawai'i home to some of the world's most beautiful backdrops, but it is also home to many colorful, rare and unique flowers. Hawai'i's flowers and leis are customarily a part of almost every ceremony and/or reception. Here's a list of the most popular (in alphabetical order):

Carnation lei

Cigar flower lei

Crown flower lei

Lei Pua Kenikeni

Tuberose lei

Carnation Lei ($4.50 & up)

Very thick and showy. The flowers are white, pink, red or striped, but can be dyed any color to match the occasion. No fragrance and best combined with tuberose when worn for weddings. Available all year.

Cigar Flower Lei ($18.50 & up)

Made with hundreds of tiny orange-red flowers strung in a rope-like style. These leis are usually worn by men. Available during the summer months.

Crown Flower Lei ($3 & up per strand)

Crown flowers are lavender or white and can be made with or without petals. This lei has no fragrance. Temperamental flower. Availability is subject to weather.

Dendrobium Orchid Lei ($6 & up single, $20 & up double)

The small dendrobium orchid comes in white, yellow, purple and lavender. Can be made double for a more substantial lei. Available year-round.

Haku Lei ($20 & up)

Made with various types of flowers, vines, leaves or seeds and are arranged and woven together and most often worn as a head piece. Available year-round.

Ilima Lei ($12.50 & up per strand)

Thousands of paper-thin ilima flower petals of yellow-orange are strung together to create this beautiful lei. Ilima lei were once only worn by the Hawaiian royalty. Available during the summer months.

Pikake and maile lei

Lei Pua Kenikeni ($5.50 & up)

The Pua Kenikeni is golden in color and has a spicy fragrance. Its unusual color and fragrance make it a popular lei when in season. Available primarily in warm summer months.

Maile Lei ($20 & up)

Fragrant and green maile leaves are traditionally worn by the groom, groomsmen and sometimes officiant. Often flowers such as pikake or ilima are woven with maile leaves. Available year-round

Maunaloa Orchid Lei ($20 & up)

White or purple vanda orchids are stacked and made with their petals lined up. Available all year.

Micronesian Ginger Lei ($9 & up single; $20 & up double)

The fragrant ginger flower is woven with stems forming a delicate lace-like pattern on the inside with the blossoms on the outside. They can be made in various styles. Available all year.

Ohai Ali'i Lei ($12–$20 single; $15–$30 double)

Bright orange or yellow in color and has a feathery appearance. Most often worn by men. Available year-round.

Pikake Lei (White Jasmine) ($5 & up per strand)

Pikake flowers resemble pearls and have a heavenly fragrance. Traditionally worn by the bride or mother of the bride. They can be entwined with other flowers such as ilima, orchids or rosebuds. We recommend a minimum of three strands. Temperamental flower abundantly available in summer months.

Plumeria ($4 & up single, $10 double; 3 cents & up per bud)

Sweet smelling flower most associated with the "smell of Hawai'i." Comes in various shades of white, yellow or pink. Can be made into a lei or used to decorate (aisle runner, tabletops, etc.).

Tuberose Lei ($7 & up single)

Delicate white flower with a sweet fragrance. It can be doubled so that only the petals show on the lei. Most often worn by mothers of the bride or groom. Available year-round.

Some other flowers found in Hawai'i that can be incorporated into your wedding decor are: hibiscus, birds of paradise, anthurium, and red ginger.

Notes

Our ceremony was a vow renewal which we took as seriously as the original wedding. Once we narrowed down the Hawaiian Islands as our site, we were open to the options of the different islands but blown away by the beauty and natural Hawaiian feel of Kaua'i. Neither of us had been to Kaua'i and the Hyatt package seemed to be calling us!

Emett Mosley & Cindy Daws

HYATT REGENCY KAUA'I

After researching the various types of wedding packages offered at several resorts in Hawai'i and the Caribbean, the choice was easy. The quality of service the Hyatt brand name promises and delivers, the variety of choices for a great price, a beautiful destination and wonderful coordinators Brenda Jose and Ella Kaohi helped us make our decision.

The planning phase was incredibly smooth. After seeing some of our friends stress out on their own wedding day, we chose our date a year in advance and made all of our plans by phone and e-mail with Brenda and Ella. When we arrived in Kaua'i, we took a tour of the property and viewed the wedding site. All I had to do was choose some flowers and show up! I had my make-up and hair done at the ANARA Spa and my mom, sisters, and I got a manicure/pedicure the day before the wedding. The Spa stylists were fabulous and very professional, and everyone in my wedding party commented on how beautiful I looked. It was a very special day in every way.

We had the Regency Club lawn as our setting and it was a dream come true with an ocean view backdrop and perfect weather. Our guests even saw a whale in the background during the ceremony.

The reception was held on the main floor balcony and we had a beautiful view while we ate! We had a late morning ceremony so the buffet included everything from pancakes to steak, which was perfect because there was something that everyone could enjoy. We are so glad we chose the Hyatt and we're looking forward to an anniversary vacation or, for that matter, any excuse to re-visit Paradise.

(For more information on the Hyatt Regency Kaua'i see page 105.)

Yours for the Asking

Once you've decided who you're going to invite, you need to decide how you are going to invite them. Your invitations should be in line with the overall theme and formality of your wedding. Your invitations are your guests' first impression of your wedding. Wedding invitations can be expensive, but you don't have to spend an excessive amount of money to convey the style and formality of your special day. There are thousands of invitations available in stationery stores, on-line and from "discount" catalogues. You can also opt to create your own—a growing trend for today's bride. Explore all these options and choose the one that best suits your style and budget. If possible, use the same kind of stationery (paper weight, style and color) for everything (invitations, save-the-date cards, RSVP, thank-you cards, etc.). Order everything at one time and order more than you think you need. Invitations are usually ordered in increments of twenty-five or fifty. If you're making your own invitations, order extra paper, velum, envelopes and anything else you need to create them. It's less expensive to order extra the first time than to have to make a small reorder because you don't have enough.

There are elements you should consider when selecting your invitations or shopping around to make your own invitations. Look at the weight of the paper, the shade, font and size of wording, size of invitation and envelopes, wording, general style and postage restrictions and costs.

QTA's (yourself before you place your order):

❏ Who is financing/hosting your wedding? (This will help dictate whose names are included on the invitation and how it's worded.)

❏ Do both sets of parents expect their names to be on the invitation? How do they want to be referred to on the invitation?

❏ How many invitations will you need? (Make sure to add at least an additional twenty-five.)

❏ Do you have all the correct information (names, dates, times, location and other details)?

❏ Are you requesting that guests wear certain attire? If so, be sure to include it on the invitations (formal wear, aloha wear, etc.).

❏ What will you use as a return address?

❏ What kind of enclosures do you want included in the invitation?

❏ What will each invitation cost you to mail?

QTA's (when deciding where/whom to order from):

❏ How long does it take to receive the invitations once you've ordered them?

❏ Can they help you with the proper wording?

❏ Do they charge extra for proofs, revisions, shipping, handling and delivery?

❏ Are there any unforeseen charges and add-ons?

❏ Do they require a deposit? If so, how much and when is it due? What forms of payment do they accept?

❏ What is their cancellation policy?

❏ Do they offer hand or machine calligraphy services? If so, what are their rates? If not, can they recommend someone?

❏ Can you order other paper products from them (thank-you cards, hold-the-date cards, maps, programs, etc.)?

Tips:

✳ Consider buying your invitations on-line. You can often find the same invitations on-line for a fraction of the price you'll pay at your local stationery stores.

Notes:

If you do not want children to attend your wedding, you can try several approaches. Do not include their names or "and family" on the invitation. Or, you can be really brave and print "Adults Only" on your invitation or RSVP card. But welcome all who come. You will be glad you did!

Notes:

❈ Even if you don't plan on buying your invitations on-line, surf the web for ideas and price points. It's a great place to research ideas without leaving your home.

❈ Tie in your invitations with your overall theme (colors, formality, verbiage).

❈ Decide what you will be ordering and including with your invitation. There is no "wrong" or "right", but typically most brides order invitations, inner and outer envelopes, a reception card, response cards and response card envelopes. Other options include: pew cards, place cards, and map/direction/accommodation information cards—even bridal registry cards.

❈ Ask to see a color proof before the final invitations are printed. Even on-line companies offer this service.

❈ If you're on a budget, keep in mind that the heavier the paper stock and the more inserts you have in the invitation, the more it's going to cost to mail it. You can expect to spend anywhere from 37–75 cents per invitation.

❈ Don't forget that you need to put stamps on your reply cards, too. You can save some money by using RSVP postcards. At press time, postcards mail for 23 cents while RSVP envelopes with cards are up to 37 cents.

❈ If you're computer savvy, you can build your own wedding website (or have someone do it for you) and have people RSVP on-line. It is efficient and can cut down on mailing costs. It's also a more convenient way for many to respond. See the vendors listed on page 202 for more information.

❈ Invitations should be mailed six to eight weeks prior to the wedding. Invitations mailed in Hawai'i to other Hawai'i residents should only take one to two days. If you're mailing invitations to the mainland, expect them to take anywhere from three to eight days. If you're mailing to foreign countries, allow ten to fourteen days for mailing time.

※ Address all invitations by hand. Write neatly. If your handwriting isn't acceptable, recruit some family or friends with nice penmanship to help you out. You can also opt to have your invitations addressed by a calligrapher.

※ Your invitations need to include everything your guests need to get to your ceremony and reception: date, time, address, exact name of site and reception room along with a map or directions, if necessary.

※ Reconfirm your ceremony and reception information before you send off your order. (i.e., reconfirm with the event coordinator at your hotel that your reception will be at the Coral Ballroom as opposed to the Grand Ballroom).

※ Make sure you have the correct spelling of absolutely everything—from names to the address and name of the location of your wedding/reception. Misspellings or typos on invitations are a bad way to set the tone of your wedding.

※ Proof, proof and reproof. And then have two or three people do the same thing. And then proof it again.

※ Spell out names and numbers in full, including those in dates, times and addresses. Do not use abbreviations or initials—except for Mr., Mrs., Ms. or Dr.

※ Things get kind of touchy when it comes to whose names are included on the invitation. Times have changed and so have some of the wording etiquette on invitations. It used to be that invitations were issued in the name of the bride's parents, even if she lived away from home or had been married before. If her parents were deceased, her guardian, a close relative or family friend may have sponsored the wedding and been listed. If only one parent was living, the invitations were issued in his/her name alone. If the bride's parents were divorced, the name of only one parent—usually the one who reared her—appeared on the invitation. If the parent remarried, the step-parent's name was listed on the first line followed by his/her daughter's to indicate relationship. These are still "safe" rules to follow but they are certainly no longer considered the "only" way to word your invitations.

❋ Print the guest's full name on the outside envelope (Mr. and Mrs. Kris Thompson or Ms. Dawn Brenneman). The inside envelope only needs to have their last name on it (i.e., Mr. and Mrs. Thompson or Ms. Brenneman).

❋ If your wedding is being held in a church, synagogue, chapel or other place of worship, the wording should read "the honor of your presence is requested." For a wedding or reception held elsewhere, your invitation should read, "the pleasure of your company is requested."

❋ If you are inviting children, write their names on a line under their parents' names on the inside envelope only.

❋ Never say anything on the invitation regarding gifts, monetary gifts or bridal registry.

❋ Although many invitation etiquette books and resources frown upon it, more and more brides are including a separate enclosure card that says where the bride and groom are registered. We don't consider this as offensive or inappropriate; more often than not we would like to know where the couple is registered. Whatever you do in reference to gifts, money or bridal registries, do it tactfully and respectfully.

❋ If you are a stickler for wedding and invitation etiquette consult a local stationer or read up on books that get down to the nitty gritty on invitation do's and don'ts.

What You Can Expect To Pay: A good rule of thumb is between 2–5 percent of the overall budget. Prices can range significantly; invitations from the local copy shop can be as economical as $1.50–$2 each, while one work of art can cost as much as $25! The point is, there are choices for every budget.

Big Red Q Quickprint Center
685 Auahi, Honolulu, HI 96813
☎ (808) 524-4126

Blueprints & Graphics
☎ (808) 853-2028
Toll Free (877) 290-8487
www.Blueprints-Graphics.cceasy.com
service@cceasy.com

Creations By You
1801 Liliha St.
Honolulu, HI 96817
☎ (808) 536-5255 / 🖷 524-0078
www.cbyweddings.com
val@cbyweddings.com
Invitations.

Dreams Unlimited
2071-C S. Beretania St.
Honolulu, HI 96826
☎ (808) 941-6164
www.weddingdreamsunlimited.com
Ctandal@aol.com
Invitations.

Hana Hou Productions
☎ (808) 383-3690
www.hanahouproductions.com
info@hanahouproductions.com

Hawaiian Creations by Mela, LLC
P.O.Box 161063
Honolulu, HI 96816
☎ 737-3867 / 🖷 734-0671
www.bymela.com
bymela@hawaii.rr.com
Hawaiian style invitations and certificates.

Hopaco
2833 Paa St., Honolulu, HI 96819
☎ (808) 831-8611
Call for store locations.

Kinohi Designs
☎ Toll Free (866) 377-1211
(808) 377-1211 / 🖷 373-2861
www.kinohidesigns.com
info@kinohidesigns.com

Leigh's Wishing Well
☎ (808) 946-1946
www.leighswishingwell.com
lww@leighswishingwell.com

Miemiko Atelier
☎ (808) 277-6999
www.miemiko.com
thepress@miemiko.com

Paper Roses
1200 Ala Moana Blvd.
Honolulu, HI 96814
☎ (808) 596-7955
www.komomaidesigns.com
komomaidesigns@aol.com

Paper Thoughts
P.O. Box 23022, Honolulu, HI 96823
☎ (808) 521-5330
www.paperthoughts.com
mail@paperthoughts.com

Paperie, The
Kāhala Mall
4211 Waialae Ave., Honolulu, HI 96816
☎ (808) 735-6464 / 🖷 735-6465

party & papier etc
1016 Kapahula Ave. #165
Honolulu, HI 96816
☎ (808) 377-8578 / 🖷 377-8578
www.partyandpapier.com
info@partyandpapier.com

Ti Leaf Collection
☎ (808)739-6097
www.tileafcollection.com/ tileaf@lava.net

It's easy to overlook one of the most important aspects of your ceremony—your wedding vows. Many couples simply defer the selection of the vows to their officiant and use "standard" vows that the officiant provides. However, it's always a nice touch to write your own vows. If you want to write your own vows but need a push in the right direction, visit your local bookstore and pick up a book on the subject (yes, they have books on writing your own vows) or go on-line. Whatever you decide, make sure the vows reflect the way you feel about each other and the commitment you are making.

Big Island:

Ali'i Printing
74-5617 Pawai Pl., Suite 102
Kailua-Kona HI 96740
☎ (808) 329-1099
Aliiprinting@turquoise.net

Big Island Printers
221 Maka'ala St.
Hilo, HI 96720
☎ (808) 961-2697 / 📠 961-2696
bip@gte.net

Celebrations and Occasions
74-5563 Kaiwi St. #134
Kailua-Kona, HI 96740
☎ (808) 329-4774 / 📠 (808) 326-3255
www.celebrationsandoccasions.com
Hundreds of specialty items: Hawaiian wedding certificates, favor boxes, cake toppers, serving and glassware.

Hawai'i Printing Corp.
☎ (808) 329-3519 (Kona)
961-6651 (Hilo)
hpckona@greensand.net

Gray Steven Print Design
☎ (808) 329-1144
tere@lino-graphics.com

Kaua'i:

A Formal Affair
PO Box 854
Kapa'a, HI 96746
☎ (808) 822-0748

Inkspot Printing
4100 Rice St.
Līhu'e, HI 96766
☎ (808) 246-0147

Mohala Wedding Services
Kapa'a, HI 96746
☎ (808) 821-8199

Notes

The Envelope Please...

♥♥

Traditional invitations and enclosures are placed in the following order: invitation, an inner envelope, response card, reception card and other enclosures. Etiquette dictates how to stuff the envelope properly. Here goes:

❧ When using an inner envelope, the invitations and all enclosure cards are put in facing the back. If the invitation is a single-fold or single card, the left edge goes in first. If it's a double-fold invitation, the folded edge goes in first.

❧ The inner envelope should be placed in the outer envelope unsealed with the flap facing down.

❧ If the invitation is a single-fold or single card, you should place the insertion cards face up in front of the invitations. In all cases, the reply card should be placed face up tucked inside the flap of the reply envelope lying against the invitation, so that the reply envelope is face down.

Hawai'i Weddings Made Simple

Dave and I chose to hold our wedding in Hawai'i because it is our home, the place that most closely represents who we are and where we're from. Our families and friends live here and they showered us with love and support before, during, and after our wedding day. We never really considered getting married anywhere else.

Dave Kusumoto & Shayna Ching

♥♥

KO'OLAU GOLF COURSE

Hawai'i is the ideal place to hold a wedding ceremony—in the sanctuary of God's creation. There is a tropical beauty unique to the Islands—from the ocean waves to the Ko'olau mountain range. We took most of our formal wedding photos outside, against a misty mountain backdrop, beside a natural stream, and surrounded by lush greens. Hawai'i provides a myriad of photo opportunities and outdoor ceremony sites.

Our Wedding Planner Was a Godsend! Our wedding coordinators were Keri Shepherd and Lynn Kelly from The Wedding Planners. I appreciated their guidance and support throughout every stage of the wedding planning process. Most wedding coordinators you hire for the day would have just come that day ready to receive directions and pass them on to everyone else. But they were with me from the beginning, helping me to brainstorm ideas, reminding me of all the little details I needed to consider, and keeping a running itinerary for the big day. They were always willing and able to jump in wherever I needed them.

Keri and Lynn gave me peace of mind in the midst of seeming chaos. Every time we met, they would not only help me plan, but offer wisdom and counsel, too. They helped me to balance the opposing opinions of others—reminding me that whatever decision I made should be for our best interests rather than for someone else's approval. They let me know that everything was to be wonderful on that day...and they were right.

'The Wedding Planners' involvement allowed me to really enjoy my wedding day. They have a knack for communicating effectively, making good decisions on the spot and directing people without stepping on their toes. Their take-charge, level-headed leadership gave our families, the ceremony site staff and catering staff a sure sense that things were under control. We were organized. We were ahead of schedule. Everything was going as planned and the one thing on our agenda was to sit back and enjoy the ride. And thanks to our wonderful wedding planners, we were able to do just that.

A Little Pick-Me-Up

Getting there is half the fun! Think about how you are going to arrive at your ceremony and/or reception site. For many, hiring a limousine service or alternative form of transportation company is considered a luxury expense. So if you're on a tight budget, this is probably one expense you'll want to forgo. However, it is relatively inexpensive and it does add some class and an air of something special to your wedding day. There are several benefits to renting a limo or special transportation. You don't have to worry about parking, designating a driver to get you to and from your ceremony and reception and you can transport your entire bridal party if necessary to ensure that you are all where you need to be, when you need to be there. Although white stretch limousines are the norm for weddings, other types of vehicles (Rolls-Royces, PT Cruisers, Stretch SUVs, sports cars, even trolleys) are available to rent.

QTA's:

❏ Do they charge an upfront percentage gratuity for the driver? If so, what is it? (10–20 percent?)

❏ If you pre-pay, do you get a discount? Do they offer multiple car discounts?

❏ How do they charge? By the hour? By the distance traveled? Are there any hidden fees?

❏ Is the transportation company familiar with how to get to and from your wedding and/or reception site?

Tips:

☀ Begin looking for your transportation company 2–3 months before your wedding. If you plan to rent specialized vehicles (like the stretch SUVs or Rolls-Royces) you may want to book your transportation earlier because vehicles of those types are limited on the island. Some vehicles may not be available on all the islands.

✳ Before you book your transportation, call the Better Business Bureau. The most common complaint lodged against transportation companies is a "no-show" or "late-show" complaint. Disreputable transportation companies will often overbook themselves or will forgo a wedding booking for a more profitable one. There are no guarantees, but checking with the BBB will help you weed out those that have a reputation for inconsistency.

✳ Book a transportation company that specializes in weddings. We don't recommend booking airport limousine companies because they have hectic, unpredictable schedules that aren't always conducive to wedding pickups.

✳ Call and do phone interviews with several transportation companies. Schedule a day to inspect the operation and vehicles you're interested in from the top few companies you've narrowed down.

✳ Have your top two preferences give you reference names and numbers of couples who have recently used their transportation services for their own wedding.

✳ Get references of good transportation companies from your other wedding vendors (photographers, wedding planners, etc.).

✳ Consider the size of your passengers, your wedding gown, and other things you may be traveling with when booking your transportation. Limos and other specialized vehicles come in various sizes (six-passenger, eight-passenger, 10-passenger, etc.) Make sure your vehicle is large enough to comfortably accommodate your needs.

✳ Always have a back-up plan for transportation in case, for some unforeseen reason, your ride does not show up. You don't want to be left stranded!

✳ Get the name and contact number of the driver or dispatch person directly involved with your booking in case of any last minute changes or emergencies.

Notes:

O'ahu:

A-1 Limousines By Neven
320 'Ōhua Ave.
Honolulu, HI 96815
☎ (808) 922-1531 / 🖷 922-1531

Ali Limousine
3203 Winam Ave.
Honolulu, HI 96816
☎ (808) 226-8944 / 🖷 737-0069
www.alilimousine.com

Alpha Limousine Service, Inc.
1441 Kapi'olani Blvd., #1413
Honolulu, HI 96814
☎ (808) 955-8898 / 🖷 955-8868
www.hawaii-limo.com
limo@aloha.net

Carey Limousine Hawaii
☎ Toll Free (888) 563-2888
(808) 572-3400
www.hawaiilimo.com
hawaiilimo@hawaii.rr.com

Cloud 9 Limousine
P.O. Box 8825
Honolulu, HI 96830
☎ Toll Free (800) 524-7999
(808) 524-7999 / 🖷 841-7292
www.cloudninelimos.com
cloudnine@hawaii.rr.com

Dang's Limousine Service
1411 Auld Lane
Honolulu, HI 96817
☎ (808) 524-5599 / 🖷 537-4634

Duke's Limousines
3134 Brokaw, 2nd Floor
Honolulu, HI 96815
☎ (808) 738-1878 / 🖷 738-1881
www.dukeslimo.com
info@dukeslimo.com

Elite Limousine Service
1059 12th Ave., Suite E
Honolulu, HI 96816
☎ Toll Free (800) 776-2098
(808) 735-2431 / 🖷 735-5159
www.elitelimoHawaii.com
info@EliteLimoHawaii.com

Hawai'i Chauffeur Services
2305 Kaululā'au
Honolulu, HI 96813
☎ (808) 522-7950 / 🖷 522-0015

Hawaiian Motion Tour Transportation
3056 E. Mānoa Rd.
Honolulu, HI 96822
☎ (808) 955-6961

Ichiban Limousine
2114 Liliha Pl.
Honolulu, HI 96817
☎ (808) 595-7733 / 478-4136
Hummer, Excalibur, Lincoln Stretch, Mercedes Sedan, Japanese and Chinese chauffeurs available.

Lowy Limousine Service
P.O. Box 6201
Honolulu, HI 96818
☎ (808) 455-2444 / 🖷 455-8460

Platinum Limousine
409 Lewers St., #129
Honolulu, HI 96815
☎ (808) 926-4466
Limo Bus, SUV Sports Limo, Japanese spoken.

Rocky's Limousine Service
2010 Kalani St.
Honolulu, HI 96819
☎ (808) 841-8488
Bilingual chauffeurs, gift certificates.
Kama'aina rates.

Sandy's Guide Tour
555 University Ave., #1707
Honolulu, HI 96822
☎ (808) 944-8094

Sharp Limousine Tours Inc.
Ilikai Towers
1777 Ala Moana Blvd., Suite 224
Honolulu, HI 96815
☎ (808) 951-6144
Bilingual chauffeurs, island-wide service.

Showtime Limousine Entertainment
P.O. Box 15365
Honolulu, HI 96830
☎ (808) 926-4444 / 🖷 395-0884
16-Passenger SUV, CD and DVD library.

Star Limousine
☎ (808) 955-2020 / 🖷 955-7435
www.hawaiistarlimo.com
starlimo@hawaii.rr.com

Tropical Fantasy Limousine
Waimānalo and Kaaiai
Waimānalo, HI 96795
☎ (808) 259-9898
🖷 486-2728

Waikīkī Limousine Service
☎ (808) 944-0970

Waikīkī Trolley
☎ (808) 593-8211 / 🖷 591-9065
www.waikikitrolley.com/charters

Wally's Tours
2105 Hoohai, Pearl City, HI 96782
☎ (808) 455-4301

Maui:

Akina Aloha Tours Inc./Akina Bus Serv.
P.O. Box 933, Kīhei, HI 96753
☎ (808) 879-2828
🖷 (808) 879-0524
www.akinatours.com
info@akinatours.com

Arthur's Limousine Service
296-A Alamaha St., Kahului, HI 96732
☎ Toll Free (877) 408-9559
(808) 871-5555 / 🖷 877-3333
www.arthurslimo.com
info@arthurslimo.com

Carey/ Town & Country Limousine, Inc.
333 Waipalani Rd., Ha'ikū, HI 96708
☎ Toll Free (888) 563-2888
🖷 (808) 573-1114
www.hawaiilimo.com
hawaiilimo@hawaii.rr.com
Contact: Kathy Barr

Wailea Limousine Service
P.O. Box 428, Wailuku, HI 96793
☎ Toll Free (800) 606-4114
(808) 875-4114
🖷 (808) 244-5762
www.wailealimo.com
info@wailealimo.com

A bridal expo can be one of the best places to gather a wealth of information in one fell swoop! The Buckles Group owns and operates the largest wedding expo in the state of Hawai'i. Traditionally held in January and July on O'ahu, you will find hundreds of wedding vendors and industry experts just waiting to answer your questions, offer advice and supply you with whatever information you need.

Expo dates vary from year to year so for specific dates and times, locations, special offers and more info log on to www.bridesclub.com

Big Island:
Hawaiian Dream Carriage Service
73-1270 Mamalahoa Hwy.
Waimea, HI 96743
☎ (808) 325-2280

Luana Limousine Service
P.O. Box 2891, Kailua-Kona, HI 96745
☎ Toll Free (800) 999-4001
(808) 326-5466 / 🖷 326-9455

Kaua'i:
Custom Limousine
P.O. Box 3267, Līhu'e, HI 96766
☎ (808) 246-6318

Kaua'i North Shore Limousine
P.O. Box 757, Hanalei, HI 96714

Plantation Carriages
3-2243 Kaumuali'i Hwy.
Līhu'e, HI 96766
☎ Toll Free (877) 877-8908
(808) 246-9529 / 🖷 246-0765
pcarriage@hawaiian.net
www.theweddingcarriage.com/wedding.htm

Notes

Lew Harrington

My husband and I decided we wanted to get married in Hawai'i early in the planning process. In fact, it was the beginning of the entire process! I dreamed of getting married "in another country," and, since he lived in Hawai'i before moving to Chicago, he asked me if Hawai'i "counted." I readily agreed! We flew from Chicago to Hawai'i months before the wedding to scout out different locations and make decisions regarding photography, flowers, reception—everything! We wanted the day and the entire trip to be a memorable one for us and our families.

We toured several locations—two larger hotels and the Bayer Estate. When we pulled up to the Bayer Estate I knew that was the place we were going to be married. The home was charming and peaceful, and the director sat with us at a table overlooking the ocean as we asked questions about the estate.

Mark Barringer & Laura McKnight

♥♥

BAYER ESTATE, 'AINA-HAINA

Those were easy decisions! We also looked at flowers and decided on having our reception on the *Star of Honolulu*.

What would we change?

❋ Skip meeting with large coordinating agencies. The ones we met with were not helpful, and they overwhelmed us rather than helped. They simply sat down with us and said, "What do you want?" Having never been married before, we didn't even know where to begin! Another offered a package—that is *not* the way to go! You don't have flexibility with what you get, and you receive their less-than-average photography.

What wouldn't we change?

❋ Spending a good chunk of money on the photographer. You get what you pay for!

❋ Having a coordinator to assist with the details—someone we could call or e-mail to help us finalize reservations and get last-minute things for us because we weren't there.

❋ Because we were coming from the mainland, we couldn't organize table centerpieces or gifts at the reception. Having our reception on the *Star of Honolulu* was the *best* way for us to go—we didn't plan a thing! Dinner, entertainment, drinks—they were all organized for us!

❋ Getting married *in* Hawaii made it special for our families. It became a vacation for all of us, and one with memories that will not be forgotten!

Dearly Beloved

If you belong to a church, synagogue or other religious establishment, you will most likely ask your clergy to perform the ceremony. If you don't belong to any religious sect or organization, you can have a judge or any other person licensed by the Hawai'i Department of Health perform your ceremony. You can also inquire at various non-denominational churches. Keep in mind some clergy will not marry people who are not in their congregation or of the same faith. Others will, but they may require you to go through some pre-marital counseling or courses. Whomever you choose, make sure they are legally able to marry you in Hawai'i. If you need more information on this, refer to pages 3-4 for more on state regulations for getting married in Hawai'i.

QTA's:

- ❏ Are they licensed by the Hawai'i Department of Health?
- ❏ How many ceremonies do they perform a month?
- ❏ Have they done other ceremonies at your site?
- ❏ Are they able to attend the rehearsal? (This is a must!)
- ❏ What do they charge?
- ❏ Do they have sample vows you can select from? Can you write your own?
- ❏ Is the clergy willing to perform the ceremony outside of a church or place of worship if that is your choice location?
- ❏ If you are using a clergy, are there any restrictions they place on the ceremony? If so, what are they?

Tips:

❊ Provide your clergy person with a wedding day itinerary so they know what kind of time frame you're working with.

❊ Most officiants have a generic timeline they work from, but they are usually able to accommodate special requests or adjustments with regards to your ceremony specifics.

☀ Ask the officiant for an outline of his/her standard ceremony (readings, prayer, ring exchange, vows, etc.). Incorporate this into your wedding day timeline.

☀ If you are hiring an officiant you do not know, meet with them in person before you book their services. Make sure you will feel comfortable with them and that they reflect your belief system.

Expect To Pay: Many officiants simply ask for a donation which can range from $100–$150. Others, like judges, court clerks, or justices of the peace may have a set price that may go as high as $300.

O'ahu:

Rev. Abigail
☏ (808) 843-2229

Aiea United Methodist Church
99-101 Laulima, Aiea, HI 96701
☏ (808) 488-5354

Aloha O Kalani Ministry
P.O. Box 4782, Kaneohe, HI 96744
☏ (808) 239-6145
www.hawaiialohaspirit.com
info@hawaiialohaspirit.com
Kahu Wendell PK Silva
Authentic Hawaiian Ceremonies

Bobby Olmstead, Senior Pastor
Hope Chapel, Hawaii Kai
☏ (808) 386-9328

**Christ Church Uniting Disciples
& Presbyterians**
1300 Kailua Rd., Kailua, HI 96734
☏ (808) 262-6911

Rev. Christina Gilman
53-567 Kamehameha Hwy.
Hau'ula, HI 96717
☏ (808) 293-0272

Church of Hawaii Nei
O'ahu's North Shore
☏ (808) 638-7841

Church of the Holy Nativity (Episcopal)
5286 Kalaniana'ole Hwy.
Honolulu, HI 96821
☏ (808) 373-2131

Rev. Clarence Liu
☏ (808) 942-2297

Cynthia Smoot, Minister
44-452 Kāne'ohe Bay Dr.
Kāne'ohe, HI 96744
☏ (808) 254-3701 / 🖷 254-6472
www.mrsminister.com
mrsminister@hawaii.rr.com

Fili Tualaulalei
VCF Honolulu
P.O. Box 19218
Honolulu, HI 96817
☏ (808) 683-0101
fili@hawaii.rr.com
Vineyard Christian Fellowship

Harris United Methodist Church
20 S. Vineyard Blvd., Honolulu, HI 96813
☏ (808) 536-9603

**Honolulu Central Seventh Day
Adventist Church**
2313 Nuuanu Ave., Honolulu, HI 96817
☏ (808) 524-1352

 Hawai'i Weddings Made Simple

Mark Kurnow (Kahu)
☎ (808) 330-1697

Our Savior Lutheran Church-Aiea
98-1098 Moanalua Rd.
Honolulu, HI 96818
☎ (808) 488-3654 / 🖷 488-4515
www.oursaviorhawaii.com
office@oursaviorhawaii.com

Reagan Miura, Senior Pastor
Second Generation Redemptive
Community Church
☎ (808) 222-0623

Rev. Ron Valenciana
☎ (808) 638-9686
www.hawaiiweddingminister.com
KissHawaii@aol.com

Ross Yamamoto, Pastor
Second Generation Redemptive
Community Church
☎ (808) 392-0755

Tedd Tennis
☎ (808) 373-7488
Bilingual (English and Japanese).

Rev. Toni Baran
44-160 Kou Pl., #2
Kāneʻohe, HI 96744
☎ (808) 235-6966
www.lovehawaii.com
lovehawaii@hawaii.rr.com

Trinity Church Windward
875 Auloa Rd.
Kailua, HI 96734
☎ (808) 262-8587

Waialae-Kāhala Chapel
1178 21st Ave.
Honolulu, HI 96816
☎ (808) 737-6611

Wedding by the Sea
1814 Poki St. #203
Honolulu, HI 96822
☎ (808) 942-7772
www.weddingbythesea-hawaii.com
revaloha@yahoo.com
Contact: Rev. Aki Mikami
Bilingual (English and Japanese).

Maui:

Rev. Alapaki
☎ Toll Free (877) 879-7149
(808) 879-7149
www.alapaki.net / alapaki@maui.net
Hawaiian minister/musician.

Judicial Services Hawaiʻi
2121 Main St., Wailuku, HI 96793
☎ (808) 244-2121 / 🖷 573-5805
boydpm@earthlink.net
Contact: Judge Boyd P. Mossman

**Kuhina Hawaiian Weddings
and Blessings**
P.O. Box 1250, Kīhei, HI 96753
☎ Toll Free (888) 565-6688
(808) 879-1499
www.kuhina.com / info@kuhina.com
*Specializing in ancient Hawaiian protocol and
traditions of yesterday.*

Wedding Fantasies of Maui
P.O. Box 10833, Lāhainā, HI 96761
☎ (808) 250-8639

Big Island:
Rev. Jack L. Ferguson, PhD
☎ (808) 325-5446

Rev. Libby Tao Kelson-Fulcher, D.D.
☎ Toll Free (866) 321-3321
(808) 322-3322 / 🖷 325-3445

Rev. Patrick Thompson
☎ (808) 322-3116

Rev. Van Buskirk
☎ (808) 933-2467

Weddings A La Heart
P.O. Box 4965, Kailua-Kona, HI 96745
☎ Toll Free (866) 321-3321
🖷 (808) 325-3445
www.weddingsalaheart.com
weddingsalaheart@hawaii.rr.com
Contact: Rev. Libby (Tao) Kelson-Fulcher

Kaua'i:

Rev. Caroline Carr
P.O. Box 690188, Makaweli, HI 96769
☎ (808) 826-0044 / 🖷 826-0038
therev@gte.net

Janet S. Oliver
☎ (808) 742-6115
marriagekauai@hotmail.com

Larry Lasota
☎ (808) 826-0044 / 🖷 826-0038
lasotas@hawaiian.net

M. Leilani K. Kaleiohi, Kahu
P.O. Box 736, Kīlauea, HI 96754
☎ (808) 821-0453
www.freewebz.com/leiofaloha/kahu.html
mlkk@aloha.net

Rev. Shalandra Abbey
P.O. Box 657
Lawai, HI 96765
☎ (808) 332-5396
www.reikikauai.com/weddings.html
reiki@reikikauai.com

Wedding Trends
♥♥

FAVORS/DÉCOR: Personalize favors. Everything from CDs with the favorite songs of the bride and groom to personalized wine bottles, glasses, place card frames.

Themed weddings with sand and seashells and Asian themed weddings are popular. Everyone wants a Martha Stewart-esque wedding. Simple. Elegant. Creative. Unique.

Centerpieces that come in like colors but various heights and sizes and shapes. Candles, flowers, floating candles, tea lights, pillars, and tapers are favorites.

FLOWERS: Simple bouquets with single or double stems of flowers. Either that or a bunch of wildflowers. Roses are still the most popular flower of choice. Other popular yet still unique are gerbera daisies, hydrangeas, colored lilies. and gardenias. Another idea for the bride is to carry one or two single-stem flowers to hand to her mother on the way to the altar, and to give her mother-in-law on the way out.

WINDOW SHOPPING: Online registry and online shopping are growing by the day. More brides are window shopping online. They will gather ideas for favors, attire, décor and then do price comparing with local shops. Brides are also using free wedding websites to help them plan their wedding or set up their own wedding website for guests to view, RSVP, and gather and give wedding information.

ESCORTS: More couples are involving other family members to walk them down the aisle. Some come arm-in-arm with a parent on each arm. Others are escorted by stepparents, mothers, brothers, grandparents, etc. It's a unique way to honor someone special, especially if you do not have a father figure to do the part.

DESTINATION WEDDINGS: Hawai'i is one of the top destination wedding and honeymoon spots in the world. Destination weddings are very popular right now. People will gather with their closest family and friends and go to an out-of-town locale and get married. It serves as both a wedding and honeymoon trip. Popular places are Hawai'i, California, wine countries, Jamaica, Bahamas, and Las Vegas.

WEDDING WEEKENDS: Special activities are scheduled for the whole weekend or for several days before, and sometimes after, the wedding. It usually begins with the wedding shower or bachelor party and continues through the rehearsal and wedding day. Events include lū'aus, golf, barbecues, and wine tastings. It often includes a brunch or breakfast the day after the wedding with immediate family members and/or the bridal party.

PHOTOGRAPHY: Digital photography is gaining popularity. More editorial or journalistic styles are also the rage. More candid photos and less posed shots or pictures that tell your wedding story are a wonderful keepsake. Group photos of all the guests and the bride and groom are also great and lots of fun if your venue and guest count permits.

othing else in life seemed as unexpected as being in Maui, dressed like a prince and princess, sipping champagne with the sounds of the ocean behind us. But there we were. The Hyatt Regency Maui Resort and Spa was the perfect choice for us. We have been all over Hawai'i during the years we have known each other, but the only place that felt right for our wedding was the Hyatt in Maui.

We decided to choose one of the resort's wedding packages and I'm so glad we did! The wedding coordinators at the resort were fabulous. They handled all the details, from top to bottom, leaving us to enjoy ourselves and our surroundings. For a very reasonable fee, every item was covered, from the cake to the minister. We decided to have the ceremony in the resort's Oriental Gardens. Surrounded by lush landscape accented with Asian art sculptures, I felt as if it were a dream. The centerpiece flowers and the bouquet were amazing, and there were rose petals sprinkled along the ceremony site and on the wedding cake.

The ceremony began with an authentic Hawaiian procession, complete with conch shell blower, hula dancer, drummer, and guitarist. After the ceremony was over, doves were released symbolizing our everlasting love for one another. It was perfect, and I didn't even have to lift a finger…except for my new hubby to slide the ring on it!

Michael Clerke & Melissa Nellsan

♥♥

HYATT REGENCY MAUI RESORT AND SPA

We took advantage of the *Kiele V* snorkel sail. The staff was friendly and knowledgeable. We couldn't believe all the variety of fish and coral. After our big day, the staff arranged a private Oceanside dining. It was unforgettable. From the service to the incredible food and the breathtaking sunset, it is something we will remember forever.

With all of the exciting things the resort had to offer, it made it easy to entertain friends and family and allow us to either participate, or have some alone-time. We were able to organize for our whole group to go to the Drums of the Pacific Lū'au, the resort's Polynesian Revue. The food was great (even the poi) and the show was a lot of fun. Later, we snuck away to the Tour of the Stars, their rooftop astronomy program, to see the Hawaiian night sky twinkle. The Romance Show with champagne and chocolate-covered strawberries was the perfect end to another perfect day.

We can't say enough great things about the staff. They were organized and a true joy to work with. Thanks to everyone at the Hyatt Regency Maui Resort and Spa for an experience none of us will ever forget!

(For more information on the Hyatt Regency Maui see page 101.)

Notes

PHOTOGRAPHY:

Worth a Thousand Words

*I*f a picture is worth a thousand words then your wedding pictures are priceless! You will never be able to recapture the moments of your wedding day, but good wedding photos can certainly help you reminisce. There are many wedding photographers to choose from. Meet with a few and you should have no problem finding the right one for you. Some specialize in black and white photographs; some have digital capabilities; others devote the entire day with you capturing every moment. Some things you'll need to consider are costs, quality and care. Your choice of photographer should fit your budget, produce quality images, proofs and enlargements, and care almost as much as you do, about providing you with photographs that will serve as memories for a lifetime. There are lots of things to keep in mind when interviewing and selecting a photographer, so get out your highlighter or take copious notes!

QTA's:

❏ How many weddings does the photographer shoot a month? Ask about his/her experience. How long has he/she been a professional wedding photographer?

❏ Does he/she carry backup equipment? How much?

❏ Does the photographer use an assistant? If so, what's the assistant's role and does the photographer take all the pictures? (Professional wedding photographers should use an assistant to help carry equipment, assist with lighting and film and help with posing or organizing photos. They may also assist in taking candid photos.)

❏ Does the photographer use soft focus techniques? (If he/she doesn't know what that is, that's a high sign he/she doesn't do many weddings!)

❏ Can you provide the photographer with a list of important photographs that you'd like taken on your wedding day?

❏ Does he/she require a deposit to reserve the date? When is the deposit due? What forms of payment does the photographer accept? (Most will require a non-refundable deposit to reserve the date. It's usually between 15 to 25 percent.)

❏ What packages are offered? What are the à la carte prices? Do you keep the proofs? Are you required to order a minimum amount of reprints? Can you book the photographer for additional time? If so, what is the additional cost?

❏ Does the photographer give price breaks for weddings on "off" times (weekdays, weekday evenings)?

❏ What happens if the photographer is ill or injured and unable to shoot your wedding? (It should stipulate in a contract that if the photographer is unable to shoot your wedding because of serious illness, accident or other reasons out of his/her control that he/she will provide another qualified photographer to shoot your wedding with the same quality and terms at no additional charge. Do not book a photographer who will not agree to this in writing.)

❏ What does the photographer guarantee? Is it in a written contract/agreement?

❏ Ask about when you can expect your proofs back. Where can you pick them up? How will they be presented? Do they come in a proof album; if so, is that included in your package? How long does it take to get your finished album, reorders and extra enlargements?

❏ Are touch-ups included in the package or do you have to pay extra for that?

Notes:

Notes:

❊ Budget at least $1,200 for your photography and wedding photos. In this field, perhaps more than any other, you usually get what you pay for. Excellent wedding photographers can charge as much as $5,500 (includes proofs, enlargements, wedding albums, negatives, digital images, touch-up services, etc.).

❊ Meet with the photographer in person. Check out his/her wedding albums and other work.

❊ Ask for references from the photographer's last three weddings. Call the brides and ask about their experience with the photographers.

❊ Package deals will cost less than à la carte.

❊ Book a photographer that you like. Personality matters and you need to be sure you "click" and that you can handle spending the most important day of your life with this person as he/she tells you where to stand, when to smile and what to do.

❊ Ask about hidden costs or additional charges (travel fees, extra film, enlargements, costs of negatives if they are not included in the package, extra costs for black and white photos, etc.).

❊ Meet with at least two photographers before booking, but don't wait too long once you find one you like. The good photographers tend to book quickly.

❊ Ask if the negatives are included in the package or if they are available for purchase.

❊ If you're looking for ways to save money, have the photographer shoot the ceremony and formals and have friends or family shoot candids of the reception.

❊ Ask for coverage of only the ceremony and formal portraits (two to three hours). Then purchase disposable cameras for your wedding party and/or guests and let them shoot candids for the reception.

✻ Pay via credit card when possible; you have sixty days after billing to dispute a charge—
it's the law.

✻ If the photographer's dress is an issue to you, ask him/her how he/she intends to dress.
If it's not up to your expectations, let him/her know what you feel is appropriate (such as
aloha shirt and khakis or a sundress, etc.).

✻ Don't settle for an oral agreement. Get all the terms in writing and make sure both
parties sign the contract as soon as you book the date. Read the entire contract (fine print
included!).

✻ As with all your vendors, check with the Better Business Bureau to see if they're members and/or if they have any complaints against them. The Chamber of Commerce is another good resource for checking potential vendors.

O'ahu:

A Special Moment
949 McCully St., #9
Honolulu, HI 96826
☏ Toll Free (866) 591-2224
(808) 591-2220
hawaiiweddingphotography.biz
vidsolve@hawaii.rr.com
Photo/Video.

Akamai Photography & Video
41-1003 Laumilo
Waimānalo, HI 96795
☏ (808) 259-6713
www.akamaiphotography.com
akafoto@aol.com

Alex Chong Photographer
444 Hobron Lane, P-18
Honolulu, HI 96815
☏ (808) 944-0883

Allen Martin Photography
1303 S. King St.
Honolulu, HI 96814
☏ (808) 596-7000
amphoto@hawaii.rr.com

Anthony Calleja Photography
P.O. Box 30431
Honolulu, HI 96820
☏ (808) 349-7917
www.anthonycalleja.com

Arna Photography
3145 Castle St.
Honolulu, HI 96815
☏ Toll Free (800) 439-9612
(808) 735-8841 / 🖷 735-8721
www.arnaphoto.com
arna@arnaphoto.com

Art Factory Hawai'i, Inc.
1946 Young St., #460
Honolulu, HI 96826
☏ (808) 943-0777 / 🖷 943-0778

Barry Maier Photography
3762 Sierra Dr.
Honolulu, HI 96818
☎ Toll Free (800) 383-5713
(808) 734-5088 / 🖨 739-5322
www.bmphoto.com / barry@bmphoto.com

Candace Freeland Photography
☎ (808) 823-8820
www.candacefreeland.com
inheaven@hawaii.rr.com

Charles F. Fasi, The Image Specialist
P.O. Box 27356, Honolulu, HI 96827
☎ (808) 521-1032
www.fasiphoto.com
charles@fasiphoto.com

Chris McDonough Photography
4329 Papu Circle, Honolulu HI 96816
☎ (808) 737-3112
www.chrismcdonoughweddings.com
info@chrismcdonoughweddings.com

Chrissy Lambert Photography
1888 Kālakaua Ave., #C307
Honolulu, HI 96815
☎ (808) 979-0001 / 🖨 979-0002
www.chrissylambert.com
info@chrissylambert.com

Christiaan Phleger,
Fine Art Wedding Photographer
4969 Maunalani Circle
Honolulu, HI 96816
☎ (808) 734-0421 / 🖨 734-2233
www.christiaanphleger.com
lexmack@lava.net
Contact: Christiaan Phleger

Contemporary Capture Photography
P.O. Box 5495, Kāneʻohe, HI 96744
☎ (808) 237-8612

Craig Stevens Studio, Inc.
1303 South King St.
Honolulu, HI 96814
☎ (808) 596-2555
Contact: James M. Takemora

Dave Miyamoto Photography
P.O. Box 25293, Honolulu, HI 96825
☎ Toll Free (888) 363-5749
(808) 396-5599 / 🖨 396-5593
www.davemiyamoto.com
davemiyamoto@hawaii.rr.com

David Murphey Photography
145 Rosebank Pl.
Honolulu, HI 96817
☎ (808) 595-0381
www.killerphotos.com
dave@killerphotos.com
Service on all of the Hawaiian Islands,
Los Angeles, San Francisco and Seattle.

Debbie Friedrich Photography
☎ (808) 271-0340
www.debbiefriedrich.com
Debbie@debbiefriedrich.com

Dorys Foltin
3705 Waialae Ave. #203
Honolulu, HI 96816
☎ Toll Free (866) 727-3663
(808) 737-3663
www.dorysfoltinphoto.com
info@dorysfoltin.com

Dream Maker
Honolulu, HI 96822
☎ (808) 537-6484
www.dreammakerhawaii.com
lutfeyj001@hawaii.rr.com

Dream Weddings Hawaii
P.O. Box 30611, Honolulu, HI 96820
☎ (808) 239-1116
www.dreamweddingshawaii.com
info@dreamweddings.com
Contact: Steve Young

Elizabeth Morgan Fine Wedding Photography
☎ (808) 358-4362
www.elizabethmorganphotography.com
info@elizabethmorganphotography.com

Eugene Kam Photography
1122 Koko Head Ave., #203
Honolulu, HI 96816
☎ (808) 737-3322
www.eugenekamphoto.com
ekp@flex.com

Floyd Honda
☎ (808) 523-1777 / 🖷 599-1493
fthpoto@aol.com

Francisco Photography
94-268 Waipahu Depot Rd.
Waipahu, HI 96797
☎ (808) 671-1128
(formerly George Dean Studio)

Garrett Nose Photography
1122 Koko Head Ave., #203
Honolulu, HI 96816
☎ (808) 732-1816 / 🖷 735-1761
www.garrettnosephoto.com
noseg@aol.com

George E. Smith Photography
1364 Manu-Mele St.
Kailua, HI 96734
☎ (808) 261-5676 / 🖷 261-2155
www.gesphoto.com
george@gesphoto.com

Gina Finkelstein Productions
758 Kapahulu Ave.
Honolulu, HI 96816
☎ (808) 674-2077 / 778-7122
www.gf-productions.com
info@ginafinkelsteinproductions.com

Love Story Weddings
☎ (808) 550-5680 / 🖷 550-5681
www.lovestoryweddings.com
lewharrington@hotmail.com

Hokuliʻi Images
575 Cooke St. #A
Honolulu, HI 96813
☎ (808) 845-4658 / 🖷 842-1186
www.hokuliiimages.com
hokulii@hokuliiimages.com
Photography by Geralyn

Hot Shots Photography
P.O. Box 10804
Honolulu, HI 96816
☎ (808) 941-8535
www.hotshotshawaii.com
hotshotshawaii@netzero.net

Island Paradise Portraits
☎ (808) 521-4447
Contact: Steven Vreeken

Ishikawa Photography
☎ (808) 946-9400
www.ishikawaphoto.com
By appointment only.

James Photography
Kapolei, HI 96707
☎ (808) 674-1829
www.jameshanphoto.com
james@jameshanphoto.com

Jayson Tanega Photography
1210 Laukahi St., Honolulu, HI 96821
☎ (808) 377-9603 / 781-7800 (cel)
www.tanega.net / j@tanega.net

Jim Creed Photography
68-281A Au St., Waialua, HI 96791
☎ (808) 637-6408

Josh Johnson Productions
☎ (808) 284-5519
joshjohnsonproductions@yahoo.com

JOSS Photography
P.O. Box 90161, Honolulu, HI 96835
☎ (808) 256-6781
www.hawaiiphotosessions.com
jossphoto@aol.com

Keely Luke Photographi'e
627 South St., #101
Honolulu, HI 96813
☎ (808) 528-5589
keely@iav.com

La-vie Photography
1888 Kalakaua Ave. #C-109
Honolulu, HI 96815
☎ (808) 941-4778 / 🖨 941-4427
www.la-viephoto.com
Hawaii@la-viephoto.com

Likolehua Photography
133 Lakeview Circle, #7
Wahiawā, HI 96786
☎ (808) 721-7022
dawny@hawaii.rr.com
Contact: Dawny Lancaster

Marcia Campbell Photography
P.O. Box 90662
Honolulu, HI 96835
☎ (808) 735-2782
www.marciacampbell.com
m@marciacampbell.com

Mark Nomura Photography
758 Kapahulu Ave. #A-504
Honolulu, HI 96816
☎ (808) 783-5269
www.marknomura.com
info@marknomura.com

Mariage Photographie
☎ (808) 754-7201
By appointment only.

Moments…Memories
47-472 Hui Kelu St.
Kaneohe, HI 96744
☎ (808) 239-2467 / 🖨 239-2593
www.momentsmemories.com
jaragaki@hawaii.rr.com

Michael Sendrey Photography
45 Ho'ola'i St., #C101-104
Kailua, HI 96734
☎ (808) 262-6015 / 🖨 262-0830
www.hawaiiphotos.com
info@hawaiiphotos.com

Mike Danzelsen Photography
1088 Bishop St., #3503
Honolulu, HI 96813
☎ (808) 536-3113
www.50photovideo.com
50@50photovideo.com

One Moment in Time
☎ (808) 739-2554
www.1momentintime.com
onemoment@hawaii.rr.com
Contact: David M. Shimabukuro

Owen and Owen Photographers
2071-A S. Beretania St., Honolulu, HI 96826
☎ Toll Free (877) 943-6936
(808) 943-6936 / 🖨 943-2191
www.owenandowen.com
owen-owen@verizon.net

Paul Hayashi Photography
235 Kuahiwi Ave., Wahiawā, HI 96786
☎ (808) 622-2346 / 🖨 621-0463
www.hayashiphoto.com
paul@hayashiphoto.com

Paul Eslit
1155 Fort Street Mall, Suite 107
Honolulu, HI 96813
☎ (808) 538-7727
www.pauleslit.com / info@pauleslit.com
Service to all islands.

Phil's Photography
95-1135 Makaikai, #65, Mililani, HI 96789
☎ (808) 255-8083
www.pphotography.com
pphotography@hawaii.rr.com

Photo Images by Rudy
565 Kokea St., #D-4, Honolulu, HI 96817
☎ (808) 847-7566
rudyarucan@aol.com

Photo Visions
☎ (808) 293-1898
www.photovisionshawaii.com
photovisions@hawaii.rr.com
Contact: Curt and Ramona Okimoto

Photography by Christie
P.O. Box 61506
Honolulu, HI 96839
☎ (808) 232-6736
www.christie-photography.com
christie@christie-photography.com

Photography by Nelson
94-801 Farrington Hwy., Suite 2-B
Waipahu, HI 96797
☎ (808) 671-5535

Picture This! Photography
☎ (808) 258-7985
www.picturethishawaii.net
picturethis@hawaii.rr.com

Sri Maiava Rusden Photography
☎ (808) 384-7029
Maiavarusdenphotography.com
ruzandsri@hawaii.rr.com

Stefanie Riedel Photography
59-519 Hoalike Rd., Haleʻiwa, HI 96712
☎ Toll Free (866) 297-9317
799-1895 (cel)
www.stefanieriedel.com
info@stefanieriedel.com

Steven A. Vreeken
P.O. Box 216, Lāʻie, HI 96762
☎ (808) 293-5047

Studio 2000
975 Kaluanui Rd., Honolulu, HI 96825
☎ (808) 396-7721
www.studio2000photography.com
studio2k@hawaii.rr.com
Contact: Dwight Iwasa

**Studio 3 Photographics
by Dwight Okumoto**
1236 Waimanu St., #B, Honolulu, HI 96814
☎ (808) 591-9044

Taylor Photography of Kailua
350 Hahani St.
Kailua, HI 96734
☎ (808) 261-0381
www.photokailua.com
info@Photokailua.com

TM Photography
298 Beach Walk, 3rd Floor
Honolulu, HI 96815
☎ (808) 497-2238 / 🖨 926-2690
murakawa@verizon.net
Photography by Toshi

Twain Newhart
☎ (808) 922-3535 / 741-3142 (cel)

Wedmemory
1585 Kapiʻolani Blvd., Suite 1204
Honolulu, HI 96814
☎ (808) 277-5328 / 🖨 943-9998

Wilber Bergado Photography
1154 Fort Street Mall #411
Honolulu, HI 96813
☎ (808) 927-5857
www.bergadophoto.com
bergado@aloha.net

Maui:

A & C Photography
P.O. Box 298
Kīhei, HI 96753
☎ (808) 875-1100 / 🖨 891-0052
www.photosbymichael.com
mike@photosbymichael.com
Contact: Michael Andrews

Action Photos of Hawaii, Inc.
333 Lilioukalani St.
Pukalani, HI 96768
☎ Toll Free (800) 373-7349
(808) 572-7081
www.apohi.com
apoh@hawaii.rr.com

**Aloha Moment Photography
& Videography**
727 Wainee St., Lāhainā, HI 96761
☎ Toll Free (800) 398-2271
🖨 (808) 667-5795
www.alohamoment.com
coordinator@alohamoment.com
Contact: David Hessemer

Blackrock Photography
P.O. Box 1163, Kīhei, HI 96753
☎ Toll Free (800) 330-1307
(808) 891-2000
www.blackrockphotography.com
brian@blackrockphotography.com

Creative Touch Photography
P.O. Box 3116, Wailuku, HI 96793
☎ (808) 244-1113 / 🖨 249-0013
www.creativetouchphoto.com
Contact: Kathryn Regier

Frames in Time
P.O. Box 2212, Kīhei, HI 96753
☎ Toll Free (877) 686-3686
🖨 (808) 877-5637
www.framesintimephotography.com
munnfoto@tiki.net
Contact: Darlene and David Munn

Gordon Nash
459 Kupulau Dr., Kīhei, HI 96753
☎ Toll Free (888) 286-5979
🖨 (808) 875-2985
www.gordonnash.com
gordon@mauiwedding.net

Hawaiian Images
2866 Ohina St.
Kīhei, HI 96753
☎ (808) 385-4436
🖨 (808) 875-0845
www.hawaiianimages.biz
david@mauivows.com
Contact: David Hessemer

Hughes Photographics
92 Iliwai Loop, Kīhei, HI 96753
☎ Toll Free (888) 829-2879
🖨 (808) 879-5518
www.hughesphoto.net
scott@hughesphoto.net
Contact: Scott Hughes

Jerry Grigory Photography, Inc.
312 Lakau Pl.
Kīhei, HI 96753
☎ Toll Free (800) 778-6284
🖳 (808) 874-8852
www.jerrygrigory.com / jgphoto@maui.net
Contact: Jerry Grigory

John Henry Photography
59 Kanoa St.
Wailuku, HI 96793
☎ (808) 242-1918 / 🖳 243-9750
www.johnhenryphotography.com
jhphoto@maui.net
Contact: John Henry

Kimberly Curtis Photography
480-A Kenolio Rd.
Kīhei, HI 96753
☎ Toll Free (800) 593-6789
🖳 (808) 879-4496
www.kcphoto.net / kimberly@kcphoto.net
Contact: Kimberly Curtis

Lizada Photography
P.O. Box 2070, Kīhei, HI 96753
☎ (808) 874-6102
lizada@maui.net
Contact: Ceasar L. Lizada

**Making Maui Memories
Photo and Video**
P.O. Box 1913, Kīhei, HI 96753
☎ Toll Free (800) 878-1583
(808) 875-8461
www.mauiphoto.com
jrocha@mauiphoto.com
Contact: Jill Ackemann

Maltese Dreams Photo/Video
P.O. Box 11743, Lāhainā, HI 96761
☎ Toll Free (800) 962-7622
(808) 665-0251
Contact: JoJo Maltese

**Maui Professional Photographers
Association**
P.O. Box 5004, Kahului, HI 96732
www.mauiprophoto.org
Directory of Photographers on Maui

Nancy Nelson Photography
792 Kupulau Dr.
Kīhei, HI 96753
☎ (808) 875 4041
www.nancynelsonphotography.com
nanel@maui.net
Contact: Nancy Nelson

Nancy Phelps Photography
P.O. Box 1071
Lāhainā, HI 96767
☎ Toll Free (877) 661-3872
(808) 661-3872
www.nancyphelpsphotography.com
phelps@maui.net
Contact: Nancy S. Phelps

Patti LeGary Photography
P.O. Box 995
Kīhei, HI 96753
☎ (808) 283-8765
www.legaryphotomaui.com
legaryphotomaui@hotmail.com
Contact: Patti LeGary

Peter Thompson Photography
P.O. Box 959, #301, Kīhei, HI 96753
☎ Toll Free (800) 550-4874
www.photohawaii.com
petert@petert.com
Contact: Peter Thompson

Photography by Bill Stockwell
638 Kumulani Dr.
Kīhei, HI 96753
☎ Toll Free (888) 676-5500
🖳 (808) 875-0872
www.billstockwell.com
awareguy@aol.com
Contact: Bill Stockwell

**Photography by Nicole –
Coolbreeze Productions**
PMB 413 P.O. Box 959
Kīhei, HI 96753
☎ Toll Free (888) 832-MAUI (6284)
🖳 (808) 874-9108
www.photographybynicole.com
imnmaui@tiki.net
Contact: Nicole L. Davis

**Reflections Photography by
Martin Wyand, Inc.**
124 Hakui Loop
Lāhainā, HI 96761
☎ Toll Free (800) 756-1796
(808) 667-9296
www.martinwyand.com
wyand@maui.net
Contact: Martin Wyand

Richard Blue Photography
601 Kaulana St.
Kahului, HI 96732
☎ (808) 667-6783 / 🖳 877-0503
www.bluephoto.com
Richard@bluephoto.com
Contact: Richard Blue

Robie Price Photography
1100 Ha‘ikū Rd.
Ha‘ikū, HI 96708
☎ (808) 575-2575
www.robiephoto.com
robie@maui.net
Contact: Robie Price

Sean Michael Hower Medias
900-A Kula Hwy.
Pukalani, HI 96768
☎ Toll Free (877) 572-1347
(808) 572-1347
www.howerphotography.com
mauiphotoR4U@aol.com
Contact: Sean M. Hower

Seventh Wave PhotoGraphics
P.O. Box 817
Pu‘unene, HI 96784
☎ Toll Free (877) 906-2843
🖳 (808) 244-1167
www.maui-angels.com
aloha@maui-angels.com
Contact: Bruce Wheeler

Steelman Studios
164 Kealaloa Ave., Makawao, HI 96768
☎ Toll Free (800) 581-6284
🖳 (808) 873-6318
www.mauibride.com
steelman@mauigateway.com
Contact: Ted Plume

Steve Strand Photography, Inc.
3500-A Malina Pl.
Kīhei, HI 96753
☎ Toll Free (866) 574-0332
🖳 (808) 879-6550
www.stevestrandphotography.com
strand@maui.net
Contact: Steve Strand

Stewart Pinsky Photography
P.O. Box 1084
Kīhei, HI 96753
☎ (808) 283-4032
www.mauiweddinggallery.com
stewpinsky@yahoo.com
Contact: Stewart Pinsky

Tad Craig Photography
120 Hana Hwy., #9, Suite 310
Pāʻia, HI 96779
☎ (808) 283-0617 / 579-9571
www.tadcraigphotography.com
Tad@tadcraigphotography.com
Contact: Tad Craig

Terry L. Rowe Enterprises
P.O. Box 1697
Kīhei, HI 96753
☎ (808) 874-5074
www.trowephoto.com
terry@trowephoto.com
Contact: Terry L. Rowe

Trade Winds Photography
P.O. Box 473
Puʻunene, HI 96784
☎ (808) 875-7587 / 🖨 875-1246
www.weddingphotographymaui.com
windfoto@mauigateway.com
Contact: Tracy Tegarden

Big Island:

Akamai Photography
74-5563 Kaiwi, Suite 139
Kailua-Kona, HI 96740-3139
☎ (808) 326-4182 / 🖨 331-1633
photos@aloha.net

Charla Photography
78-6740 Aliʻi Dr. #4
Kailua-Kona, HI 96740
☎ (808) 322-7727 / 🖨 322-7713
www.charlahawaii.com/
charla@kona.net

Hawaiian Images Photography & Video
75-1027 Henry St., #111A
Kailua-Kona, HI 96740
☎ (808) 329-7880 / 🖨 334-0331
www.hawaiianimages.net
himages@aloha.net

Kaleo Napua O Hawaiʻi
65-1269 Kawaihae Rd.
Kamuela, HI 96743
☎ (808) 885-4045

Linc Rydell Photography
248 Aina Lani Pl.
Kapaʻa, HI 96746
☎ (808) 822-2520

Mark Wilson Photography
HC 2 Box 4600
Kamuela, HI 96743
☎ (808) 885-7556

Pono Studio
☎ (808) 822-4671

Rainbow Photography
P.O. Box 1143
Kīlauea, HI 96754
☎ Toll Free (888) 828-0555
(808) 828-0555 / 🖨 828-0550
www.rainbowphoto.com
rainbo@aloha.net

Aloha Where?

♥ ♥

For those of you looking to add an aloha flair to your wedding, Hilo Hattie is a great place for aloha wear, wedding favors, centerpieces, and more.

They have white-on-white men's, women's, and kids' fashions for weddings and/or receptions. They provide volume discounts on wedding favors, fashions, and gift baskets for centerpieces among other things. They can also provide aloha shirt invitations and other stationery.

And if you're on the mainland and can't quite make it to Hawai'i for your wedding, they can help bring some Hawai'i to you. They arrange Hawaiian entertainment and Hawaiian food for the wedding receptions through their mainland stores. You can call them at (800) 233-8912 or check them out on the web at HiloHattie.com for store locations and other services.

Toby Hoogs Photography & Video
75-6009 Alii Dr., Unit# V-1
Kailua-Kona, HI 96740
☎ (808) 329-6591
photo@tobyhoogs.com
www.tobyhoogs.com

Video Productions Hawai'i
732 Ala Kula Pl., Hilo, HI 96720
☎ (808) 959-2244
kalehao@verizon.com

Kaua'i:

**Coconut Coast Weddings
and Photography**
1191 Kuhio Hwy. #20
Kapaa, HI 96746
☎ Toll Free (800) 585-5595
🖷 (808) 822-2201
www.kauaiwedding.com
coconut@kauaiwedding.com

Photo Spectrum
2987 Umi St., Līhu'e, HI 96766
☎ (808) 245-7667
www.photo-spectrum.com
info@photo-spectrum.com

Portraits of Hawai'i
2381 Kipuka St., Koloa, HI 96756
☎ Toll Free (800) 745-7414
🖷 (808) 742-7392
www.portraitsofhawaii.com
poh@aloha.net

Lāna'i:

Asher Productions
P.O. Box 631332
Lāna'i City, HI 96763
☎ (808) 564-2200
🖷 564-2200
www.Lanaiweddings.com
ash-inc.@aloha.net
Contact: Jeffery Asher

There is no doubt that our wedding day was the happiest day of our lives! In fact, I think we may have given Disney a run for his money in that our wedding may have been the happiest place on earth on October 8, 2005.

My husband pastors a church of 2000+ members and still growing. Everyone is family to us and in Hawai'i, we call that ohana. As soon as we announced our engagement, our wedding plans were no longer our own and with wonderful hearts and brilliant ideas, our ohana planned our wedding in 6 months!

Michael Lwin & Lynnette Kelly

♥♥

NEW HOPE LEEWARD MINISTRY CENTER IN WAIPAHU, HAWAI'I

The 6-month engagement was just enough time to plan for 2,500 invited wedding guests! Mike and I aren't much for doing things in typical fashion and likewise with our wedding. We love to create memories, and we realized that the planning process was as much a celebration as our wedding day. We involved as many people in the details, decision-making, preparation, and execution of our wedding day as we could. We had mini committees in charge of every area and detail including parking, food service, VIP hostesses for our families, guest check-in, a complete tech team to run lights, cameras, and sound, a decorations team, floral design, stage design, and so much more! Over 100 volunteers dedicated hours of labor and love to create extraordinary wedding day memories! We even had a team of very creative gals that custom designed, baked, and decorated our Mickey & Minnie wedding cake of twinkies! That's right—TWINKIES!

The day was perfect from the very beginning as the girls gathered at 5 a.m. for hair, make-up, and the dress-up routine! The butterflies jumped and fluttered in my stomach and became all the more active as I heard my bridal processional music start and the time came to walk down the aisle to meet my waiting and soon-to-be husband. "Deep breaths," I told myself as I continued to focus and just keep walking. As

(continued on next page)

I approached the stage, I could see Mike, his tear-filled eyes and the look of awe and wonder in his face! What a joy-filled and blessed moment!...I drank in the amazing realization that THIS was the day the Lord had made and this man the gift that the Lord had given me and entrusted me with for the rest of my life!

We escaped to our very own home for our wedding night get-away—an absolutely perfect finish to a perfect day! The week that followed was spent with family in multiple receptions hosted at our home along with lots of Hawaiian-style playtime as we hosted tours for our visiting family from the mainland and all over the world.

The honeymoon continued as several weeks later we headed to Maui for a relaxing do-nothing weekend of sunshine and naps by the pool and luxurious spa massages, facials, and pampering. Married life is a blast! In all the little details and routines of everyday life, we'll joyfully celebrate the blessing of marriage and continue the "honeymoon" forever!

The Reel Deal

More and more couples are opting to include a video as a part of their reception program. Today's technology allows videographers to edit in photos, special video clips and music along with video excerpts of wedding day prep, photos, the ceremony and more. A well-done wedding video can tell the couple's love story, capture their fondest memories and share some of their favorite moments. It's a good way to have guests get to know the bride and/or groom, it serves as a nice addition to your reception program and it's a great keepsake for years to come.

QTA's:

❑ How many cameras do they use during the ceremony?

❑ Do they use updated, high quality, professional video equipment? Do they have editing and dubbing equipment to edit on-site?

❑ What type of editing do they do? Is it post-edited or in-camera edited?

❑ How do they charge? Is it a flat fee? Hourly? If it's a flat fee, how many hours does that include?

❑ Are editing, titles and music included in the quoted price? Any other costs or additional expenses you should budget in?

❑ If you purchase a package deal, how many tapes does that include? How much are additional tapes?

❑ Can you buy the unedited master tape?

❑ Can you select the music you want?

❑ How far in advance do you need to provide them with photos and or video clips you want included in the video?

❑ Are they familiar with your wedding/reception site?

Tips:

☀ Ask for references from friends or family who have recently used a videographer for their wedding or special event.

☀ Ask to see some actual wedding videos shot by the person who will be doing your recording.

☀ Make sure the person who is shooting your wedding is the one you meet with and whose work you have seen.

☀ Get a written agreement of exactly what type of video coverage you want, number of cameras and videographers, type of editing, music, special graphics and effects, names of camera persons and editors, the date, time and location of the ceremony.

☀ Ask them to meet you at the actual ceremony site to go over any specifics you want.

Expect To Pay: Prices vary. You'll pay anywhere from a few hundred to several thousand dollars.

O'ahu:

Aloha Friday Productions A/V
94-434 Kilani St.
Mililani, HI 96789
☎ (808) 781-2684 / 672-7280
www.afphawaii.com
info@afphawaii.com

Crane Media
98-1277 Kaahumanu St.
Aiea, HI 96701
☎ (808) 383-7090 / 🖷 989-0581
www.crane-media.com
james@crane-media.com

Digital Expressions
☎ (808) 674-0020
www.digitalexpressionshawaii.com
info@digitalexpressionshawaii.com

Digital Vision Studios
737 Bishop St., Suite 1430
Honolulu, HI 96813
☎ (808) 224-4406

Digital You
☎ (808) 677-3311
www.digitalyouvideo.com
sales@digitalyouvideo.com

Ikaika Kimura
94-515 Uke'e St., #304
Waipahu, HI 96797
☎ (808) 678-3010 / 🖷 678-3050
ikaika@excitemediagroup.com

Images in Motion
98-200 Kamehameha Hwy., #401
Aiea, HI 96701
☎ (808) 486-7465 / 🖷 486-6941

Imagine Wurks Productions
☎ (808) 788-4361
www.imaginewurks.com
info@imaginewurks.com

Innervision Video Productions, Inc.
☎ (808) 735-5869 / 🖷 732-5507
www.innervision-video.com
info@innervision-video.com

Innovative Images by Warren
1952 Nehoa Pl., Honolulu, HI 96822
☎ (808) 536-4038 / 🖷 599-4574
iibw@hawaii.rr.com

Javier Videoworkz
☎ (808) 255-3715 / 277-7100
javiervideoworkz@hawaii.rr.com
Contact: Ringo and Arlene Javier

Magnus Hawaii
851-H Pohukaina St.
Honolulu, HI 96813
☎ (808) 589-1234 / 🖷 589-8989
www.lthi.com
info@magnushawaii.com

Marc Charles Michael
350 Ward Ave., #106
Honolulu, HI 96814
☎ (808) 392-9000
www.beunforgettable.com

Mike Danzeisen
1088 Bishop St., #3503
Honolulu, HI 96813
☎ (808) 536-3113
www.50photovideo.com
50@50photovideo.com

Noel Enterprises, Inc.
1221 Kapiʻolani Blvd., Suite 345
Honolulu, HI 96814
☎ (808) 596-2249
www.noel-inc.com
noelvideo@hawaii.rr.com
Contact: Royden

**North Shore Video Productions
& Photography**
47-679 Hui Alala St.
Kaneohe, HI 96744
☎ Toll Free (888) 800-0436
(808) 239-2461
www.northshorevideo.com
kamail002@hawaii.rr.com
By appointment only.

Picture Perfect Productions
680 Ala Moana Blvd. #407
Honolulu, HI 96813
☎ (808) 371-6112
www.magjipro.com / magjipro@aol.com

Studio West Hawaiʻi
856 Ilaniwai St., Studio 201
Honolulu, HI 96813
☎ (808) 593-9942 / 🖷 593-9943
www.studiowesthawaii.com

The Big Picture Productions
1188 Bishop St., #1506
Honolulu, HI 96813
☎ (808) 550-8208

Video Designs
1240 Ala Moana Blvd., #310
Honolulu, HI 96814
☎ (808) 593-8866
www.videodesigns.net
videodesigns@hawaii.rr.com
Contact: Douglas Kazama

Video by Jen Productions
94-266 Waipahu Depot St.
Waipahu, HI 96797
☎ (808) 678-1313 / 🖷 677-6937
www.videobyjen.com
videobyjen@hawaii.rr.com

Visionworks
1188 Bishop St., #2102
Honolulu, HI 96813
☎ (808) 943-0037

Maui:
About You Videos
3676 L. Honoapiʻilani, #D303
Lāhainā, HI 96761
☎ (808) 669-1044

Bright Light Productions
P.O. Box 84, Wailuku, HI 96793
☎ (877) 881-4888 / 283-2488
www.mauidigitalvideo.com
cindy@mauigateway.com
Contact: Cindy Paulos

DMI Video
P.O. Box 12617, Lāhainā, HI 96761
☎ (808) 250-3473 / 🖨 667-5354
dmivideo@hotmail.com
Contact: Dan or Jeane McMahon

Hawaiʻi Video Memories
230 Hana Hwy., Suite #11
Kahului, HI 96732
☎ Toll Free (888) 255-7080
🖨 (808) 871-8366
www.HawaiiVideoMemories.com
info@HawaiiVideoMemories.com
Contact: Todd Perkins

Millenium Films
P.O. Box 183, Kīhei, HI 96753
☎ (808) 874-0995 / 🖨 879-8822
www.millenium-films.com/wedding.htm
mike@millenium-films.com
Contact: Mike Knowles

Surefire Productions
1680 S. Alaniu Pl., Kīhei, HI 96753
☎ (808) 874-8230
www.surefireproductions.com
mike@surefireproductions.com
Contact: Michael DeJean

Big Island:
Aikane Video Productions
P.O. Box 468, Holualoa, HI 96725
☎ (808) 326-7223

Captured Memories Video Productions
Hilo, HI 96720
☎ (808) 938-9835
www.capturedmemorieshawaii.com
capturedmemories@hawaii.rr.com

Hawaiʻi Wedding Videography & Photo
732 Ala Kula Pl., Hilo, HI 96720
☎ (808) 959-2244
kalehao@verizon.com

Toby Hoogs Photography & Video
75-6009 Alii Dr., Unit# V-1
Kailua-Kona, HI 96745
☎ (808) 329-6591 / 🖨 329-7293
photo@tobyhoogs.com
www.tobyhoogs.com

Kauaʻi:
Hawaiian Creative Video
☎ (808) 822-5784

I-Do Video Productions
4934 Alani Pl., Kapaʻa, HI 96746
☎ (808) 823-6130
idovideo@aloha.net

Profile Productions
P.O. Box 223038, Princeville, HI 96722
☎ Toll Free (866) 481-8825
🖨 (808) 826-0038
www.kauaiwedddingvideos.com
lasotas@hawaiian.net
Contact: Larry and Elaine LaSota

Video Lynx
276 Aina Pua Pl., Kapaa, HI 96746
☎ (808) 821-1367 / 🖨 821-1368
www.videolynxkauai.com
sales@videolynxkauai.com

SPECIALTY PRODUCTS AND SERVICES:

Isn't That Special!?

Hawai'i, and its melting pot of traditions and cultures, can make for an eclectic mix of products and services that you may not find in traditional "mainland" weddings. See our chapter on ethnic weddings and traditions on pages 23-30 for more. We will list the people, places and things that can assist you in everything from handmade crafts and origami cranes to personalized gifts.

We would like to think that we have listed absolutely every one you would ever need to contact to plan your wedding in Hawai'i, but there may be someone or something we've overlooked. If you find additional resources you think we should mention in the next printing of this book, please feel free to forward them to us at keri@wedding-planners.net. We encourage you to use all the resources you can find. Scour the internet and bookstores for books and magazines. There are literally hundreds of thousands of wedding resources at your fingertips—especially on-line.

There is a quaint little wedding shop in Mānoa Marketplace on O'ahu called The Wedding Cafe. It's a great place to peruse through hundreds of wedding books and magazines. They have lots of local vendors who advertise their services in and around the shop. You can sign up for free workshops (like how to make specific wedding favors or photo and makeup tips) or hold your wedding shower there. It's a great place to meet with friends and mull over your many wedding decisions in a comfortable, contemporary shop. They even serve great food at reasonable prices. (See address and contact on page 204.)

Other great resources for planning your wedding in Hawai'i are the bridal expos and Hawai'i bridal magazines. The only drawback with these are that you are only receiving information from people who pay to participate in the expos or advertise in the magazines, so you do not get a complete listing of all the vendors and services available. But you're getting a good sampling and it's a great place to start.

Internet:

Bridesclub.com
www.bridesclub.com
Website with many wedding links

Hawaii Wedding Source.com
www.hawaiianweddingsource.com/isles.htm
Resource site for all islands.

Live Internet Weddings.com
☎ Toll Free (888) 859-5455
(808) 946-2290
www.Liveinternetweddings.com
Liveinternetweddings@hawaii.rr.com

the knot
www.theknot.com
Vast resources with many links for Hawai'i and the mainland.

Pacific Rim Weddings Magazine
☎ (808) 242-6835 ex 0
www.pacificweddings.com

The Wedding Host
www.theweddinghost.com
questions@theweddinghost.com
Your wedding details on the web for all your friends to enjoy.

O'ahu:

Aloha Nannies
1400 Kapiolani Blvd., C4-261
Honolulu, HI 96814
☎ (808) 394-8438
www.alohanannies.com
alohanannies@yahoo.com
On-site childcare for your wedding and special events.

Auntie Nalani's Cookies
P.O. Box 223, Honolulu, HI 96810
☎ (877) 851-8453 / (808) 841-4615
🖷 (808) 841-4746
www.auntienalaniscookies.com
meltinyourmouthcookies@yahoo.com
A little taste of Hawai'i for your guests. Hand woven lauhala baskets with delicious cookies.

Butterfly Kisses
95-211 Ho'oni Pl., Mililani, HI 96789
☎ (808) 671-2617 / 227-2617
www.butterflykisseshawaii.com
sheri@butterflykisseshawaii.com
Butterfly release, centerpieces, favors, etc.

Chamber of Commerce of Hawai'i
1132 Bishop St., #402
Honolulu, HI 96813
☎ (808) 545-4300 / 🖷 545-4369
www.cochawaii.com / info@cochawaii.org
Are you one of the lucky people who will visit the islands for your dream wedding? The Chamber of Commerce of Hawai'i can help you find the information you need.

Chocolate Sushi
Enchanted Lake Shopping Center
1020 Keolu Dr., #D-4
Kailua, HI 96734
☎ (808) 263-7878
Specializing in chocolate favors.

Classic Cranes
91-335 Hoowalea Pl.
Ewa Beach, HI 96709
☎ (808) 455-4455
www.origami-tsuru.com
information@origami-tsuru.com
Contact: Cathy Lancaster

Creations By You
1801 Liliha St., Honolulu, HI 96817
☎ (808) 536-5255 / 🖷 524-0078
www.cbyweddings.com
Beads, specialty papers, wedding & craft supplies

Creative Native Crafts
259B Mokauea St., Honolulu, HI 96819
☎ (808) 842-9100/ 🖷 843-8686
www.creativenativecrafts.com
info@creativenativecrafts.com
Hawaiian themed stationery, crafts and supplies.

Deco Clay Craft Academy
764 Kapahulu Ave., Honolulu, HI 96816
☎ (808) 735-7800
www.decoclay.com
*A unique craft experience offering classes,
supplies and custom-created designs.*

Designs by Kimiko
P.O. Box 22045, Honolulu, HI 96823
☎ (808) 542-5428
www.designsbykimiko.com
satoc007@hawaii.rr.com
*Finely handcrafted tiaras, combs, jewelry and
accessories for every occasion.*

Diamond Head Winery
330 Sand Island Access Rd., #106
Honolulu, HI 96819
☎ Toll Free (877) 841-9463
(808) 841 9463 / 🖷 847-3144
www.diamondheadwinery.com
diamondheadwnry@comtelweb.com
*Make your own wine and labels
for your special occasion.*

Elvira Chocolat
826 Queen St., #200
Honolulu, HI 96813
☎ (808) 591-8826
chocolat_email@yahoo.com
Hawaiian macadamia nut chocolate candies.

Everything Nice
P.O. Box 147, Kailua, HI 96734
☎ (808) 227-3702
Contact: Melissa Makuakane
www.everything-nice.net
*Custom handmade crystal jewelry for brides,
bridesmaids, and flower girls!*

Forever Creations
2766 S. King St., Apt. #6, Honolulu, HI 96826
☎ (808) 330-1711

Gee Yung Lion Dance
1024 Smith St., Honolulu, HI 96817
☎ (808) 599-4690

Haliʻa Aloha
P.O. Box 4782, Kāneʻohe, HI 96744
☎ (808) 239-6145
www.hawaiialohaspirit.com
info@hawaiialohaspirit.com
*Authentic Hawaiian wedding ceremonies
and celebrations.*

Hawaiian Candle Supplies Co.
720 Moowaa St., #J, Honolulu, HI 96817
☎ (808) 848-2402 / 🖷 848-2403

Hawaiian Island Prints
47-347 Lulani St., Kāneʻohe, HI 96744
☎ (808) 239-2003
www.HawaiianIslandPrints.com
art-shayna@hawaii.rr.com
Certificates in both Hawaiian and English.

Honolulu Horse & Carriage
☎ (808) 924-7895 / 🖷 696-4199
www.honolulucarriage.com/Weddings.htm
hnlhorse@aol.com
*"A horse-drawn carriage is not expensive—
It's Priceless."*

It's About Time
☎ (808) 591-2004
*Specializing in 1001 origami cranes. By
appointment only.*

Keepsakes Hawaii
812-A Kawaiahao St., Honolulu, HI 96813
☎ (808) 951-5337 / 596-2245
www.keepsakeshawaii.com
keepsake@pixi.com
Preservation of wedding bouquets and other precious flowers. Located in the heart of Honolulu, they service weddings on all of the islands.

Rainbow Pigeons
1503 Nanakai St., Pearl City, HI 96782
☎ (808) 455-5990
Release colorful homing pigeons at your wedding.

Something Etched
☎ (808) 265-9629
etchedinglass@verizon.net
Hawai'i's largest manufacturer of etched glassware.

Sugar Rush by Frances
P.O. Box 62166, Honolulu, HI 96822
☎ (808) 265-9629 / 🖷 (808) 265-9629
www.sugarrush-byfrances.com
fpons4948@aol.com
Sugar Rush by Frances is the premier provider of upscale miniature pastries and desserts on O'ahu. Elegant in appearance but packed with delicious homemade goodness, Sugar Rush pastries are "scratch-baked" in small batches in Honolulu by chef and owner Frances Pons. Please call for an appointment.

Sumoca Arts
P.O. Box 104, Honolulu, HI 96810
☎ (808) 226-2882
www.sumocaarts.com
sumoca.arts@verizon.net
Custom 1001 origami cranes.

sunshine, smiles, & flowers
☎ (808) 258-1166
www.sunshinesmilesandflowers.com
support@sunshinesmilesandflowers.com
Affordable, quality, custom-beaded jewelry ideas for bridal and everyday wear.

Sweet Aloha Chocolates
292C Mokauea St., Honolulu, HI 96819
☎ Toll Free (866) 246-2658
(808) 841-0991
www.chocolatehawaii.com
sales@chocolatehawaii.com
Custom & personalized favors, gifts, cookies, etc.

Tsurus by Akemi
☎ (808) 947-1579
Origami cranes.

Wedding Cafe, The
2752 Woodlawn Dr., #5-209
Honolulu, HI 96822
☎ (808) 988-1005
www.theweddingcafe.net
love@theweddingcafe.net
Great place to meet with coordinator, have bridal showers and get info on wedding.

White Doves of Ko'olau
45-561 Ko'olau View Dr.
Kāne'ohe, HI 96744
☎ (808) 247-1599
www.whitedovesofkoolau.com
hawaiidoves@aol.com
Ceremonial dove release.

Maui:

Aloha Ice Sculpting Company
794 Kauhikoa Rd., Ha'ikū, HI 96708
☎ (808) 575-9493
www.alohaicesculptingcompany.com
icedesigns@hawaii.rr.com

Doves of Love—White Dove Releases
☎ (808) 870-5450 / 🖷 669-1559
crossk002@hawaii.rr.com
Contact: Kitty & Mark Schmier

Marry Me Hawaii.com
www.marrymehawaii.com
info@marrymehawaii.com

Maui Dove Release
100 Luluka Pl.
Kīhei, HI 96753
☎ Toll Free (866) 537-8888
🖷 (808) 874-1832
www.mauiweddingcakes.com/doves.htm
info@mauiweddingcakes.com
Contact: Casey and Cheryl Logsdon

Maui Doves—White Doves Release
P.O. 1078, Makawao, HI 96768
☎ (808) 573-1717 / 🖷 572-4126
www.mauidoves.com/home.html
MauiDove@verizon.net

Maui Wedding Association
P.O. Box 684, Kīhei, HI 96753
☎ (808) 573-3337
www.mauiweddingassociation.com

Merry Monarch Butterfly Ranch
☎ (808) 878-3553

Big Island:

Attco
73-5580J Maiau St.
Kailua-Kona, HI 96740
☎ (808) 326-2332
www.attcoinc.com
Props and backdrops to create themes like garden, nautical, Hollywood, oriental, Polynesian, paniolo, pirates, etc.

Baskets by Vinel
P.O. Box 225, Hakalau, HI 96710
☎ (808) 963-5466
avsugino@excite.com

Celebrations and Occasions, Inc.
74-5563 Kaiwi St. #134
Kailua-Kona, HI 96740
☎ (808) 329-4774 / (808) 326-3255
www.celebrationsandoccasions.com
Hundreds of specialty items: Hawaiian wedding certificates, favor boxes, cake toppers, serving and glassware.

Chamber of Commerce
75-5737 Kuakini Hwy., #207
Kailua-Kona, HI 96740
☎ (808) 329-1758 / 🖷 329-8564
www.hawaiiislandchamber.org
info@kona-kohala.com

Kona Wine Market
75-5626 Kuakini Hwy.
Kailua-Kona, HI 96740
☎ Toll Free (800) 613-3983
(808) 329-9400 / 🖷 329-1522
konawinemarket.com

Maile Charters
P.O. Box 44335, Kamuela, HI 96743
☎ Toll Free (800) 726-7245
(808) 326-5174 / 🖷 882-1820
www.adventuresailing.com
sailing@adventuresailing.com
Offers romantic weddings and honeymoons at sea.

Kaua'i:

Butterflies Over Hawai'i
505 Pu'u'ōpae Rd., Kapa'a, HI 96746
☎ (808) 332-8006
www.butterfliesoverhawaii.com
art@butterfliesoverhawaii.com

Kaua'i Wedding Professional Assoc.
P.O. Box 761
Kapa'a, HI 96746
www.Kauaiwedpro.com
A listing of "all things wedding on Kaua'i."

Sri Maiava Rusden

When we saw Shriners Waimānalo, we knew this was the place we wanted to get married. The simplicity and natural Hawaiian setting were two elements that we wanted in our wedding.

Don Ynigues & Lisa Miyashiro

♥♥

SHRINERS ON WAIMĀNALO BEACH

The week of our wedding was rainy and gloomy. Waimānalo was flooding and cars could barely get through Waimānalo town. The rehearsal practice was a total disaster! My future husband, being the nice guy he is, promised his groomsman that he would pick him up before the rehearsal, only allowing himself an hour to get to Waikīkī from Pearl City. As a result, he was 2 hours late to the practice. I felt like I was right in the middle of a "Sex and the City" episode where Charlotte was getting married and everything was going wrong. But, with God's blessings, everything worked out for the best.

The day of our wedding was magnificent! There were a few raindrops in the horizon, but the weather held to a nice sunny day. My wedding party and I got ready at the Outrigger on the Beach as the "boys" and the set-up crew got the wedding site ready. When I arrived at Shriners, I was so taken aback by how beautiful the site was! The reception area was covered with red roses with personal sayings scattered on all the tables. The chandelier that my wedding decorator had created for the head table was exquisite with glass red beads and red roses dangling from the ceiling. The red velvet wedding cake that my close friend had made was beautiful! It was truly everything I imagined my wedding to be!

As I started to walk down the aisle, I told my father…"I'm losing it!" I lost it even before I turned the corner. I was so overcome with emotions I couldn't help but cry As Na Leo Pilimehana's song, "The Rest of Your Life" played, I walked closer to my future and felt an overwhelming sense of warmth and love.

The ceremony went beautifully despite some looming black clouds. We had to laugh when in the middle of the ceremony, the drops got heavier and my husband's son (also his best man) was given an umbrella to hold for us so we wouldn't get wet. Instead of holding it for us, he held the umbrella over his head. Our groomsman had to give him a friendly nudge and "mouthed" quietly, "It's for them." Right after we said our vows and walked down the aisle…the skies opened and there was a downpour of rain. After the rain stopped, we took our pictures on the beach where it was totally deserted.

Our wedding turned out to be everything we wanted…food, decorations, family, friends. I remember a good friend telling me, "Savor this moment…it passes fast." I will forever savor the moments because it was truly a magical day!

Suggested Wedding Songs

Popular Hawaiian Songs or Songs by Local Musicians:

- ❏ *What Are You Doing for the Rest of Your Life* (Na Leo Pilimehana)
- ❏ *Over the Rainbow* (Bruddah Iz)
- ❏ *Lei Pikake* (Hapa)
- ❏ *For Your Love* (Leahi)
- ❏ *Right Before My Eyes* (Na Leo Pilimehana)
- ❏ *The Road that Never Ends* (Kealii Reichel)
- ❏ *In This Life* (Bruddah Iz)

Other Hawaiian Songs Sung by Various Local Artists:

- ❏ *Lei Aloha*
- ❏ *Lei Makamae*
- ❏ *Paoakalani*
- ❏ *Moon of Manakoora*
- ❏ *Beyond the Rainbow/Waipio*
- ❏ *Pua Maeole*
- ❏ *Lovely Hula Hands*
- ❏ *Hawaiian Wedding Song*
- ❏ *Beautiful Kahana*
- ❏ *Makalapua*
- ❏ *I'll Remember You*
- ❏ *Mapuana*

Traditional Selections for Prelude Music (Non-Hawaiian):

- ❏ *Canon in D* (Pachelbel)
- ❏ *Jesu, Joy of Man's Desiring* (Bach)
- ❏ *Only Time* (Enya)
- ❏ *I Will Be Here* (Steven Curtis Chapman)

Trumpet Voluntary:

- ❏ *Ave Maria* (Schubert)
- ❏ *"Air On the G String"* from Orchestral Suite No. 3 (Bach)
- ❏ *"Air"* from Water Music (Handel)
- ❏ *Forever in Love* (Kenny G)
- ❏ *My Heart Will Go On* (Celine Dion– Titanic Soundtrack)
- ❏ *The Four Seasons* (Vivaldi)
- ❏ *Clair de Lune* (Debussy)
- ❏ *Joyful, Joyful, We Adore Thee* (Organ)
- ❏ *"Waltz"* from Sleeping Beauty, Act 1 (Tchaikovsky)

Interlude:

- ❏ *Ave Maria* (Schubert)
- ❏ *Ave Maria* (Gounod)
- ❏ *Cavalleria Rusticana* (Intermezzo Mascagni)
- ❏ *"Duettino"* from Lakme (Delibes)
- ❏ *Greensleeves* (Barber's Adagio)
- ❏ *Hymn - Finlandia* (Grieg)
- ❏ *Jesu, Joy of Man's Desiring* (J.S. Bach)
- ❏ *Joyful, Joyful We Adore Thee* (Ode to Joy) (Beethoven)
- ❏ *I'll Walk with God* (Handel)
- ❏ *London Trio #3 - Adante* (Haydn)
- ❏ *Lord's Prayer* (Handel)
- ❏ *O God of Life* (Panus Angelicus Franck)
- ❏ *O mio babbino caro* (Gianna Schicchi) (Puccini)
- ❏ *"Quando Men' Vo"* (Musetta's Waltz from La Boheme) (Puccini)
- ❏ *Romanza* (Beethoven)
- ❏ *Serse: Largo* (Handel)
- ❏ *Sheep May Safely Graze* (J.S. Bach)

Suggested Wedding Songs (cont.)

Unity Candle:

- *From This Moment* (Shania Twain & Bryan White)
- *Grow Old With Me* (Mary Chapin Carpenter)
- *The Wedding Song* (Kenny G)
- *One Hand, One Heart* (West Side Story)
- *Keeper of the Stars* (Tracy Byrd)
- *Ave Maria* (Schubert)
- *Flesh of My Flesh* (Leon Patillo)
- *Me and You* (Kenny Chesney)
- *I Believe In You and Me* (Whitney Houston)
- *It's Your Love* (Tim McGraw & Faith Hill)
- *When I Said I Do* (Clint Black & Lisa Hartman-Black)
- *Canon in D* (Pachelbel)
- *Here and Now* (Luther Vandross)
- *Household of Faith* (Steve & Anne Paynter)
- *Because You Loved Me* (Celine Dion)
- *Give Me Forever, I Do* (John Tesh)
- *When You Say Nothing at All* (Allison Kraus)
- *All My Life* (K-Ci and Jo-Jo)
- *This I Promise You* (NSync)
- *You Light Up My Life* (Leann Rimes)
- *Always* (Atlantic Starr)
- *I Do* (Paul Brandt)
- *Wherever You Go* (David Haas)
- *Circle of Life* (Elton John's Theme–Lion King Soundtrack)
- *If I Should Fall Behind* (Bruce Springsteen)
- *Faithful Friend* (Marsha Stevens & Debbie Hardy)
- *I'll Always Be Right There* (Bryan Adams)
- *Love of my Life* (Sammy Kershaw)
- *Once in a Lifetime Love* (Alan Jackson)
- *Amazing Grace* (Lari White)
- *True Companion* (Marc Cohn)

Father/Daughter Dance:

- *Butterfly Kisses* (Bob Carlisle)
- *Father's Eyes* (Amy Grant)
- *Daddy's Little Girl* (Mills Brothers)
- *Through the Years* (Kenny Rogers)
- *Unforgettable* (Nat King Cole/Natalie Cole)
- *Have I Told You Lately* (Rod Stewart/ Van Morrison)
- *Wonderful Tonight* (Eric Clapton)
- *Unchained Melody* (Righteous Brothers)
- *What a Wonderful World* (Louis Armstrong)
- *You Are So Beautiful* (Joe Cocker)
- *Stardust* (Various)

Mother/Son Dance:

- *A Song for My Son* (Mikki Viereck)
- *Through the Years* (Kenny Rogers)
- *Unforgettable* (Nat King Cole/Natalie Cole)
- *Have I Told You Lately* (Rod Stewart/ Van Morrison)
- *Wonderful Tonight* (Eric Clapton)
- *What a Wonderful World* (Louis Armstrong)
- *You Are So Beautiful* (Joe Cocker)
- *A Song For Mama* (Boyz II Men)
- *Wind Beneath My Wings* (Bette Midler – Beaches Soundtrack)
- *Because You Loved Me* (Celine Dion)
- *Sunise, Sunset* (Fiddler on the Roof)
- *In My Life* (The Beatles)
- *Nothing but Love* (The Wilkinsons)
- *Greatest Love of All* (Whitney Houston)
- *Hero* (Mariah Carey)
- *You're the Inspiration* (Chicago)

Faster Selections for (Entry, Departure, etc.):

- *All My Friends Are Getting Married* (Skyhooks)
- *Boom Boom* (Paul Lekakis)
- *Bridge to Your Heart* (Wax)

- *I Knew The Bride When She Used to Rock & Roll* (Nick Lowe)
- *Let's Stick Together* (Brian Ferry)
- *Never Gonna Give You Up* (Rick Astley)
- *Power of Love* (Hewy Lewis)
- *Simply the Best* (Tina Turner)
- *If I Could Turn Back Time* (Cher)
- *Two Strong Hearts* (John Farnham)

First Dance, Cutting Cake, Entry and Leaving:

- *All of You* (Diana Ross & Julio Ingelesius)
- *All I Ask of You* (Cliff Richard & Sarah Brightman)
- *All My Life* (Linda Ronstadt & Aaron Neville)
- *And I Love You So* (Perry Como)
- *Because I Love You* (Stevie B)
- *Best of My Love* (Eagles)
- *Blue Eyes* (Elton John)
- *Can You Feel the Love Tonight* (Elton John)
- *Can't Help Falling in Love* (Elvis Presley)
- *Can't Fight This Feeling* (REO Speedwagon)
- *Cherish* (Kool & the Gang or Madonna)
- *Could I Have This Dance* (Anne Murray)
- *Crazy for You* (Madonna)
- *Do That to Me One More Time* (Captain & Tennile)
- *Don't Know Much* (Linda Ronstadt & Aaron Neville)
- *Endless Love* (Diana Ross & Lionel Richie)
- *Endless Love* (Mariah Carey & Luther Vandross)
- *Endless Summer Nights* (Richard Marx)
- *Every Woman in the World* (Air Supply)
- *Friends and Lovers* (Gloria Loring)
- *Greatest Love of All* (Whitney Houston or George Benson)
- *Groovy Kind of Love* (Phil Collins)
- *Hawaiian Wedding Song* (Elvis Presley)
- *I Swear* (All 4 One)
- *I Wanna Wake Up with You* (Boris Gardiner)
- *Just the Way You Are* (Billy Joel)
- *Lady in Red* (Chris de Burg)
- *Looking Through the Eyes of Love* (Melissa Manchester)
- *Move Closer* (Phillis Nelson)
- *Nothing's Gonna Stop Us Now* (Starship)
- *Now and Forever* (Anne Murray or Richard Marx)
- *Power of Love* (Celine Dion or Jennifer Rush)
- *Right Here Waiting* (Richard Marx)
- *Stuck on You* (Lionel Richie)
- *Suddenly* (Billy Ocean or Olivia Newton John)
- *Stand By Me* (Ben E King)
- *Take My Breath Away* (Berlin)
- *That's What Friends Are For* (Dionne Warwick)
- *Tonight I Celebrate My Love for You* (Peabo Bryson & Roberta Flack)
- *Touch of Paradise* (John Farnham)
- *Unforgettable* (Nat King Cole/Natalie Cole)
- *Unchained Melody* (Righteous Brothers)
- *Up Where We Belong* (Joe Cocker & Jennifer Warnes)
- *We've Got Tonight* (Kenny Rogers & Sheena Easton)
- *We've Only Just Begun* (Carpenters)
- *Welcome to My World* (Elvis Presley or Jim Reeves)
- *What a Wonderful World* (Louis Armstrong)
- *When a Man Loves a Woman* (Michael Bolton or Percy Sledge)
- *Wind Beneath My Wings* (Bette Midler)
- *When I Fall In Love* (Rick Astley or Celine Dion)
- *Woman* (John Lennon)
- *Wonderful Tonight* (Eric Clapton)
- *You Are So Beautiful* (Joe Cocker)
- *You Send Me* (Michael Bolton or Sam Cooke)

This was my second marriage and the first for my husband. He wanted to keep it simple and I, of course, wanted something special to remember. Since we knew we would be paying for the wedding ourselves we figured out about how many people we wanted to invite and set our budget. We wanted a beautiful wedding but we had to stick to a budget. I spoke with my bridesmaid and maid of honor for advice and they suggested having our wedding reception at sea. I thought that this was a wonderfully unique idea. I am a local girl so having my wedding in Hawai'i was very important. My husband is originally from Minnesota, so I knew there would be many friends and family traveling to Hawai'i from the mainland. What a great idea to have our wedding ceremony on land and then to set sail at sunset for dinner and dancing at our wedding reception. As I gathered more information about Atlantis Cruises' *Navatek I* Dinner Cruise, I found that my night could be very affordable and attainable.

Julia Canionero & Rann Campbell

♥♥

HAWAII MARITIME MUSEUM & ATLANTIS CRUISES' NAVATEK

We chose to have the ceremony at the Maritime Museum located near the Pier 6, where the *Navatek I* docks. Hawai'i in August certainly lived up to its expectations because the day couldn't have been more picturesque. My son walked me down the aisle as our family and friends were all seated around us. The *Navatek I's* captain performed our simple but beautiful ceremony and then we all made our way to the boat.

We boarded and set sail right before the sun set. I had planned a special surprise for my husband; I wanted to perform the hula for him to the Hawaiian Wedding Song. He had never really seen me dance the hula and I wanted to share this local tradition with him and his family. After enjoying our meal, a DJ provided music for dancing which I know that everyone enjoyed.

Right as the sun was setting the crew made an announcement and we all went out on the deck. Watching the sunset over the ocean was unbelievably romantic. When the sun had almost completely gone, someone in our party noticed that three dolphins were following the boat. They swam, jumped, and played with the boat all the way to the pier. I know that if we had chosen any other locale we wouldn't have had these wonderful escorts!

One of the best features of having the reception on the boat was that almost everything was already taken care of. The food was catered and we didn't have to clean up at all. The boat's safety was explained thoroughly to us by the crew members so everyone felt comfortable and at ease. The staff was very friendly and accommodating and really helped make our wedding memorable and special. I am very glad that we chose to have our wedding reception at sea on the *Navatek I*.

WORKSHEETS

Bridal Gown

Bridal Shop:

Contact Person: Phone: Fax:

Consultation (Date/Time):   Wedding Day Appointment (Date/Time):

Website: E-mail Address:

Designer/Manufacturer: Style:

Color/Fabric: Train Length:

Size: Cost:

Alterations Contact: Phone: Fax:

Alterations Specifications:

Fitting Dates:

First Fitting (Date/Time):   Second Fitting (Date/Time):

Final Fitting (Date/Time):   Pick Up (Date/Time):

Cost:

Headpiece/Veil

Style: Color: Length:

Cost:

(continued on next page)

Bridesmaids' Attire

Company:

Contact Person: Phone: Fax:

Address:

Website: E-mail Address:

Designer/Manufacturer: Style:

Color/Fabric: Size: Cost:

Accessories:

Alterations Contact: Phone: Fax:

Alterations Specifications:

Fitting Dates:

First Fitting (Date/Time):   Second Fitting (Date/Time):

Final Fitting (Date/Time):   Pick Up (Date/Time):

Cost:

Flower Girl's Dress

Designer/Manufacturer: Style:

Color/Fabric: Size: Cost:

Accessories:

Groom's Formal Wear

Formal Wear Shop:

Contact Person: Phone: Fax:

Local Address:

Website: E-mail Address:

Designer/Manufacturer: Style:

Color/Fabric: Accessories:

Measurements:

Coat: Sleeve: Neck: Waist: Inseam:

Shoes:

Size: Style: Color: Cost:

Alterations Specifications:

Fitting: Final Fitting/Pick-Up Date/Time:

Groomsmen's/Ushers'/Fathers' Formal Wear

Formal Wear Shop:

Contact Person: Phone: Fax:

Local Address:

Website: E-mail Address:

Designer/Manufacturer: Style:

Color/Fabric: Accessories:

Measurements:

Coat: Sleeve: Neck: Waist: Inseam:

(continued on next page)

Shoes:

Size: Style: Color: Cost:

Alterations Specifications:

Fitting: Final Fitting/Pick-Up Date/Time:

Ringbearer's Formal Wear

Formal Wear Shop:

Contact Person: Phone: Fax:

Local Address:

Website: E-mail Address:

Designer/Manufacturer: Style:

Color/Fabric: Accessories:

Measurements:

Coat: Sleeve: Neck: Waist: Inseam:

Shoes:

Size: Style: Color: Cost:

Alterations Specifications:

Fitting: Final Fitting/Pick-Up Date/Time:

Total

Total Number of Formal Attire Rentals: Total Cost:

Less Deposit Amount: $ Paid On (Date):

Balance Due: $ Date:

Hair

Salon/Company:

Appointment With: Phone: Fax:

Consultation Date/Time: Wedding Day Appointment Date/Time:

Address:

Website: E-mail Address:

Deposit Amount: Total Cost of Services Provided:

Makeup

Salon/Company: Appointment With:

Consultation Date/Time: Wedding Day Appointment Date/Time:

Contact Person: Phone: Fax:

Address:

Website: E-mail Address:

Deposit Amount: Total Cost of Services Provided:

(continued on next page)

Nails

Salon/Company: Appointment With:

Appointment Date/Time:

Contact Person: Phone: Fax:

Address:

Website: E-mail Address:

Desired Services:

Total Cost of Services Provided:

Spa

Salon/Company: Appointment With:

Appointment Date/Time:

Contact Person: Phone: Fax:

Address:

Website: E-mail Address:

Desired Services:

Cost of Services Provided:

Caterer

Contact Person: Phone: Fax:

Address:

Website: E-mail Address:

Type of Service Needed:

❑ Buffet   ❑ Sit-Down   ❑ Pūpū ❑ Cake & Punch

❑ Other:

❑ Specialty Foods/Service:

Menu Selection:

(continued on next page)

Caterers (cont.)

Services

Kitchen Facilities: _______________________________ Cost: _______________

Food Prep & Equipment: _______________________________ Cost: _______________

Servers Provided: _______________________________ Cost: _______________

Gratuity Included: _______________________________ Cost: _______________

Beverage Services: _______________________________ Cost: _______________

Setup: _______________________________ Cost: _______________

Clean-up: _______________________________ Cost: _______________

Cake: _______________________________ Cost: _______________

Cake Knife Set & Supplies: _______________________________ Cost: _______________

Linens/Napkins: _______________________________ Cost: _______________

Ice Carvings: _______________________________ Cost: _______________

Other: _______________________________ Cost: _______________

Other: _______________________________ Cost: _______________

Total Cost: _______________

Type of Service Needed:

Per Person: _______________ Estimated Guests: _______________ Total Cost: _______________

Menu Selection Due Date: _______________ Final Head Count Due Date: _______________

Deposit Due Date: _______________ Deposit Amount: _______________

Balance: $ _______________ Balance Due Date: _______________

Reception Site:

Contact Person: Phone: Fax:

Address:

Website: E-mail Address:

Name of Room/Area:

Room/Area Capacity: Date Confirmed:

Reception Start Time: End Time:

Head Count By: Final Head Count:

Cocktails/Pūpū Time: Meal Time:

Color of Linens: Color of Napkins:

Special Instructions:

Total Cost:

Less Deposit: $ Date of Deposit:

Balance: $ Due Date of Balance:

(continued on next page)

Service Includes: (Servers, Bartenders, Valet, Parking, Setup, Clean-up, Meal, etc.)

Equipment/Supplies Included in Cost: (Tables, Chairs, Linens, Decorations, etc.)

Other Information:

Consultants/Wedding Planners

Consultant Company:

Contact Person: Phone: Fax:

Address:

Website: E-mail Address:

Type of Service Needed:

- ❏ Reception location
- ❏ Reception coordination
- ❏ Ceremony location
- ❏ Ceremony coordination
- ❏ Bridal gown rentals and sales
- ❏ Custom sewing and alterations
- ❏ Bridesmaid dresses
- ❏ Formal wear
- ❏ Caterer
- ❏ Beverage service

- ❏ Photographer
- ❏ Videographer
- ❏ Beauty
- ❏ Flowers
- ❏ Cake/Baker
- ❏ Party Equipment Rental
- ❏ Favors/Decorations
- ❏ Invitations/Stationery
- ❏ Bridal Registry
- ❏ Entertainment/Music

- ❏ Transportation
- ❏ Honeymoon
- ❏ Jewelry
- ❏ Attendant Gifts
- ❏ Rehearsal
- ❏ Rehearsal Dinner
- ❏ Other ______
- ❏ Other ______
- ❏ Other ______
- ❏ Other ______

Terms of Payment (Select One):

❏ Flat Fee Based on Services Agreed Upon:

❏ Hourly:

❏ Percentage (Percentage of Budget):

Deposit Due Date: Deposit Amount: $

$ Balance Due on:

(Be sure to have your terms of agreement contract with your wedding planner attached to this worksheet. It should have a detailed account of all services provided and costs.)

Equipment & Party Rentals

Company:

Contact Person: Phone: Fax:

Local Address:

Website: E-mail Address:

Delivery:

Ceremony Location: Date: Time:

Reception Location: Date: Time:

Type of Service Needed:

WEDDING ITEMS	QUANTITY	COST	WEDDING ITEMS	QUANTITY	COST
Aisle Runner:		$	Hurricane Lamps:		$
Arches:		$	Kneeling Benches:		$
Buffet Tables:		$	Pillars:		$
Cake Table:		$	Round Tables:		$
Candelabra:		$	Stations:		$
Chairs:		$	Table Mirrors:		$
Chair Covers:		$	Tents/Canopies:		$
Dance Floor:		$	Other:		$
Flower Stands:		$	Other:		$
Gazebos:		$	Other:		$
			Subtotal:		**$**

(continued on next page)

BEVERAGE ITEM RENTALS	QUANTITY	COST
Bar:		$
Beer Taps & Kegs:		$
Beverage Fountains:		$
Champagne Buckets:		$
Coffee Makers:		$
Coolers:		$
Other:		$
Subtotal:		**$**

LINENS

	QUANTITY	COST
Napkins:		$
Color		
Buffet Table Covers:		$
Color		
Cake Table Covers:		$
Color		
Subtotal:		**$**

SERVICEWARE/FLATWARE

	QUANTITY	COST
Cake Knife Set:		$
Coffee & Tea Service:		$
Punchbowl:		$

SERVICEWARE/ FLATWARE (CONT.)	QUANTITY	COST
Punchbowl Glasses:		$
Serving Utensils:		$
Trays:		$
China:		$
Flatware:		$
Glassware		$
Subtotal:		**$**

MISC. RENTALS

	QUANTITY	COST
Balloons & Helium Tank:		$
Lavaliere:		$
Podium:		$
Sound System:		$
Standing Mic:		$
Lighting:		$
Other:		$
Other:		$
Subtotal:		**$**

	QUANTITY	COST
Subtotal (All):		**$**
Tax:		$
TOTAL:		**$**

Florist:

Contact Person: Phone: Fax:

Local Address:

Website: E-mail Address:

Delivery:

Location: Deliver To:

Date: Time:

	QUANTITY	COST PER	TOTAL
Ceremony Flowers			
Bridal Bouquet/Flowers:		$	$
Bridal Throw:		$	$
Headpiece/Haku:		$	$
Bridesmaids' Bouquets/Flowers:		$	$
Bridesmaids' Headpieces/Hakus:		$	$
Flower Girl's Basket:		$	$
Flower Girl's Headpiece/Haku:		$	$
Mother-of-the-Bride Corsage:		$	$
Mother-of-the-Groom Corsage:		$	$
Fathers' Boutonniere/Lei:		$	$
Groom's Boutonniere/Lei:		$	$
Groomsmen's Boutonnieres/Leis:		$	$
Ushers' Boutonniere/Leis:		$	$
Stepparents' Corsages/Leis/Boutonnieres:		$	$

(continued on next page)

	QUANTITY	COST PER	TOTAL
Ceremony Flowers (continued)			
Grandparents' Corsages/Leis/Boutonnieres:		$	$
Parents' Thank You Bouquets/Leis:		$	$
Groom's Boutonniere/Lei:		$	$
Special Guests' Flowers/Leis:			
Out of Town Guests:		$	$
Emcee/Entertainment:		$	$
Guest Table Attendant:		$	$
Officiant:		$	$
Wedding Planner:		$	$
Misc.:			
Ceremony Decor:		$	$
Lattice/Archway:		$	$
Aisle:		$	$
Altar Arrangements:		$	$
Pew Arrangements:		$	$
Communion Table:		$	$
Unity Candle:		$	$
Candelabra Arrangements:		$	$
Chairs:		$	$
Other:		$	$
Other:		$	$

TOTAL: $

Florist:

Contact Person: Phone: Fax:

Local Address:

Website: E-mail Address:

Delivery

Location: Deliver To:

Date: Time:

Reception Flowers

	QUANTITY	COST PER	TOTAL
Head Table:		$	$
Family Table:		$	$
Buffet Table:		$	$
Cake Table:		$	$
Cake Topper:		$	$
Guest Table:		$	$
Centerpiece Arrangements:		$	$
Favors:		$	$
Podium:		$	$
Other:		$	$
Other:		$	$
Other:		$	$

TOTAL: $

(continued on next page)

Other Reception Decorations

Centerpieces: Cost: $

Supply Store:

Local Address:

Website: E-mail Address:

Supplies Needed:

Favors: Cost: $

Supply Store:

Local Address:

Website: E-mail Address:

Supplies Needed:

Other Decorations/Misc. Supplies:

Wedding Day Transportation

Company Name:

Contact Person: Phone: Fax:

Address:

Website: E-mail Address:

Cost Per Hour: Minimum Hours: Overtime Rate:

Type of Vehicle(s):

	PICK-UP TIME	PICK-UP LOCATION	DRIVER'S NAME/ NUMBER
To Ceremony Site:			
Bride			
Bridesmaids			
Groom			
Groomsmen			
Bride's Parents			
Groom's Parents			
Other Guests			
Other Guests			
Other Guests			
Other Guests			
Other Guests			

(continued on next page)

	PICK-UP TIME	PICK-UP LOCATION	DRIVER'S NAME/ NUMBER
To Reception Site:			
Bride and Groom			
Bridesmaids			
Groomsmen			
Bride's Parents			
Groom's Parents			
Other Guests			
Other Guests			
Other Guests			
From Reception Site:			
Bride and Groom			
Bridesmaids			
Groomsmen			
Bride's Parents			
Groom's Parents			
Other Guests			
Other Guests			
Other Guests			
Other Guests			

Photography

Photographer/Studio:

Photographer's Name: Phone: Fax:

Address:

Website: E-mail Address:

Assistant's Name:

Type of Service Needed:

❑ Rehearsal   ❑ Pre-Wedding   ❑ Ceremony   ❑ Reception

❑ Other:

Report Times/Locations:

Rehearsal Date: Start Time/Location:

Pre-ceremony: Start Time/Location:

Ceremony: Start Time/Location:

Reception: Start Time/Location:

(continued on next page)

Package Includes: (Number of Proofs, Enlargements, Touch-ups, Negatives, Number of Hours, Travel Fee, Albums, Costs for Additional Prints, etc.)

Photos:

Date Proofs Will Be Ready:

Date Final Prints Will Be Ready:

Date Album Will Be Ready:

Cost:

Cost of Total Package:

Deposit Amount/Due Date:

Final Payment Amount/Due Date:

(Make sure you attach your signed contract with all the stipulations, specifics and terms of agreement to this worksheet. Be sure to review the tips and questions to ask carefully before signing a contract.)

Video Service:

Videographer's Name: Phone: Fax:

Address:

Website: E-mail Address:

Assistant's Name:

Type of Service Needed:

☐ Rehearsal ☐ Pre-Wedding ☐ Ceremony ☐ Reception

☐ Slide Show Video

☐ Other:

Report Times/Locations:

Rehearsal Date: Start Time/Location:

Pre-ceremony: Start Time/Location:

Ceremony: Start Time/Location:

Reception: Start Time/Location:

(continued on next page)

Package Includes: (Number of Videotapes, Number of Hours, Videotape Length, Turnaround Time for Slide Show Video, Extra Charge for Additional Tapes)

Cost:

Cost of Total Package:

Deposit Amount/Due Date:

Final Payment Amount/Due Date:

(Make sure you attach your signed contract with all the stipulations, specifics and terms of agreement to this worksheet. Be sure to review the tips and questions to ask carefully before signing a contract.)

Rehearsal and Dinner

This day is important for several reasons. It gives you a chance to do a dry run and work out any kinks in your ceremony timeline. It's important you invite key people involved in your ceremony. It also serves as a nice time to thank family and friends who have been an important part in your wedding planning and in your lives and introduce family members who may not have already met.

Ceremony/Rehearsal Site:

Rehearsal Date: Time:

Contact: Phone:

Address: E-mail:

Parking Info:

Confirmed Rehearsal Site/Date/Time: ☐ Yes   ☐ No

Number of People Attending:

Dinner Site:

Dinner Date: Time:

Contact: Phone:

Address:

Parking Info:

Made Reservations: ☐ Yes   ☐ No

Number of People Attending:

Total Cost: $

(continued on next page)

Guest List: (Be sure to include officiant, bridal party, flower girl, ring bearer, musicians if necessary, family, friends, special guests)

GUEST(S)   RSVP

Guest Book Attendants/Gift Table Attendants: Setup and/or man the guest book table. These people should be responsible, organized and reliable. They will attend to the guest book, make sure cards are firmly attached to gifts, gather cards, check-in guests and inform them of any other pertinent information.

Name: ________________________   Contact Number: ________________________

Name: ________________________   Contact Number: ________________________

Name: ________________________   Contact Number: ________________________

Name: ________________________   Contact Number: ________________________

Name: ________________________   Contact Number: ________________________

Name: ________________________   Contact Number: ________________________

Name: ________________________   Contact Number: ________________________

Ceremony Decorations Coordinator: Oversees all details at your ceremony site including musicians, florists, photographer, videographer, ushers. If you have a wedding planner or coordinator he/she will usually handle this responsibility, or sometimes this person is provided by your ceremony site.

Name: ________________________   Contact Number: ________________________

Photographer/Florist Helper: This person(s) needs to be familiar with both sides of the family. He/she can assist with getting the flowers to family members who need them (leis, corsages, boutonnieres, etc.) and expedite the family photos by letting the photographer know who's who and having them around for the photos.

Name: ________________________   Contact Number: ________________________

Name: ________________________   Contact Number: ________________________

Name: ________________________   Contact Number: ________________________

Name: ________________________   Contact Number: ________________________

(continued on next page)

Gift/Card Person: This person will work with the gift table attendants and will transport all the wedding gifts and cards from the ceremony and/or reception site to a safe, secured location; usually needs a large vehicle.

Name: _________________________________ Contact Number:_________________

Greeters/Ushers: These people will greet guests as they arrive, hand out wedding programs, bubbles, flower petals and inform guests of any pre-ceremony activities. Seat guests.

Name: _________________________________ Contact Number:_________________

Name: _________________________________ Contact Number:_________________

Name: _________________________________ Contact Number:_________________

Name: _________________________________ Contact Number:_________________

Name: _________________________________ Contact Number:_________________

Decorations Crew: These people help with any additional decorations that aren't done by the florist or site coordinators.

Name: _________________________________ Contact Number:_________________

Name: _________________________________ Contact Number:_________________

Name: _________________________________ Contact Number:_________________

Other Ceremony Delegations:

Duties: ____

Name: _________________________________ Contact Number:_________________

Duties: ____

Name: _________________________________ Contact Number:_________________

Guest Book Attendants/Gift Table Attendants: (See Delegating Ceremony Duties Sheet) Also serve as hosts or hostesses who welcome guests, invite them to have refreshments and/or answer other questions.

Master of Ceremonies: Orchestrates the program part of the reception. Announces bridal party, first dance, slide show, cake cutting, etc. Musicians can also serve as the program emcee.

Name: _________________________________ Contact Number:_________________

Photographer/Florist Helper: (See Ceremony Delegations Sheet)

Gift Person: (See Ceremony Delegations Sheet)

Decorations Crew: These people help with any additional decorations that aren't done by the florist or site coordinators. Duties can include placing favors and centerpieces on tables, decorating head table, chairs, etc.

Name: _________________________________ Contact Number:_________________

Name: _________________________________ Contact Number:_________________

Name: _________________________________ Contact Number:_________________

Name: _________________________________ Contact Number:_________________

Name: _________________________________ Contact Number:_________________

Rental Equipment: This person is in charge of anything that was rented by an outside vendor and needs to be collected and returned. Items can include cake knives, cake pillars, lights, tiki torches, etc. Many rental companies will deliver and pick up rented items unless they are small in size or amount.

Name: _________________________________ Contact Number:_________________

Name: _________________________________ Contact Number:_________________

Name: _________________________________ Contact Number:_________________

Name: _________________________________ Contact Number:_________________

(continued on next page)

Cleanup: These people will help with any breakdown and cleanup needed. They're more crucial in out-door weddings or weddings held without banquet help. They need to be the last to leave and be aware of any terms of the cleanup agreement you have with your place of reception.

Name: ___________________________ Contact Number: ___________________

Name: ___________________________ Contact Number: ___________________

Name: ___________________________ Contact Number: ___________________

Name: ___________________________ Contact Number: ___________________

Other Reception Delegations

Duties: ____

Name: ___________________________ Contact Number: ___________________

Duties: ____

Name: ___________________________ Contact Number: ___________________

Duties: ____

Name: ___________________________ Contact Number: ___________________

Duties: ____

Name: ___________________________ Contact Number: ___________________

Duties: ____

Name: ___________________________ Contact Number: ___________________

Duties: ____

Name: ___________________________ Contact Number: ___________________

Here's a traditional breakdown of various roles that family and friends play in your wedding planning process. I don't want to sound like a broken record, but the keri-wedding-philosophy bears repeating. It's not about right or wrong; just what's right or wrong for your dream wedding. So do what you wish with this list of traditional roles and responsibilities (to include, but not limited to, ripping out this sheet and tossing it).

Maid/Matron of Honor
- ❏ Assists bride in selecting wedding attire (wedding gown and bridesmaids' dresses)
- ❏ Plans bridal shower
- ❏ Assists bride in putting together list and collecting items for wedding day
- ❏ Assists bride in getting dressed
- ❏ Arranges bride's veil and train before the processional and recessional
- ❏ Holds bride's bouquet during the ceremony
- ❏ Serves as witness for marriage license signing
- ❏ Offers wedding toast
- ❏ Assists bride in changing into going away clothes
- ❏ Mails wedding announcements after the wedding

Best Man
- ❏ Responsible for organizing ushers' activities
- ❏ Plans bachelor party for groom
- ❏ Drives or travels with groom to ceremony site
- ❏ Brings marriage license to the ceremony
- ❏ Holds onto wedding rings until needed at ceremony (unless the rings are tied to the ring bearer's pillow)
- ❏ Assists groom in arranging formal wear rental, fittings and pick-up
- ❏ Pays the officiant, musicians, photographer and any other service providers the day of the wedding (unless there is a wedding coordinator)
- ❏ Drives newlyweds to reception if applicable
- ❏ Offers wedding toast
- ❏ Oversees return of tuxedo rentals for groom and groomsmen

Bridesmaids
- ❏ Assist maid/matron of honor in planning bridal shower
- ❏ Assist bride with addressing invitations
- ❏ Assist bride in running errands, making favors, centerpieces or other wedding elements
- ❏ Encourage single women to participate in bouquet toss

Groomsmen/Ushers
- ❏ Help best man with bachelor party
- ❏ Distribute wedding programs and other printed information to guests as they arrive
- ❏ Seat guests at the ceremony
- ❏ Direct guests to reception site if applicable

Bride's Mother
- ❏ Assists with preparing guest list for bride and her family
- ❏ Assists in planning the wedding ceremony and reception

(continued on next page)

Bride's Mother (continued)
- ❏ Assists with bridal shower
- ❏ Helps bride select bridal gown
- ❏ Selects own dress
- ❏ Assists bride's out-of-town guests with travel accommodations
- ❏ Last person seated before processional
- ❏ Participates in receiving line if applicable
- ❏ Assists in hosting the reception
- ❏ Pays for majority of wedding costs

Bride's Father
- ❏ Assists with preparing guest list for bride and her family
- ❏ Selects attire to complement groom and groomsmen
- ❏ Walks bride down the aisle
- ❏ Gives the bride away
- ❏ Participates in receiving line if applicable
- ❏ Dances with bride for father/daughter dance
- ❏ Assists in hosting the reception
- ❏ Offers wedding toast
- ❏ Pays for majority of wedding costs

Groom's Mother
- ❏ Assists with preparing guest list for groom and his family
- ❏ Selects own dress (to complement mother of the bride's dress)
- ❏ Assists groom in planning rehearsal dinner
- ❏ Assists groom's out-of-town guests with travel accommodations
- ❏ Participates in receiving line if applicable
- ❏ Dances with groom for mother/son dance

Groom's Father
- ❏ Assists with preparing guest list for groom and his family
- ❏ Selects attire to complement groom and groomsmen
- ❏ Assists groom in planning rehearsal dinner
- ❏ Offers toast to bride at rehearsal dinner
- ❏ Participates in receiving line if applicable

Flower Girl (with some help from her parents)
- ❏ Responsible for renting/purchasing dress selected by bride
- ❏ Attends wedding rehearsal
- ❏ Walks during processional

Ring Bearer (with some help from his parents)
- ❏ Attends wedding rehearsal
- ❏ Responsible for renting attire selected by couple
- ❏ Walks during processional with rings on pillow (or fake rings)

Working Budget

	BUDGET	ACTUAL	COMMENTS
Total Wedding Budget:	$	$	

A. Attire

Bride:

	BUDGET	ACTUAL	
Bride's Gown	$	$	
Headpiece/Veil	$	$	
Jewelry	$	$	
Undergarments	$	$	
Stockings	$	$	
Shoes	$	$	
Alterations	$	$	
Garter	$	$	
Other:	$	$	

Bridesmaids:

	BUDGET	ACTUAL	
Bridesmaid's Dress	$	$	
Headpiece	$	$	
Jewelry	$	$	
Shoes	$	$	
Alterations	$	$	
Other:	$	$	

(continued on next page)

	BUDGET	ACTUAL	COMMENTS
Bridesmaids (continued):			
Flower Girl Dress	$	$	
Other:	$	$	
Ring Bearer Attire	$	$	
Other:	$	$	
Groom:			
Formal Wear Rental*	$	$	
Shoes*	$	$	
Other:	$	$	
Other:	$	$	
Groomsmen:			
Formal Wear Rental	$	$	
Shoes*	$	$	
Other:	$	$	
Other:	$	$	
SUB-TOTAL A	$	$	

(continued on next page)

245

	BUDGET	ACTUAL	COMMENTS
B. Beauty			
Hair/Makeup Artist	$	$	
Manicures	$	$	
Pedicures	$	$	
Spa Services	$	$	
Massage	$	$	
Other:	$	$	
SUB-TOTAL B	$	$	
C. Cakes/Bakers			
Wedding Cake	$	$	
Cake Delivery/Setup	$	$	
Cake Topper	$	$	
Cake Knife	$	$	
Sheet Cake	$	$	
Other:	$	$	
Other:	$	$	
SUB-TOTAL C	$	$	

(continued on next page)

D. Ceremony/Reception

	BUDGET	ACTUAL	COMMENTS
Site Fee	$	$	
Ring Bearer Pillow	$	$	
Chairs	$	$	
Archway	$	$	
Guest Book/Pens, etc.	$	$	
Pūpū (Hors d'Oeuvres)	$	$	
Main Meal/Caterer	$	$	
Beverages	$	$	
Bartending	$	$	
Bar Setup Fee	$	$	
Corkage Fee	$	$	
Pouring Service	$	$	
Gratuity	$	$	
Parking Fees	$	$	
Other:	$	$	
Other:	$	$	
Other:	$	$	
Other:	$	$	
SUB-TOTAL D	**$**	**$**	

(continued on next page)

E. Consultants/ Wedding Planners

	BUDGET	ACTUAL	COMMENTS
Consultant Fee	$	$	
Other:	$	$	
Other:	$	$	
SUB-TOTAL E	$	$	

F. Entertainment

	BUDGET	ACTUAL	COMMENTS
Ceremony Musicians/Music	$	$	
Pre-Reception Musicians/Music	$	$	
Reception Musicians	$	$	
DJ	$	$	
Emcee	$	$	
Sound System	$	$	
Other:	$	$	
Other:	$	$	
Other:	$	$	
Other:	$	$	
SUB-TOTAL F	$	$	

(continued on next page)

	BUDGET	ACTUAL	COMMENTS
G. Equipment Rentals			
Tent/Canopy	$	$	
Tables	$	$	
Chairs	$	$	
Lighting	$	$	
Setup/Breakdown	$	$	
Delivery	$	$	
Dance Floor	$	$	
Linens	$	$	
Beverage Items/Accessories	$	$	
Serviceware	$	$	
Tableware	$	$	
Other:	$	$	
Other:	$	$	
Other:	$	$	
Other:	$	$	
Other:	$	$	
Other:	$	$	
Other:	$	$	
SUB-TOTAL G	**$**	**$**	

(continued on next page)

	BUDGET	ACTUAL	COMMENTS

H. Flowers & Decorations

	BUDGET	ACTUAL	COMMENTS
Ceremony Flowers (see page 225)	$	$	
Reception Flowers (see page 227)	$	$	
Centerpieces	$	$	
Favors	$	$	
Gift Table	$	$	
Flower Girl Basket	$	$	
Delivery/Setup (Florist)	$	$	
Delivery/Setup (Centerpieces/Favors)	$	$	
Balloons	$	$	
Candles	$	$	
Other:	$	$	
Other:	$	$	
Other:	$	$	
SUB-TOTAL H	**$**	**$**	

I. Invitations/Stationery

	BUDGET	ACTUAL	COMMENTS
Invitations	$	$	
Response Cards	$	$	

(continued on next page)

	BUDGET	ACTUAL	COMMENTS

I. Invitations/Stationery (continued)

	BUDGET	ACTUAL
Reception Cards	$	$
Ceremony Programs	$	$
Announcements/ Save-the-date Cards	$	$
Thank You Cards	$	$
Postage	$	$
Calligrapher	$	$
Paper Napkins	$	$
Matchbooks	$	$
Hawaiian Wedding Certificate	$	$
Other:	$	$
Other:	$	$
SUB-TOTAL I	**$**	**$**

J. Limousines/Transportation

	BUDGET	ACTUAL
Transportation	$	$
SUB-TOTAL J	**$**	**$**

K. Officiants

	BUDGET	ACTUAL
Officiant Service/Gratuity*	$	$
SUB-TOTAL K	**$**	**$**

(continued on next page)

L. Photographer

	BUDGET	ACTUAL	COMMENTS
Engagement/ Announcement Photos	$	$	
Formal Bridal Portrait	$	$	
Wedding Package	$	$	
Negatives	$	$	
Additional Prints	$	$	
Travel Fee	$	$	
Enlargements	$	$	
Touch-Ups/Chrome Work	$	$	
Other:	$	$	
Other:	$	$	
SUB-TOTAL L	$	$	

M. Videographer

	BUDGET	ACTUAL	COMMENTS
Wedding Day Video	$	$	
Extra Tapes	$	$	
Photo Montage	$	$	
Other:	$	$	
Other:	$	$	
SUB-TOTAL M	$	$	

(continued on next page)

	BUDGET	ACTUAL	COMMENTS
N. Specialty Products & Services			
Hawai'i Weddings Made Simple	$	$	
Bride's Gift*	$	$	
Bridesmaids' Gifts	$	$	
Groom's Gift	$	$	
Groomsmens Gifts*	$	$	
Rehearsal Dinner*	$	$	
Marriage License*	$	$	
Bridal Gown Preservation	$	$	
Name Change Fees	$	$	
Honeymoon	$	$	
Crane/Tsuru Design	$	$	
Other:	$	$	
Other:	$	$	
Other:	$	$	
Other:	$	$	
Other:	$	$	
Other:	$	$	
SUB-TOTAL N	**$**	**$**	

(continued on next page)

Working Budget (cont.)

	BUDGET	ACTUAL	COMMENTS
O. Miscellaneous			
	$	$	
	$	$	
	$	$	
	$	$	
	$	$	
	$	$	
	$	$	
	$	$	
	$	$	
	$	$	
	$	$	
	$	$	
SUB-TOTAL O	$	$	

Total

	BUDGET	ACTUAL
SUB-TOTALS A–D	$	$
SUB-TOTALS E–G	$	$
SUB-TOTALS H–M	$	$
SUB-TOTALS N–O	$	$
TOTAL	$	$

*Groom usually pays for these items

** Groom pays for *some* of these items

Alterations/Seamstress:

Name: Phone:

Contract Date: Amount: $ Deposit Date: Amount: $

Final Payment Date: Amount: $

Bridal Salon:

Name: Phone:

Contract Date: Amount: $ Deposit Date: Amount: $

Final Payment Date: Amount: $

Balloonist:

Name: Phone:

Contract Date: Amount: $ Deposit Date: Amount: $

Final Payment Date: Amount: $

Bakery (Cakes):

Name: Phone:

Contract Date: Amount: $ Deposit Date: Amount: $

Final Payment Date: Amount: $

Bartending Services:

Name: Phone:

Contract Date: Amount: $ Deposit Date: Amount: $

Final Payment Date: Amount: $

(continued on next page)

Calligrapher:

Name: Phone:

Contract Date: Amount: $ Deposit Date: Amount: $

Final Payment Date: Amount: $

Caterer:

Name: Phone:

Contract Date: Amount: $ Deposit Date: Amount: $

Final Payment Date: Amount: $

Centerpieces:

Name: Phone:

Contract Date: Amount: $ Deposit Date: Amount: $

Final Payment Date: Amount: $

Ceremony Musicians:

Name: Phone:

Contract Date: Amount: $ Deposit Date: Amount: $

Final Payment Date: Amount: $

Ceremony Site:

Name: Phone:

Contract Date: Amount: $ Deposit Date: Amount: $

Final Payment Date: Amount: $

(continued on next page)

Consultant/Wedding Planner:

Name: Phone:

Contract Date: Amount: $ Deposit Date: Amount: $

Final Payment Date: Amount: $

Decorations:

Name: Phone:

Contract Date: Amount: $ Deposit Date: Amount: $

Final Payment Date: Amount: $

Equipment Rentals:

Name: Phone:

Contract Date: Amount: $ Deposit Date: Amount: $

Final Payment Date: Amount: $

Favors:

Name: Phone:

Contract Date: Amount: $ Deposit Date: Amount: $

Final Payment Date: Amount: $

Florist:

Name: Phone:

Contract Date: Amount: $ Deposit Date: Amount: $

Final Payment Date: Amount: $

(continued on next page)

Gift Suppliers:

Name: Phone:

Contract Date: Amount: $ Deposit Date: Amount: $

Final Payment Date: Amount: $

Ice Sculpture:

Name: Phone:

Contract Date: Amount: $ Deposit Date: Amount: $

Final Payment Date: Amount: $

Officiant:

Name: Phone:

Contract Date: Amount: $ Deposit Date: Amount: $

Final Payment Date: Amount: $

Photographer:

Name: Phone:

Contract Date: Amount: $ Deposit Date: Amount: $

Final Payment Date: Amount: $

(continued on next page)

Reception Site:

Name: Phone:

Contract Date: Amount: $ Deposit Date: Amount: $

Final Payment Date: Amount: $

Reception Musicians:

Name: Phone:

Contract Date: Amount: $ Deposit Date: Amount: $

Final Payment Date: Amount: $

Reception Entertainment:

Name: Phone:

Contract Date: Amount: $ Deposit Date: Amount: $

Final Payment Date: Amount: $

Rehearsal Dinner:

Name: Phone:

Contract Date: Amount: $ Deposit Date: Amount: $

Final Payment Date: Amount: $

Tuxedo Rental:

Name: Phone:

Contract Date: Amount: $ Deposit Date: Amount: $

Final Payment Date: Amount: $

(continued on next page)

259

Transportation:

Name: Phone:

Contract Date: Amount: $ Deposit Date: Amount: $

Final Payment Date: Amount: $

Videographer:

Name: Phone:

Contract Date: Amount: $ Deposit Date: Amount: $

Final Payment Date: Amount: $

Other:

Name: Phone:

Contract Date: Amount: $ Deposit Date: Amount: $

Final Payment Date: Amount: $

Other:

Name: Phone:

Contract Date: Amount: $ Deposit Date: Amount: $

Final Payment Date: Amount: $

Other:

Name: Phone:

Contract Date: Amount: $ Deposit Date: Amount: $

Final Payment Date: Amount: $

Index:

                                    Hawai'i Weddings Made Simple

Other Valuable Resources in Planning Your Wedding

Weddings For Dummies
Marcy Blum and Laura Fisher Kaiser

The Knot Ultimate Wedding Planner
Carley Rooney

The Big Wedding on a Small Budget
Planner and Organizer
Diane Warner

The Good Honeymoon Guide
Lucy Hone

I'm Getting Married, Now What?!
Andrea Rotondo Hospidor

Planning A Wedding To Remember
Beverly Clark

Easy Wedding Planning Plus
Elizabeth and Alex Lluch

Pacific Rim Weddings Magazine

Hawai'i Bride & Groom Magazine

The Hawai'i Bridal Directory

Helpful Websites for Planning Your (Hawai'i) Wedding (in addition to those listed throughout the book)

www.theknot.com
www.weddingspot.com
www.usabride.com
www.weddingchannel.com
www.bridalplanner.com
www.gohawaii.com
www.bridesclub.com
www.getawayweddings.com (good source for
   destination weddings)